Also by James Conaway

The Big Easy, a novel (1970)

Judge: The Life and Times of Leander Perez (1973)

THE TEXANS

THE TEXANS

James Conaway

Alfred A. Knopf
New York
1976

THIS IS A BORZOI BOOK
PUBLISHED BY ALFRED A. KNOPF, INC.

Copyright © 1972, 1975, 1976 by James Conaway
All rights reserved under International and Pan-American
Copyright Conventions. Published in the United States by
Alfred A. Knopf, Inc., New York, and simultaneously in
Canada by Random House of Canada Limited, Toronto.
Distributed by Random House, Inc., New York.
"The Source: Oil and Patriots" and "A Question of
Maids" were originally published as "Oil: The Source"
and "El Paso," in a slightly different form,
in the *Atlantic Monthly*.

LIBRARY OF CONGRESS CATALOGING IN PUBLICATION DATA

Conaway, James.   The Texans.
Includes index.
1. Businessmen—Texas.   2. Business and politics—
Texas.   3. Elite (Social sciences)—Texas.
I. Title.
HC107.T4C65 1976   338'.092'2 [B]   75-36787
ISBN 0-394-49169-6

MANUFACTURED IN THE UNITED STATES OF AMERICA
FIRST EDITION

For Brennan

A republic of outlaws loosely allied with
the United States, Texas survives, and survives
quite well, by breaking the rules.

—Peter Gent,
North Dallas Forty

Contents

THE TEXANS

Prologue

Texas hangs somewhere between saddle-worn cliché and ongoing natural wonder. The notoriety it received during the years of Sam Rayburn's and Lyndon Johnson's reigns in Washington overshadowed the state's truly extraordinary character, which is not political, but commercial. Certainly the latter aspect often employs the former, but it is big business that has generally set the tone, affecting all levels of society. The emblematic figures are not Rayburn and Johnson, but former Governor Allan Shivers and John Connally, representative of a loose and genial collection of wealthy men whose power extends considerably further than state boundaries, and whose influence and activities have been effectively hidden. The group is known—when it is known at all—as the Texas establishment.

Another oil-producing state, Louisiana, harbors a bemused tolerance of corruption in high places. Texas, however, has come to expect great wealth among its leaders. The paradox is that most Texans are not wealthy. They are descendants of German, Danish, French, Mexican, and not a few Yankee settlers, and of white Anglo-Saxon Protestants from the South who early became the movers in the economics and politics of the state. They made fortunes from cotton, wearing out the black soil in east Texas, and from cattle, producing ranches and legends of great size and tenacity. Abolitionists charged in 1835 that the Texas revolution was a "slaveocracy conspiracy" to expand the number of slave states, when it was really a Protestant uprising against the Latin Catholics.

Texas became a one-party state in 1860 because it contained a substantial number of slaves, but that number declined rapidly. The Civil War never excited the Texas imagination. The racial politics that dominated the rest of the South was replaced in the Lone Star State by a preoccupation with money—the best ways to produce it and protect it.

"A modified class politics seems to be evolving," wrote V. O. Key, Jr., in *Southern Politics,* "not primarily because of an upthrust of the masses that compels men of substance to unite in self-defense, but because of the personal insecurity of men suddenly made rich who are fearful lest they lose their wealth."

Populist sentiment was strong in Texas around the turn of the century, when the railroads, banks, trusts, and merchants all needed regulation. The concern for agrarian reform lessened with the oil boom, and the liberal cause became synonymous with political obsolescence after the Second World War.

The establishment has been instrumental in electing every governor of Texas since the political demise of James V. Allred in 1938, a former attorney general who had consistently opposed monopolies and enforced the anti-trust laws. Allred's successor was W. Lee "Pappy" O'Daniel, marketer of Hillbilly Flour and master of ceremonies on a radio program featuring the Light Crust Doughboys, who ran on a platform of the Ten Commandments and opposition to a sales tax. A favorite slogan was "Less Johnson grass and politicians, more smokestacks and businessmen."

The governors following O'Daniel—Coke Stevenson, Beauford Jester, Shivers, Price Daniel, Connally, Preston Smith, and Dolph Briscoe—have all been essentially establishment candidates, which is not at all the same thing as being the product of a political machine. Connally was its flower, and best represents what Texas has become: urban, industrial, "capital-intensive," and sophisticated, a symbol not of ideological power play or frontier virtue, but of the greatest possibilities and excesses of making it in America.

The debate over the establishment's existence persists. Walt Rostow, President Johnson's adviser, who was brought by him to Texas where he teaches at the state university, says, "The term establishment stems from the English concept of support for the king and the established church. An establishment can't be maintained by an occasional phone call. It requires a system of communications, and a staff."

Powerful Texans would greet the idea of such a formal arrangement with horror and derision, for it would appear undemocratic, and would be both vulnerable and less effective than the present loose coalition. Much better is the *subrosa* accord established among like-minded men, the effects of which are felt with some financial encouragement here, some legal or political expertise there, until the society reflects the values of its unseen plutocracy.

Rostow's haven in the hills outside Austin is one eloquent tribute to that plutocracy and its widespread influence, for it helped make Vietnam as much a Texan as an American war. Another tribute is the fact that Bill Moyers, Johnson's press secretary and an opponent of the war, felt he could not return to Texas because the power structure was hostile to him, and to his sentiments.

The old order is passing, but those taking its place have essentially the same values. Scratch a Texan and you'll find an entrepreneur. John Connally, H. Ross Perot, George Brown, Bunker Hunt, Lloyd Bentsen—they are some of the best known, and most emulated, but today no one man speaks for Texas. The mythic type is in eclipse, his exuberance, individuality, and rampant disregard for convention replaced by restraint, conformity, and a careful display of good taste. The basic appetites of a Lyndon Johnson have been refined and honed down in a Connally, and reduced to essentials in a Bentsen. Gut reaction gives way to systems analysis, human concerns to cost effectiveness, ass-grabbing to a courtly sobriety and—above all—a distance.

These are the attributes of corporate statesmen, a group whose definition is, in the end, academic.

"The establishment is the country-club set," says Frank Erwin, former regent of the University of Texas, and a political agent for both Johnson and Connally. "You know, those handsome men who run the state."

1 ☆ THE GIANTS

Et in Arcadia Ego

That April, 1972, afternoon their planes floated high above the old Spanish land grants, sunlight glinting from glazed windows and the tips of silver wings, the sky loud with their power. They were the wealthiest and the most influential of Texans, already dressed for dinner, and their talk was of that event, the delicious incongruity of it, what it all meant. This aerial convergence of status and money was not the stampede described in that famous novel about Texas, which some of them had read, and all hated. But the present similarity between fiction and fact was not lost upon the passengers of those graceful, jet-driven symbols of mobility and utter independence.

"They were merely private vehicles," wrote Edna Ferber two decades before, "bearing nice little alligator jewel cases and fabulous gowns and overbred furs. No sordid freight sullied these four-engine family jobs whose occupants were . . . women in Paris gowns from Neiman-Marcus." The men, however, no longer wore Stetsons and shirt sleeves with little pearl snaps on the cuffs, but black ties and the air of dour anonymity that had come to represent this corporate state since *Giant* first appeared. There were no more diamond stickpins or belt buckles among Texas's best, no more handmade dress boots and raw ole good times—no more show of heart—for Texas had changed.

An old-fashioned barbecue done in proper style was still fitting. It recalled another era of prosperity, and touched a chord of memory—perhaps more cinematographic than real—of childhood promise, and belief in that grand vague term that is so Texan: greatness. The President of the United States would be at Picosa, John Connally's ranch, no extraordinary event for the bankers and oilmen, the insurance executives, contractors, real-estate mandarins, the master entrepreneurs of electronics and data processing and a hundred other endeavors that rode the rim of the economic frontier. But one did not pass up the opportunity to talk with the President, even if he wasn't a Texan (he was the next-best thing), or a Democrat.

It was to be not only the party of the year, but also the harbinger of the '70s—an inaugural of sorts of Texas's restored power at the highest level. That the White House could move to Floresville was not an idle dream to many of the guests, who had seen it move to an unlikelier spot in Texas, though they would only speak of that in the privacy of their fuselages, and then with discretion.

San Antonio lurked off to the west, devoid of the virgin skyscrapers that graced the favored citadels of Houston and Dallas, a depressing reminder of the state's racial diversity and stolid agrarian tradition. The guests might all own spreads with registered herds, weekend ranches or citrus groves, or at least soybean futures—certainly a share of a club with a golf course expansive enough to suggest pastoral exclusion. But their allegiance was to the newer, urban mills of wealth and its amenities.

No, the view did not inspire men of vision. Neither prairie nor good range, but a dirt farmer's country cluttered with scrub cottonwood, hackberry, and mesquite. Heavy red soil washed red in the gullies. President Nixon would not know the difference, but the Texans who had never seen Picosa had doubts about its possible appeal.

Then suddenly it appeared—three thousand acres of vernal profusion, a literal oasis. Already planes were stacked high above the green coastal Bermuda grass, almost artificial in its vibrancy, like so much Astroturf. They settled lower and lower toward the stone ranch house set among ancient live oaks, the striped yellow-and-white awning clearly visible to the eager guests, resplendent in the setting sun. A herd of sleek, cherry-red Santa Gertrudis cattle crowded the fence, watching the planes come in low over the lip of the crimped ribbon of a runway, and taxi into a formation that seemed almost military.

Cowboys posed on horses, within view of the house and the arriving guests. Their bandannas were whipped by the wind, their mounts restive but controlled. The spectacle was not entirely for the benefit of the President, whose massive Marine Corps helicopter stood isolated, flanked by purposeful young men in business suits and sunglasses. The men and women disembarking with handbags and tentative smiles felt a pride of heritage in the sight of those equestrian silhouettes, as remote and unreal as a Charles Russell canvas. Some joked among themselves about cowhands cutting the little planes out from among the bigger Lears, Falcons, and even a four-engine Jetstar, the only one in private ownership.

Some of the planes were less than great, holdovers from an earlier magnificence. There was the Murchisons' Flying Jenny, a white, propeller-driven DC-3, specially fitted with a picture window. John Murchison and his brother Clint, Jr., scions of one of the great oil fortunes, owners of the Dallas Cowboys and untold investments, found the old Jenny comfortable. But hours later, after the festivities were over and the planes had dispersed toward Houston and Dallas, Fort Worth, Amarillo, Austin and Midland, Victoria, Denton, Marathon, Sherman and Corpus Christi, members of the Hunt party would hear the Murchisons' pilot on the radio, angrily contending with a thunderstorm, a mere mile above the ground. The Hunts' Lear—a demonstrator on loan from a hopeful salesman—would streak safely against a star-speckled sky, thirty thousand feet above the clouds.

The guests knew from the formation of planes which among them were missing. Lyndon Johnson was at home in the hill country, recovering from a heart attack, but he would not have attended anyway. James Aston, president of the Republic National Bank of Dallas, was present, but his plane had landed at San Antonio instead of Picosa. Aston and his passengers—editors from the Dallas *Morning News,* the most influential paper in the state—had been forced to come the rest of the way by limousine, which threaded the gauntlet of state police, Texas Rangers, and FBI agents guarding the road and the gate to the ranch. The week before, Aston's pilot had driven to Picosa just to inspect the runway, and he disapproved of the amount of gravel on the tarmac.

Bundles of white chrysanthemums hung from the oaks about the patio in enormous pots. Caterers brought from as far away as Fort Worth—three hundred miles to the north—attended the smoking banks of beef tenderloin, and roasted corn, on butane-fired barbecue pits, while strains of subdued string music issued from costumed mariachis.

The center of attention, oddly enough, was not the President and the First Lady, but their host, the former Secretary of the Treasury, and chairman of Democrats for Nixon, an efficient and partisan organization that would carry Texas for Nixon for the first time in the upcoming 1972 election. It was Connally's finest hour, and he radiated confidence and respectability. Gone was the vermilion ranch suit, with the hand-sewn darts, of his early days as Governor of Texas, replaced by more formal attire acceptable in any capital of the world, where his elegant silver hair and slightly dissolute good looks would have been instantly recognized.

The Nixons seemed more relaxed than usual—almost ebullient in their own constricted way, he wearing the enameled American flag in the lapel of his soft blue blazer, she in a full-length backless gown gaily checked in red and white. They seemed content in Connally's shadow as he proudly showed them about the house of Lueders stone, pointing out the bits of Georgian and French Provincial architecture incorporated in the ranch style so dear to the President. Connally took obvious delight in calling Nixon's attention to details—the marble mantel, and the black Brazilian granite floors, the stair railing of antique brass, an Oriental chandelier bought in New Orleans, massive hand-carved teakwood doors ("They weigh three hundred and sixty pounds apiece, Mr. President"), and an entire marble floor imported from an eighteenth-century London mansion.

The First Lady was carefully attended by Nellie Connally, a short, attractive woman with a pleasant smile, who seemed slightly distraught on this momentous occasion. She had prepared for it for two solid weeks, assisting the help in washing lettuce and shucking corn, supervising all the flower arrangements. Nellie Connally even went into the fields herself to pick bluebonnets, Indian pinks, fireweels, and daisies for Pat Nixon, and then in the excitement forgot to present the bouquet to her.

The receiving line took shape with no apparent effort. The women's voices were eager and high-pitched as the men quietly urged them forward. The faces of most of the men would have been unknown to the average Texan,

for they performed their tasks in the boardrooms and
clubs and office suites of the cities, environments soft-
ened by assorted chinoiserie. They preferred the irre-
futable worth of ancient Oriental screens and vases, or
paintings by Melvin Warren and Porfirio Salinas, although some displayed Monets, Picassos, and an occasional Braque. For the most part, these men remained
out of the public view and, in Texas, mercifully free of
undue scrutiny by the press. Their power did not issue
from a podium or a platform, but was a natural accrual
through interlocking directorships of the largest banks,
corporations, and law firms, a sympathy between business and government by means of contacts established
and cultivated for years. The sympathy was based upon
friendship or mutual need or money, or—as was usually
the case—friendship and mutual need and money. They
were not lobbyists—they hired others to handle the
grosser aspects of political persuasion—and invited the
best lobbyists to their parties. Nor were they politicians
in the mundane sense of those who simply run for public
office. Yet they exercised a unified power in the state
unparalleled in America.

The white-haired figure shaking the President's hand
with patrician reserve was George Brown, head of one
of the world's largest construction firms, and a primary
backer of both Johnson and Connally. His company,
Brown & Root, had participated in all the major construction in Vietnam, on Project Mohole in the Pacific
Ocean, on the National Aeronautics and Space Administration's Houston Space Center, and on countless other
massive projects around the world, many of them related
to war. Brown's eyesight had begun to fail, but his political acumen remained intact, as did his elevated position among his peers.

Quite different in appearance was the short, plump
Nelson Bunker Hunt, a heavy supporter of Nixon's, who
wore a shy, gap-toothed grin. The third son of H. L.

Hunt, Bunker was a formidable force in his own right in financial America, and not unknown to controversy. He and other members of the Hunt family were presently involved in a federal wiretapping suit. His oil interests in Libya were threatened with nationalization. Neither of these would prevent his buying another thoroughbred racehorse, or his later attempt with his brother, Herbert, to buy up a large portion of the world's available silver.

There were many names famous in oil, hard-bitten wildcatters unaccustomed to sartorial elegance, survivors of the chaotic oil boom like Jake Hamon and Monty Moncrief who had no illusions about politicians. Second-generation oilmen were smoother, some said effete. Amon Carter, Jr., displayed a lack of enthusiasm for his father's legacy, whether it was the oil wells or the publishing empire of the Fort Worth *Star-Telegram*, but he enjoyed the gathering. Likewise Corbin Robertson, son-in-law of one of the wealthiest oilmen, Hugh Roy Cullen, and Paul Haas, the host's friend and oil operator from Corpus Christi.

Perry Bass, nephew of perhaps the most famous wildcatter of all, Sid Richardson, was also present. Richardson had been Connally's financial mentor, and Bass had been Connally's partner in settling the Richardson estate, which netted Connally close to a million dollars while he was governor.

The stocky czar of the Houston insurance empire, Gus Wortham, moved through the ceremony with characteristic abruptness. He had built up American General Insurance from scratch, and still ran it and other enterprises with an iron hand. Johnson had often visited Wortham's cattle auctions at the 9-Bar Ranch while he was President, slipping secretly away from Washington in Air Force One. They frequently talked by telephone in those years. Once Johnson had asked to speak to Wortham's black chauffeur, Lester. "Do you know who this is?" Johnson had asked, and when Lester said he did not, Johnson told him it was the President. Then Johnson prompted, "Lester, what does it feel like to be talking to the President of the United States?"

The courtly, gaunt H. B. Zachry represented most of the political money in San Antonio. He backed Connally in 1961, helping him carry south Texas. Zachry's construction firm did millions of dollars' worth of business in Texas annually; his name was well known, but not his face or his opinions. "A dictatorship is the best form of government," he would say in a later interview, musing about politics. "That is, it's best if you have a real good dictator. But the system always falls apart after the first one."

Pollard Simons, the Dallas developer and builder of one of the world's largest shopping malls, was warmly received by both the President and the host. Connally was Simons's close friend and business associate. Simons had given him the highest hill in his thousand-acre Jamaican resort, Tryall, where Connally built a house described by his Dallas decorator as "Oriental contemporary," with sliding doors and a sunken bathtub. That was Connally's headquarters for golfing expeditions undertaken in the well-known patent-leather shoes in orange and white (the official colors of the University of Texas), and for the cattle venture said to be his and Simons's joint effort near Montego Bay. Connally entertained men of position in Jamaica, including Gerald Ford and Senator Lloyd Bentsen.

Simons, himself a millionaire many times over, shared Connally's penchant for luxury. He began his career with a loan of $150 from the First National Bank in Dallas to rent a parking garage. (He originally asked for $300, and was told that if he could make it on $300, he could also make it on $150.) He and Connally enjoyed the distinctions among life's necessities that seemed lost upon their mutual friend Nixon.

H. Ross Perot, a young man who resembled a Marine recruit in costly civilian dress, his smile quick and slightly uncertain, was as warmly received as any of the guests. Although he was the founder of Electronic Data Systems and a pace-setter in the Texas electronics and data-processing boom, he did not seem experienced enough to be one of America's richest men. It was known that he derived joy from employing money well, and believed absolutely in its powers. His efforts to free the prisoners of war in North Vietnam had earned him the reputation of maverick philanthropist and latter-day Don Quixote. The guests would have applauded his patriotism, but they were secretly horrified that he drew so much attention to himself and his milieu, that he did not go through proper channels. Nixon understood his zealotry well. Through Connally, he later appealed to Perot to save the Wall Street firm of du Pont, Glore, Forgan, and therefore the nation. And Perot agreed, thus losing, it is said, more money on paper in the stock market in one day than any other American in history.

The bankers present were in many cases also lawyers. James A. Elkins, Jr., son of the late Judge James Elkins, founder of the First City National Bank of Houston, smoked his cigarettes in an elegant holder after passing them through a hole in a gold disk to pack the tobacco, a flourish the Judge would have disdained. Judge Elkins had been a member of the powerful, unofficial 8-F Crowd, cronies including Herman and George Brown, Wortham, and others, who met regularly in a suite in Houston's Lamar Hotel and exerted great influence in city and state politics. Before his death, Judge Elkins founded the law firm that had become Vinson, Elkins, Searls, Connally & Smith.

Other senior partners of the firm were also present at the barbecue. (Three of Houston's law firms were among the largest half-dozen in America, and their influence and interests ranged widely across the country.)

Vinson, Elkins, Searls, Connally & Smith maintained stocks of stationery with Connally's name missing from the letterhead to facilitate his forays into government.

The bright satellites of leadership passed quickly through the receiving line: Anne Armstrong, Nixon's adviser from Texas, and a favorite on the national Republican luncheon circuit; Erik Jonsson, Dallas's facile mayor, and the political force behind the creation of the world's largest airport; Ima Hogg, aging daughter of the notorious Texas governor Jim Hogg, once slandered by an opponent who falsely claimed he had a second daughter named Ura; the former mayor of San Antonio and an old Connally supporter, A. A. McAllister.

The presence of Lyndon Baines Johnson was never missed. Johnson had certainly served the interests of those present, but he had lacked the necessary polish, that quality of separateness spawned by the corporate process. He had remained his own basic, profane self even in the highest office, as large and irrepressible as his mistakes, as complicated and unreliable as his constituency. And he was too hidebound Democratic to eat canapés as a boost to incumbent Republicanism. He would later confide to a friend—after Nixon was reelected, and Connally switched parties—regarding his apprentice and long-time political right arm, "I should have kept my eye on that boy."

Connally was undeniably tailored to the image of success. He embodied a unique blend of tenacity, charm, and thickness of hide that made him the confidant and troubleshooter for rich and powerful men. He was a winner in an age when leaders were bred to campaigning, unencumbered by moral imperatives, and imbued with celluloid brilliance. Forget party affiliation, the vestigial fin of the old order, and the host of the barbecue became an ideal candidate for anything.

Symmetry was inherent in the gathering. Emerging from the house onto the patio, and moving among the groups of guests, Allan Shivers was a reminder of the more exuberant 1950s. His jacket of green checks was a bit overstated, but his presence was important. Exactly two decades before, Shivers had as Democratic governor led the campaign in the state for the election of Dwight Eisenhower. The Shivercrats were early proof that dominant Democrats in Texas more closely resembled national Republicans than Democrats. Shivers had headed the Texas delegation to the 1952 Democratic Convention after a bitter struggle within the state party that proved to be a watershed. Rayburn and Johnson made sure the Shivercrats were seated as the official delegation, Eisenhower carried Texas, and the liberals never recovered.

Members of the press stayed close to the bar, or talked with the men whose job it was to act as mediators between the public and the powerful. George Christian, whose simple manner belied brains and grit, had served as Johnson's press secretary, a member of Connally's Capitol corps, and a key adviser in the Democrats for Nixon. He shifted easily among the anointed candidates. He would eventually act as an adviser, with Warren Woodward, another ubiquitous political operative, to Bentsen in his campaign for the 1976 Democratic Presidential nomination. Another political packager present, Julian Read, had coordinated Connally's television presentations during his first race in 1961, the most expensive gubernatorial campaign in Texas history. Tall and resolute, Read emulated Connally in most things, dressed as Connally did, walked and spoke in the same manner, and eventually became the only one of the guests to follow him into the Republican fold.

Editors representing various newspapers around the state remained separate from mere reporters. The editor of the Houston *Chronicle,* Everett Collier, was a modest newsman, but an avowed promoter of Connally and his closest friends. He headed Houston's most conservative paper, although some would argue that the difference between it and the Houston *Post* was discernible only to the trained eye. Collier had been one of many to beg Connally to run for a fourth term as governor, so great was the anxiety among his peers that the carefully constructed state machinery might fall into insensitive hands.

Approval by half a dozen such newspapers around the state, and their counterparts in television, was almost tantamount to the success of an issue or a candidate, and Connally had it from all of them. Once he telephoned Collier and asked him to write an editorial urging Crawford Martin to run for the position of attorney general. Collier said he didn't mind writing endorsements, but that no editorial had ever appeared in the *Chronicle* urging someone to run. "There's always a first time, Everett," Connally said.

The guests who had assembled at the barbecue would agree on most candidates and most issues, sometimes publicly. One such cause had been the proposal to divert the Mississippi River to Texas. Without first asking the permission of Louisiana, Governor Smith had three years before formed a Committee of 500, with Connally serving as co-chairman, and lined up the support of Texas congressmen. The scheme was truly Texan: 12 million acre-feet of water transported through concrete ditches 300 feet wide and 40 feet deep, equipped with eighteen dams. A quarter of a million acres in east Texas was to be flooded, and the water piped to other parts of the state. The cost was estimated at slightly less than $14 billion, six times the cost of TVA during the first thirty years of its existence. The federal government would be asked to pay two-thirds of the cost. The desert would bloom, and a few contractors, developers, and speculators would make new fortunes. To everyone's surprise, the voters failed to approve floating the necessary bonds, but the issue was still far from dead among those gathered at Picosa.

It was not incidental that the host's favorite film was *Giant*. So impressed was he by spectacle that he overlooked Hollywood's misrepresentations. He was himself an actor, and a romantic. That the theme song of *Giant* should become an integral part of his 1961 campaign for governor had been preordained, the music swelling and filling hundreds of high-school auditoriums across Texas as Connally mounted the stage.

"People frequently were annoyed by the fact that as they talked to him he appeared not to be listening," Ferber had written of Bick Benedict, idealized heir of the Reata spread. "He listened to nothing that did not vitally interest him. . . ."

Superficially, that description might have suited the gentleman rancher who finally led the President, seemingly a stranger in his own body, off the pavement and onto the grass to view prize bulls. Connally was clearly dominant. Nixon's affection and admiration for him were well known—favor that amounted almost to adulation. Texans present at the White House when Connally took the oath as Treasury Secretary were pleased to see Nixon deferring to him, and at the same time amazed that the President of the United States would allow himself to be so overshadowed. Now Connally elicited from Nixon a mild attempt at wit—"I grew up on Santa Gertrudis Street in East Whittier. But we didn't have any Santa Gertrudis cattle"—and would later present the President to his dinner guests as the willing recipient of their inquiries, a rare stance for Nixon, the leader of a great world power.

They had much in common, however. Both men were Southwesterners, born of large, poor families, who decided early to achieve material success, debating and acting their way through school. Both spent their entire adult life involved in politics, both were the beneficiaries of the actions and backing of older, influential men. They were inordinately ambitious. But perhaps the most important similarity between Connally and Nixon was their Sunbelt conservatism, based upon privilege rather than individual rights.

Indeed, Texas could boast of nurturing this new conservatism. Government rather than the marketplace was considered the prime source of revenue for the large corporations, although their officers would continue to laud free enterprise. Political favor was recognized as more effective—and more desirable—than economic proficiency in meeting with success. Money given to politicians espousing this conservatism—though in fact it was far from being traditionally conservative—was new, money donated for specific purposes by the new barons accustomed to speculating, and solicitous of security in all things.

A daughter—not present at the barbecue—of two of its most prominent guests had become troubled by the political nature of the relationships she observed among her parents' peers. A product of privilege in Texas—she became a friend of Connally's while he was governor and she was a student at the university—she wrote a novel about the society she knew well. It was never published. The notes she jotted down while planning the novel reveal the nature of her anxiety.

"When rich people get bored," she wrote, "they often take to killing things, usually fish, fowl, other mammals, and sometimes each other. . . . A small group of men in power whose private lives are unlike anything the public thinks they are . . . The agony of a decent sensibility discovering great and accepted lies, the fraud and illusion by which much of life is conducted and actions rationalized . . . I read about the poor like I read about the space shots, 'How interesting!' . . . How does a subject become politicized? Why does a man poison his relationships with others by politicizing them?"

The lights blinked on along the runway's edge. The President paused on the patio to allow brief exposure to the press before its members were dispersed; Nixon spoke to them of sports. Then, in a conscious effort to match the occasion, he raised a hand and swept it jerkily across the view. "The sweep of the country," said the President. "This is big country, it produces big men."

The symmetry persisted. The short, stout, weather-beaten man trying unsuccessfully to make conversation with the President was Robert J. Kleberg, Jr., head of the fabulous King Ranch, a million acres spread over Texas's southern tip that was supposedly the model for Ferber's Reata. The Klebergs were the first among the big ranching families; their money was older, and Connally admired their style of life most of all. Kleberg himself worked from six in the morning until dark, and lived in a hacienda of twenty-five rooms on the ranch's Santa Gertrudis division, for he had developed that breed of cattle. Oil produced another $16 million a year for the ranch, and Kleberg had negotiated leases with seven successive presidents of Humble, now Exxon. He owned land in countries as distant as Morocco and Argentina, including 12 million acres in Australia. Within three years, Kleberg would be dead of cancer, and the ranching empire's future would be uncertain.

An element of gaiety became apparent as the guests moved on to dinner, protocol satisfied, hearts warmed by various liquors. The élite character of the gathering would arouse criticism, but they expected that, would not be surprised when a liberal Democratic congressman said of them a few days later, "Like the infamous Appalachian Conference of November 14, 1957, the guest list was kept secret. . . . There can never be tax reform in America as long as the fat cats are protected and pampered by the President of the United States."

In fact, it amused them, for the guests knew only too well that the pampering was mutual. Connally planned to raise at least $2 million through Democrats for Nixon, and already many of them had made contributions before the federal disclosure law had gone into effect earlier that month. These included executives of George Brown's Texas Eastern Transmission Corporation, who gave $30,000, while the same company's employees donated another $30,000. The Murchison brothers gave $50,000, Perry Bass $20,000, Jake Hamon $25,000, James Elkins, Jr., $15,000. And there would be much, much more.

They would not have been surprised if Nixon had chosen Connally as his running mate in the election. If the jettisoning of Vice-President Spiro Agnew proved unacceptable to the Republicans, then Connally could hope to receive Nixon's blessing and support for his own race for President in 1976—no small advantage. And Nixon strengthened such speculation by telling the gathering that his host was "a man who had demonstrated that he is capable of holding any job in the United States."

Connally stood before them following dinner, proving himself accomplished both as statesman and impresario. He was fond of metaphors involving fishing—a favorite was "Don't mess with the top waters," a reference to the small fry that swim close to the surface, in the light —and he indulged himself, and his guests. "I have never learned much in politics," he began, and the smile was appropriately self-deprecating. "But I always learned that you had to fish with live bait. And we are not without some in this gathering this evening."

A significant portion of the bait, money aside, was Texas's twenty-six electoral votes, a fair cushion against

the possible loss of another big state that had not supported Nixon in 1968.

Connally then graciously suggested that the President
might answer questions from the guests.

"I can assure you," said Nixon, rising, "if I don't
know the answers, John will."

"Mr. President," began the inquiry that best expressed
the sentiments of the assembled and now replete Texans,
"Do you anticipate any developments in Vietnam other
than those courageous statements we heard on television
the other night?"

Nixon welcomed the opportunity to speak at length on
this subject. He said that South Vietnam was fighting
well, but required naval and air support from America,
and that he, the President of the United States, planned
to provide it as long as it was required, an assertion that
drew discreet applause. Not to provide support, he
added, would lead to a Communist takeover. That would
weaken the office of the Presidency, his first concern, and
would also damage respect for America abroad, confidence at home, and would lead to other Communist ad-
ventures.

The guests stood almost as one, and toasted their
President, raising high glasses of Moët & Chandon cham-
pagne. So pleased was Nixon that he spoke out forcefully
against busing, and was again toasted and applauded.

Yet irony was a concomitant of success that April
evening. Sitting among the best of Houston's lawyers,
standing with them to drink to the President's health
and the triumph of his policies, was a man who looked
more like a two-fisted ward heeler than a senior partner
in one of the nation's most influential legal firms. He
was Leon Jaworski, a former chairman of Connally's
Governor's Committee on Public Education, who would
play a crucial role in America's most momentous litigation—today no more than a lonely epiphany in the minds
of dreamers and the politically disaffiliated.

And standing on the periphery of the gathering, lamp-tanned and always agreeable, was the Austin attorney and lobbyist Jake Jacobsen. He had long been an associate of the host's, and would play a key role in a controversy that would radically alter the import of that day at Picosa.

The wind had risen, pressing the grass flat and disturbing the heavy, gnarled branches of the oaks that groaned in the darkness. The President and the First Lady were not concerned about the weather, for they were to sleep in the Connallys' master bedroom before continuing on to Washington the next day. But the guests dispersed, with lively shows of gratitude.

The planes warmed with the sound of thunder, passed along the corridor of lights, and ascended into the vast Texas sky. Their passengers had not been disappointed that evening. They were able to take with them the radiant image of their host, and the words of their President.

"Now I have seen," said Nixon, "what Texas is supposed to be."

Interlude

FLORESVILLE

State Highway 181 angles southeast from San Antonio, across uneventful country. Latin fatalism prevails here even among the Anglos, evident in the unpainted clapboard houses with roofs of corrugated iron, the skeletal windmills, the trailers set in weeds, the graveyards for refrigerators and abandoned cars. The billboard advertising Lone Star beer is an adornment. Beyond it stretches the county reservoir, where a man sits on a stump, his cane pole thrust out over dark, motionless water.

Floresville is the seat of Wilson County, and Connally's hometown. "A growing bedroom city," says the sign erected by the Chamber of Commerce, in the hope that San Antonio executives will come this far to build their ranchettes. The little Floresville courthouse was constructed during the Depression, and when I first saw it my eye was drawn not to a statue or a cannon mounted on the lawn but to a six-foot concrete reproduction of a peanut, Wilson County's most profitable crop.

The façade of the Ben Franklin 5 & 10 has been faded by the sun and driven dust, but the bank—said to be owned by Connally—is made of impervious new stucco.

The drugstore has been renovated—it contains a rack of glamour products—and a library has been built behind the courthouse, but the town itself has not changed much in half a century. Men in straw cowboy hats drink draught beer in the cool shadows of the tavern across from the John Deere dealership, and next door the Floresville Recreation Center boasts of half a dozen pool tables with patched felts.

Here in Floresville, Connally's father worked, at various times, as a barber, a butcher, a bricklayer, and a tenant farmer, all without success. John Bowden Connally, Sr.'s, forebears fled the Irish potato famine, and arrived in Wilson County by way of Alabama. His wife was a Wright, and a Methodist, one of the toiling, persevering women of the Southwest who come to exercise a greater influence over the children than the fathers do. The big family was dirt poor. Connally, Sr., borrowed enough money to start a bus line—an Oldsmobile with jump seats—running between San Antonio and Corpus Christi, called the Red Ball Express. Competition was keen, and agents for the big lines often dragged the independent drivers and their passengers from the buses and beat them. Connally held on long enough to sell his line profitably to Greyhound, and bought a ranch outside of Floresville that is now a small part of the Connally estate.

Small-towners are not always kind to the impoverished in their midst, especially if the poor happen to live in the country. The Connallys were considered uppity by Floresville's burghers for buying the land; the term "white trash" wasn't unknown to Connally and his brothers. They never played at sports after school because there was work to be done. Connally remembers cutting knee pads from old tires to wear while dragging a sack among the rows of cotton; as an adult, he once spoke of "breaking the land with a turning plow. Believe it or not, that's a fine sensation. . . . I used to take off my shoes because the soil behind the plow just felt good to walk in."

He probably hated the work, the diet of beans and bread—what he considered degradation. Early on, he discarded the childish ambitions of being a cowboy, a Mountie, a Texas Ranger, and settled upon being a lawyer, an extraordinary objective for a gangling farm boy whose father had no more than a sixth-grade education. His ambition to get up and out was so strong that there was no denying it, and it became manifest in a need to win and upgrade, and not mess with top-water distractions.

A high-school classmate who now sells eggs in a narrow room stacked with cardboard cartons, his radio plugged into a light socket, remembers Connally's ambition. "I never liked being on his volleyball team," the man says reflectively, staring out into the dusty Floresville street. "If somebody made a mistake, he gave 'em hell. . . . Connally was always trying to be high society. My idea of a good time on Saturday night was to get a bottle, but he never did. Connally always wore a tie, and liked to debate."

He lost a debating contest to the son of a Floresville judge. One of Connally's four brothers, Merrill, recalls that John "was by far the better of the two speakers. It was the same old story. The superintendent of the schools was beholden to the district judge, who was part and parcel of the county unit. There was nothing we could do. It was a closed corporation."

Those who know Connally well say he determined to win everything from then on. The experience taught him something about politics; it also confirmed that poor people are natural victims, are losers. Today Connally does not like to hear his family described as "poor"—he prefers "of modest means"—and it is only in the presence of the poor that he ever appears ill at ease.

Connally was cocky, dramatic, given to fits of ire. He

hit a disgruntled cow in the neck with a two-by-four; he and a friend disguised themselves as Mexican bandits and disrupted their church league picnic, causing a sponsor to jump into a washtub full of sandwiches. He was vain. The editors of his high-school annual remarked, "What would happen if Johnnie lost the part in his hair?" His classmates called him "Senator," and applied to him the epigram "They always talk who never think."

Merrill says his brother was "aggressive, not an avid reader, totally normal. The gold Cadillacs and the homburgs aren't part of his real beginnings; people like to put him in the Madison Avenue image. . . . John has no burning desire to be wealthy—he just wants to be *comfortable*, like everybody else. Of course, comfort," he adds, "depends upon the length of your measuring stick."

The road leading out to Picosa passes through the Mexican-American neighborhood, past the Mission Bautista Church, the Wayne Feed Yard, the dump, and across the San Antonio River. After nine miles, the plain of dense coastal Bermuda grass begins, planted as an experiment by the Connallys in forage, and a stark contrast to the other ranches in the area where stands of mesquite have not been jerked out of the earth by huge chains dragged behind Caterpillars. A sign—"CONNALLY HOME RANCH"—has been added to the old place, as has a picket fence, and fresh white paint to the clapboards, now the home of a Mexican-American caretaker. Here ten thousand people sat on hay bales and ate barbecue during Connally's first gubernatorial campaign.

Across the road stands Merrill's contemporary ranch house, set on a watering tank for which he built a dam. The big outboard-inboard parked in his front yard bears the large inscription across the stern "THE CONNALLYS OF FLORESVILLE." Merrill is in the cattle and liquid-fertilizer business with John. He resembles his brother, although he is taller and ascetic-looking. Merrill helped manage his brother's 1962 campaign, displaying organizational talent, and a self-reflection that is alien to John. Merrill once entertained serious political ambitions, but his brother's presence and fierce competitiveness consigned Merrill to contending for minor offices.

"It's a good, clean, independent life," he says, sweeping his hand across the view. "Cattle is the freest of government control of any industry. There's something about a rural, small-town upbringing that builds character, something that goes back to the soil. It's the bootstrap operations, getting somewhere without being given a lot. Americans respect a man who gets out there and takes hold of a job. Like Teddy Roosevelt, or John Wayne. John Connally's a hard-liner in a lot of ways. If he did get to be President, we wouldn't have these little nations kicking at our shins."

Darkness comes suddenly, acquires a grainy, windswept quality. Car radios are popular antidotes to loneliness, filling the air with skittering Mexican violins, or the admonitions of the "Old-Fashioned Gospel Hour." ("I dee double hog-tie dare anyone this side of Heaven or Hell to check our income-tax returns. . . .") It is easy to imagine a poor and ambitious young man quoting Joaquin Miller's "The Defense of the Alamo" to some rancher's daughter, while his 1935 Chevy rattled across the empty land.

2 ☆ SUCCESS IN AMERICA

Connally as Avatar

His mother's image in fair face,
The infant love of all his race.
　　　　　—Lord Byron,
　　　　The Prisoner of Chillon

The University of Texas brought recognition of Connally's real talents. Austin proved to be everything Floresville wasn't: a pleasant foothill city on the Colorado River, free from both the stifling heat and the prejudices of home. He never really looked back until he was able to buy Picosa—and even that set no demons to rest.

He adopted his father's middle name, Bowden, because he had not been given one. Attending UT was not so much an educational experience as a social one, a heady communion of the state's potential leaders, essential for reasons both practical and vaguely patriotic. On campus one made one's contacts for later life, one learned about the *real* Texas. A year or two at an Ivy League school for cotton and cattle scions was all right, but it was downright foolish to graduate up East if one had political aspirations.

It was the UT experience that mattered—the unbridled enthusiasm, the social triumphs, the aura of endless possibility that is so Texan. College remains the zenith for an extraordinary number of Texans, who forty years after graduation insist upon recalling in detail the vagaries of some fraternity election or the unfolding of a football game on a breezy Saturday afternoon.

Connally decided to make it in Austin long before he came in view of the university campus. He was too poor to pledge a fraternity, but would make up for that by defeating the "Greek" candidates for student-body president, and marrying the university sweetheart. He decided to engage in a regimen of what in another age would be called self-improvement. He joined the Wesley Players, the Methodist Church drama group at UT, and the Curtain Club. That Connally would play the coveted lead in Lynn Riggs's *Green Grow the Lilacs,* upon which *Oklahoma!* was based, seemed inevitable. "Connally was a born actor," says a member of the Curtain Club who became curator of the Hoblitzelle Library theater collection. "He could play any part that he wanted, and could have made a career of the theater."

The line separating dramatics and politics was almost nonexistent. He became president of Wesley Players and the Curtain Club, and of the Athenaeum Literary Society, a debating group whose support was essential to a non-Greek candidate for president of the Student Assembly. The friends he made were to help him then and later, men like Robert Strauss, Jake Pickle, Joe Kilgore, Walter Jenkins. Campus politics was a struggle within a composite of the state's social hierarchy; the exposure it and acting provided would be of great benefit as Connally's peers took over law firms or banks or rose with the tide of federal money that flowed into Texas after

World War II. A score of prominent men would years afterward claim to have been Connally's roommate.

Jake Pickle, later to become a United States congressman, was the independent candidate for the presidency of the Student Assembly in 1937. Connally managed Pickle's campaign, advising him to adopt the stance of mock reformer and oppose the influence of fraternities —known as the "clique"—in campus affairs. Pickle won, and the following year he and Connally changed roles. The *Daily Texan* identified Connally with the "machine." He and Pickle divided the campus into the equivalent of precincts, and attempted to limit opposition by proposing that potential candidates be forced to post a five-dollar bond. This failed, but Connally did manage to have his name placed first on the ballot, the best position in a crowded race. Through superior organization—Connally would later bring many of his same people into the National Youth Administration, into Lyndon Johnson's campaigns, and eventually into his own—and hard politicking, Connally became Student Assembly president.

Only to quit. One advantage of being president was that it paid thirty dollars a month, a welcome addition to the money Connally made from selling vacuum cleaners, mints, and chewing gum. But his grades were not as high as those required for the office, since he studied sporadically, aided by a mind of near-photographic capability—a distinct advantage in law school, and a carefully guarded secret. He was bored with the job, and quit, just as he would resign the presidency of the Curtain Club, establishing early a pattern of attaining relatively exalted positions and then abandoning them.

Other traits surfaced—a romantic sense of mission without a specific objective, the rhetorical flourish, an overweening respect for those already in power. He refused to take a stand on censorship of the student newspaper; he agreed with the dean in the administration's battle with the Athenaeum over a meeting hall, earning the nickname "Bow Down Connally"—a reference to his middle name. His favorite novel was *The Count of Monte Cristo,* his favorite poem Byron's *The Prisoner of Chillon*—a fact he often pointed out to reporters in later years, to counter what he considered to be the debilitating provincialism of a man like Lyndon Johnson.

The university was not known for its intellectual rigor; Connally was not so much contemptuous of ideas as he was unburdened by them. He quickly learned that what one says is not nearly so important as how one says it. He could stand up in front of a crowd and be anyone he chose, from a robot in Karl Čapek's futuristic *R.U.R.* to a student candidate with the safest of issues— the cleanliness of the cafeteria. He displayed to many that ineffable quality labeled "leadership" that could as easily pass as hustle. A program for the 1936 university production of S. N. Behrman's *Biography* bears a photograph of Connally in the role of Richard Kurt, his mouth set and eyebrows arched, mannerisms that became as habitual as breathing, and now instantly recognizable.

The New Deal brought Connally to the attention of Lyndon Baines Johnson. In 1936, Connally helped run the campaign of a candidate for attorney general and was subsequently recommended to Johnson, who was head of the National Youth Administration in Texas. They were formally introduced by the independent oilman J. R. Parten, and Johnson told them he would run for Congress with the purpose of "helping Roosevelt pack the Supreme Court."

Johnson was a product of the dour and elemental hill country, but he never experienced deprivation comparable to that known by the Connally family. He recognized what the New Deal could mean to Texas in terms of jobs and such amenities as electricity. But his service as secretary to Congressman Richard M. Kleberg, of the King Ranch, had provided him a firsthand view of

Washington and of political leverage. His fervor for Roosevelt's policies was partly genuine populist sentiment, mostly expediency.

When the Austin congressional seat became vacant, Johnson declared against half a dozen anti-Roosevelt candidates, and won, although the sentiment against Roosevelt in Texas had begun to build. The lesson wasn't lost on Connally. During the campaign, he hung around the office, stuffing envelopes and running errands, and displaying an uncommon poise and assertiveness for a college student. For him the New Deal meant jobs, for himself and many of his friends, and Connally associated himself with what he saw as a winning combination of strong government and "progressive" rhetoric. His later speeches would contain reverberations of New Dealism—phrases such as "greatness for Texas" and "the America of tomorrow"—hollow vessels cut loose from the old moorings of substantive social concern.

Johnson asked Connally to come to Washington as his secretary. The man who was later to manage Johnson's radio and television empire, J. C. Kellam, was asked by Johnson to interview Connally about the job, and Kellam says he advised Johnson not to hire Connally because he was "too able. He won't stay with you." Connally was an impressive young man. Gus Wortham says of Connally, whom he met at this time, "John was the most attractive man I knew. He was sweet, but strong as horse radish. He's not just a promoter, though he is interested in business. We wouldn't have been interested in him if he wasn't."

Connally was hired despite such ableness, and he dropped out of law school to take the job. He had already passed the Texas state bar examination, but didn't complete his course work and obtain a degree until the grade requirements were lowered in 1941. For two years Connally helped run Johnson's office. He became intimately acquainted with Washington, learning Johnson's method of organization, his preference for push over compromise, his attention to detail. According to Connally's brother Merrill, "John was in there with the big boys from the beginning. He didn't have a lot of time to grow up."

Connally returned to Austin to complete his studies, but was soon running Johnson's first campaign for the Senate. He brought in his friends from the university, and from the NYA—men like Kilgore, later a congressman, Pickle, and Strauss. Johnson's opponent was "Pappy" O'Daniel, who attacked the New Dealers as a "gang of back-slapping, pie-eating, pussy-footing professional politicians who couldn't run a peanut stand." Johnson countered by plugging the "military preparedness" theme, his primary appeal to the state's businessmen and future contractors.

Johnson lost, but Connally proved himself as a highly effective organizer who was not afraid to act on his own decisions. He could also stand up to LBJ's temperamental excesses, from which his staffs suffered over the years. Connally was independent enough to provide a valuable foil. He once announced, against Johnson's orders, that Johnson could not meet speaking engagements because of laryngitis. When Johnson and Sam Rayburn became involved in a heated argument in the back seat of a car in Washington that Connally was also riding in, he reportedly stepped out of the car at a stop light and walked away.

Connally seemed willing to overextend himself in Johnson's interest. His political instincts combined with a kind of combative recklessness were invaluable, and Johnson would often use him over the years as a sounding board, and as a hatchet man. George Christian describes their relationship as "a sort of big-brother, little-brother thing."

Connally, says Kilgore, "seemed to know everybody. You'd take a ride with him, and he'd wave at every car."

He was fond of cowboy clothes, and long, dramatic silences. A writer for the Austin *American* spoke of his "wealth of black hair that waves over his head and ends in a senatorial twist at the neck. He has a heavy beard, and although he keeps it cut, its blackness gives him that heavy-jowled look that belies his age, which is only 24."

He joined the Navy after Pearl Harbor, and came out as a lieutenant commander, ready to make money. All he needed to be a success was credit, according to a friend, and he got that credit from the Capitol National Bank in Austin, where one of the principals was Herman Brown, financial backer of Johnson's campaigns. The money—$25,000—bought Connally an interest in KVET, a radio station organized by veterans, including Pickle, Kellam, and Merrill Connally; Walter Jenkins, later Johnson's Presidential assistant; Robert Phinney, who became district collector for the Internal Revenue Service; the Austin lawyer Ed Clark; and Willard Deason, who would become a member of the Interstate Commerce Commission. They formed the nucleus of Johnson's second race for the Senate, and would all provide invaluable contacts for Connally through the years.

A photograph taken at the time shows Connally wearing a set of earphones, working as a disk jockey, shortly before he managed Johnson's 1948 campaign for the Senate. By then he was well acquainted with the brawling tradition of Democratic politics in Texas, and good at it. Johnson had trouble making up his mind to run, and the threat of a Connally candidacy instead helped bring him round. Connally was already a political pro, personable, and his whole family would have campaigned for him. Johnson's opponent, Coke Stevenson, would have won the election if 203 votes had not been discovered at the last minute and added to the returns from Box 13 in Alice after the polls had closed.

That all those votes but one had been cast for Johnson was considerably more than a coincidence, and earned him the nickname of "Landslide Lyndon." The historical significance of the extra votes in Box 13 has probably been exaggerated, since Johnson was an undeniable force in the state, and would have surfaced elsewhere if he had not been elected then. But the charade in Alice was a typical act of expediency in American politics, and proved that Johnson and his lieutenants would go to great lengths to win.

Connally served for a while as Senator Johnson's administrative aide, but returned to Austin soon to pursue his own fortune. He was taken on by the law firm of Alvin J. Wirtz, the man who introduced Johnson to Herman Brown, and the good angel of the budding establishment in Texas. But Connally left the firm after Wirtz's death. For a short period he was unemployed, waiting for the right break, drinking coffee with the pols and the lobbyists from the state capitol, a young man with good connections and a habitual pair of khaki trousers, who seemed oddly at loose ends. He carried a cigarette lighter which, if his critics and some friends are to be believed, he used only to light the cigarettes of rich men. It was a crucial time in an already full and singleminded career.

Oil served as the conduit between potential and realization. Sid Richardson, Texas wildcatter and one of the richest men in the country, told his friend Johnson that he needed someone to help look after his varied interests, particularly in relation to Washington. Johnson recommended Connally. Richardson's primary interests were related to oil and gas—the oil depletion allowance, and regulation of the price of natural gas by the Interstate Commerce Commission—and Connally understood the workings of Congress.

Richardson invited Connally to visit him at the Fort Worth Club, where the two of them talked well into the night. Richardson lacked most social graces, and was impressed by the young man's poise. Connally was hired for his good common sense, according to the official version of their meeting, and told by Richardson that he would be put "in the way to make some money."

Richardson and his nephew Perry Bass had large investments besides those in oil and gas, including real estate, broadcasting, retailing, and ranching. Connally moved to Fort Worth, learned to play golf as an aspiring diplomat must learn bridge, and acted as a general manager and political overseer of the Richardson holdings. He loved the work, which was easier than operating for Lyndon, and certainly more lucrative.

Most of all, he loved the money, its presence, and the company it kept. For him rich people really were different, and in their interests he developed a facility with the bromide and an assertiveness that characterized him while he was still a young man. He also developed a toughness as impressive as his theatrical appearance, a toughness associated not with principle but with political advantage. The endless caucuses, and now board meetings, bolstered an ambition without specific objective other than wealth.

Connally arrived as Richardson's emissary to Washington, wearing wing-tip two-tone shoes, and a straw boater with a brightly colored band. He regularly used Johnson's Capitol Hill office to entertain prominent figures in the oil and gas industry, or his own suite at the Mayflower. He refused to register as a lobbyist, even at Johnson's urging, claiming that he had his own investments, and was looking after his own interests.

He was one of the most effective lobbyists during the 1956 debate over freeing the price of natural gas from federal control. He became known as one of the Gold Dust Twins, the other twin being Connally's friend, and a Texan, Elmer Patman, lobbyist for William Keck's Superior Oil. Both men worked diligently in favor of the

Senate bill for decontrol, a bill introduced by Majority Leader Johnson.

Meanwhile, the oil industry had become so inured to dispensing money for political favors that it had become sloppy. A veritable blizzard of cash blew through Congress during the deregulation debate, and $2,500 of it landed unadorned on the desk of Senator Francis Case, a Republican from South Dakota. Case announced the bribery attempt, thereby breaking the unwritten rule that no senator even mentions anything that might embarrass another senator—particularly when he happens to be the Majority Leader.

Connally left Washington the day of Case's announcement. He did not return to Texas, but flew instead to Las Vegas. A few days later he met another prominent oil lobbyist in the airport coffee shop. According to the lobbyist, Connally asked if he intended to implicate Connally in the scandal. "I can take the heat," the lobbyist told Connally. "That's what I'm paid to do."

An investigation became unavoidable. Johnson got his vote on the bill, and he also managed to get a separate Senate inquiry that limited the scope of the investigation of the bribe attempt, which had threatened to cover contributions "by any persons directly or indirectly favoring passage of the gas bill." Johnson called the Senate into surprise session an hour early, passing the measure restricting the investigation. A special committee was carefully weighted against producing further revelations damaging to certain senators, or to the oil industry.

However, he still had the standing Senate Elections Subcommittee to worry about, which he had to prevent from asking embarrassing questions. In this he received help from an unlikely source—Vice-President Richard Nixon. Nixon had his own reasons for wishing to limit any investigation of the oil and gas industry: Oilmen were his biggest contributors. Most of the money in his secret slush fund—the subject of his Checkers speech—

came from oilmen. So Nixon agreed to entertain the first meeting of the special committee in his own office, where it was hastily ruled that the standing Elections Subcommittee had no jurisdiction in the case.

Then Johnson called Senator Thomas Hennings of Missouri, head of the Elections Subcommittee, into his office, and told Hennings he was in contempt of the Senate for attempting to investigate the attempted bribery of Case. Johnson proclaimed that the special committee, not Hennings's subcommittee, would "put the influence peddlers in a strait jacket." It did considerably less than that. Connally's friend Elmer Patman and John Neff, another Texan and lobbyist for Superior Oil, were simply accused of "galloping irresponsibility." William Keck, president of Superior, was absolved of blame.

The official story was that Patman had brought twenty-five hundred-dollar bills to Neff, who then delivered the money to Case's campaign headquarters in Sioux Falls. Both claimed the money was a contribution, not a bribe. The special committee welcomed that fine distinction, but the public did not. The Justice Department eventually prosecuted Patman, Neff, and—oddly enough—Superior Oil instead of Keck. Patman and Neff were fined $2,500 apiece, and Superior Oil $10,000, after company representatives pleaded guilty to aiding and abetting violations of the federal lobbying laws. Patman and Neff were given suspended sentences by a judge who could not see how any "useful purpose" could be served by imprisonment.

The natural-gas bill passed, but Eisenhower was forced to veto it because of the adverse publicity.

At home in Texas, Connally was known as Johnson's emissary, and his opinions carried weight. The Democratic party in Texas had less and less in common with the national Democrats. It was Connally who announced in 1960 that John Kennedy was suffering from a "fatal" disease, and being kept alive by large doses of cortisone

—an attempt to offset knowledge that Lyndon Johnson had a bad heart. This was the first public manifestation of Connally's dislike of the Kennedys. During the 1960 convention, when Robert Kennedy advised Johnson to withdraw because of opposition within the party to his candidacy, Connally snapped at Kennedy, "Who's the candidate, you or your brother?" In Texas, Connally raised money for Johnson's Presidential candidacy primarily by attacking John Kennedy as having interests contrary to those of wealthy Texans.

An obvious source of Connally's antipathy was the fact that the Kennedys were Eastern "liberals," and less than enamored of Lyndon Johnson. But there was another reason. The Kennedys had inherited their wealth, and its advantages; they had not spent most of their lives scrambling and plotting their rise. Yet they had great popular appeal, as well as their father's money, a combination Connally must have found difficult to forgive.

Kennedy's appointment of Connally as Secretary of the Navy was an act of appeasement—of Johnson and Sam Rayburn, and of oil money in Texas. Connally stayed in that office for less than a year.

Connally's options were limited in 1961. He had served in the shadow of bigger and richer men; one was subservient to a Kennedy, the other, Richardson, had died in 1959. Although Connally was well thought of by Richardson's heirs, he was not family. The $800,000 he received as executor of Richardson's estate and the contacts he had made in Richardson's service were his reward. A high political office at home was a way of utilizing these contacts, and excellent preparation for making one's own fortune—one that could count in Texas. He decided to run for governor.

"I never expected John to run for office," said John

Singleton, once a member of LBJ's youth corps, and now a federal judge in Harris County, appointed by Johnson. "I told him he would have to get down on the level of the people, that I couldn't see him shaking hands, and kissing babies and Negroes. Lyndon loved people, but not Connally. I just couldn't think of him as a candidate. He was always the man coming in the back door."

A feeling existed among rich Texans that the Democratic party in the state was becoming too Democratic, too closely identified with the working people and labor unions. Also, the Republicans threatened to become a reality, with John Tower seen as the unlikely living proof. A candidate was needed who could smite the Republicans, and at the same time render the Democrats respectable and thoroughly safe for the establishment.

Connally secured pledges and money from among friends in Fort Worth, Dallas, and Houston. When he met with his prospective backers and organizers at Dolph Briscoe's Catarina Ranch in south Texas, his mind was already made up to run. Some of his friends still had doubts, after watching Connally step off the plane from Washington wearing a homburg and a vest, that he had any possibility of being elected.

Briscoe's ranch was a frequent meeting place for politicians and organizers. Briscoe himself led hunts in jeeps equipped with special controls, so that the community chase became a kind of automated shooting gallery conducted over many of his 165,000 acres. Among those attending Connally's initial planning session were Lloyd Bentsen, Frank Erwin, and Ben Barnes, then a member of the Texas legislature and the brightest young face in state politics. Eugene Locke, a wealthy Dallas attorney picked by Connally to manage his campaign, spent much of the evening on his hands and knees in the middle of the floor, pointing to maps and attempting to convince the others that the campaign should be organized around the state's big shopping centers.

Connally and Robert Strauss would raise close to a million dollars for the campaign. Money was no problem; learning the system was. Early in the campaign, he appeared before the Texas Automobile Dealers Association and gave a speech that one member considered "the worst I ever heard. I never knew a man who knew less about state government. . . . We held another breakfast meeting for him about two months later, and I never heard a man who knew more about state government."

Campaign publicity was handled by Julian Read, who had earlier lent his talents to the Eisenhower effort in Texas, and would make Connally's the first sophisticated, homogenized gubernatorial campaign.

"Before that time," says Read, "campaigns were amateurish. Now our plan was to utilize the media in the best possible way for this candidate. Until then, we hadn't even had coordination of graphics, but with Connally's star quality we could do things. There was a dramatic quality about him that made everything play better. His best quality was assimilation of information —everything seemed to come out of *him*. We didn't have to be fearful of what he would say. Even if he said something unwise, it sounded good. . . . John Connally may be the best candidate in the history of politics."

Connally's avowed platform was Texan greatness, his real platform the preservation of the one-party system and the entrenched powers that would profit by control and direction in the statehouse. The young editor of the *Texas Observer*, Willie Morris, wrote that the impact of Connally's winning "would be far-reaching and disastrous. His present political power, a lesson from the Lyndon Johnson primer, comes from the top down, through the big law firms, the banks, Brown & Root.

Johnson never had, as such, an extensive precinct organization. He has traditionally played the various
political groupings one against the other, using the liberal or the conservative organizations to his advantage
as the times demanded."

Connally narrowly defeated Don Yarborough (no relation to Ralph) in the election. But his first term was
not promising. It was a time of apparent insecurity in
his relations with politicians on the mere state level, and
of floundering on issues of policy. Connally could not
seem to accustom himself to dealing with the legislature,
a dull and demeaning process.

His appointments were predictable and uninspired.
Strauss went to head the state banking board, Erwin to
the university board of regents. The governor of Texas
does not possess great power, and Connally acted to offset this by carefully picking the heads of commissions
and regulatory boards. He combined the old Game and
Fish Commission and the state parks board into a new
body called the Parks and Wildlife Commission. It had
jurisdiction over the vast public lands and waterways of
the state, and absolute control over the shell-dredgers of
the Gulf, big contributors and loyal friends who gained
access to some $100 million worth of new spoils during
Connally's administration.

The wounding of Connally during the assassination of
President Kennedy rendered Connally unbeatable in
Texas, and identified him with a brief, radiant Kennedy
era for which he had no sympathy. Kennedy's trip to
Texas was in part an attempt to heal the rift in
the Texas Democratic party, split between the liberal
faction led by Ralph Yarborough and the dominant
Johnson-Connally conservative wing. Kennedy also
wished to appear as representative of all the people, un-
affected by party or ideological squabbles, and it was
just that image of the President that Connally could not
abide.

Connally's resistance to the visit was broadly based. He did not want an outsider he disliked attracting more attention than himself in Texas. More important, Connally did not want it made apparent that he was not in control of all the Democrats at home.

The atmosphere at the statehouse prior to the visit was one of smoldering resentment. The advance man sent from Washington to Austin to make arrangements was given a chair at the end of a long conference table and served a sandwich, while Connally, wearing cowboy boots, took a chair at the other end and ate a thick steak. When the advance man explained that the final decisions about the visit must be made in Washington, Connally jumped up from the table and telephoned directly to the White House. He told Kenny O'Donnell, Kennedy's appointments secretary, what the Governor of Texas wanted done, and then stalked out of the room.

Connally agreed to appear with Kennedy at a luncheon at the Trade Mart, which had ceilings high enough to permit the building of tiers on the dais that would elevate Connally and the President above the Yarborough faction. The selling of tickets to various fund-raisers was casual and desultory, for making Kennedy look weak in Texas was both a personal gratification to Connally and a shrewd political move.

During Kennedy's visit, Connally pushed ahead of him to shake hands with spectators. His popularity was at a low level, as a poll in the Houston *Chronicle* indicated, his chances of re-election just about even. The assassination changed all that. Connally and Nellie rode in the limousine with Kennedy and Jackie, and the bullet that passed through Connally's lung would almost certainly have killed him if he hadn't slumped forward and stemmed the flow of blood.

The tenor of Connally's statehouse changed after he recovered from his wounds. It became mock-regal, a bit smug, with the Governor's inaccessibility a matter of pride. The sartorial bias changed from ranch suits and boots to a more Eastern sheen, with the men about the Governor reflecting his concern with grooming and his determination not to be too closely identified with things Texan. His second and third terms were uneventful—a gradual consolidation of power, and the stimulation of business and industry.

Connally spoke out against Medicare, opposed federal anti-poverty programs, and civil-rights laws. In the 1962 campaign against Don Yarborough, he had denounced him as part of a "diabolical plan" of the "left-wing radical Americans for Democratic Action" and Eastern labor organizers, who were supposedly out to seize control of Texas. He then attacked his Republican opponent in the election as a "renegade turncoat opportunist" because he had once been a Democrat.

Spending was one outstanding policy of Connally's three terms as governor, during which time the state budget rose from $1.46 billion to $2.5 billion. Much of that went to education, and to promotion of industry and tourism. He turned San Antonio's HemisFair, supposedly a tribute to Texan cultural diversity, into a paean to big business, and raised bank interest rates. Texas still had no minimum-wage law, and the lowest weekly benefits to injured workers in America.

Connally's reaction to a march in 1966 by farm laborers was a personal one, and representative of those who supported him. The laborers were seeking $1.25 an hour in wages, and marching up from south Texas to Austin to dramatize their request. But before they arrived, on Labor Day, Connally took his attorney general and Ben Barnes and drove south toward the marchers, meeting them in New Braunfels. Connally got out of the car long enough to tell the leaders of the march that he would not "lend the dignity, the prestige" of the governor's office to their cause by receiving them at the Capitol.

By the end of his third term, Connally was excruciat-
ingly bored with the governorship. He was rarely available to anyone outside his close circle of advisers. Office
workers signed much of his correspondence, and once a
mail clerk was brought up to Connally's office to pose as
the Governor, and shake hands with a prominent Japanese businessman.

His decision not to run for a fourth term threw his
supporters into a crisis. In that novel written about the
establishment by the young woman who belonged to it,
the Governor of Texas, Michael Chambers, is determined not to run for another term in spite of the fact
that "a number of men had spent significant amounts of
money on him, directly and indirectly, and had grown
used to commanding respect . . . in the governor's office.
. . . They would miss having a friend in power."
Chambers tells his young friend that he is going home
"and raise cows. I'm going to party and screw around
and play with power and get rich."

Connally was Texas's favorite-son candidate at the 1968
Democratic Convention in Chicago. His choice for his
own successor at home was Eugene Locke, a smooth but
indifferent candidate with little appeal beyond the
nineteenth hole. When Locke held a fund-raiser in Dallas
featuring a symphony orchestra, establishment figures
began to wonder how he would go over in Lubbock. The
largesse of Herman Brown and others finally settled on
Preston Smith, a malapropic but more appealing former
lieutenant governor who had proved malleable, and was
elected in spite of himself.

Connally took his 1968 convention role personally. The
day Johnson announced he would not seek another term
as President, Connally called a midnight meeting at
the governor's mansion. It included Frank Erwin and
Connally's brother Merrill, who had been left to manage

Locke's foundering campaign. Connally was determined to block any move by Robert Kennedy to get the Democratic nomination.

He also had his own aspirations. After the state executive committee unanimously endorsed Connally as favorite son, he went on statewide television to claim that he had no "personal ambitions" to be President of the United States, but that there would be "no more John Nance Garner, or Lyndon B. Johnson to help Texans. . . . My deep concern for the loss of Texas leadership in Washington . . . caused me to agree to become a favorite-son candidate." He then spoke of the necessity of bringing about "an honorable end to the war in Vietnam."

The murder of Robert Kennedy in Los Angeles removed the primary object of his maneuvering. Connally flew to Chicago three days before the convention began with a double motive: to get himself picked as Vice-President on the ticket with Hubert Humphrey, and to prevent a denunciation of the war in Vietnam. He pushed the platform committee toward a strong affirmation of Johnson's policies, which also reflected upon him and upon Texas, at the same time condemning the most prominent of the doves, Eugene McCarthy and George McGovern.

Texas became the target at the convention of all who were opposed to the war. The delegation was challenged as unrepresentative, and the rules committee voted to abolish the unit rule whereby a state may vote as a unit, disregarding minority votes within the delegation.

Connally, tight-lipped, ashen-faced, met with Humphrey in the latter's suite at the Conrad Hilton, where Connally told him they weren't "going to change the rules in the middle of the game." He said that the violence outside the convention hall was giving Democrats a bad name, and that Humphrey should stand up for law and order, publicly commending Mayor Daley's forces.

The message was brutally delivered, and although Humphrey commended no one, he did remain above the struggle.

In the fetid, surreal atmosphere of Chicago in 1968, some unlikely things occurred. One was the official proposition that Connally run as McCarthy's Vice-President, put to Connally in Robert Strauss's suite by Richard Goodwin, McCarthy's aide. They spent four hours together—much too long for an unequivocal refusal. Connally later said to friends, "Well, I hope you're not mad. I just gave away half the patronage in the country."

The Texas delegation was challenged on the floor of the convention, and Texas's speakers were booed. The liberals' challenge was defeated, but Connally did not consider that victory enough. He felt soiled by association with Chicago in 1968. Angry and embarrassed by the ill will shown to Texans, and wary of the possibility that Edward Kennedy might be drafted, he finally released his Texas delegates. He left bruised and defiant —and almost a Republican.

When Humphrey visited Texas the following September, Connally ignored him. But he did find time to visit with the state Republican chairman, oilman William P. Clements, Jr., and Ben Carpenter, Dallas patriarch and chairman of Texans for Nixon. Connally advised them that the country would be "better off" if Nixon was elected, and provided the names of rich Democrats he felt would contribute to Nixon's campaign.

Shortly before the election, Connally did agree to appear briefly with Humphrey and Ralph Yarborough. That required the best efforts of his friend Strauss, in the interest of the hoary illusion of unity among Democrats, and a hole card in the off chance that Humphrey was elected. Connally would later pay for "cratering"— Texas political jargon for caving in under pressure. An associate of President Nixon's said of Connally shortly after the election, "If that fellow had a few more guts, he'd be Secretary of Defense today."

Within weeks of the expiration of his third term as governor, Connally joined one of the most prestigious of the big Houston law firms, which thus became Vinson, Elkins, Searls, Connally & Smith. His salary was a quarter of a million dollars a year; and his effectiveness was soon to be greatly enhanced by his role in the Nixon administration.

Connally's appointment as Treasury Secretary in December, 1970, astounded many people both at home and in Washington. Nixon was attempting by this appointment to accomplish in the country at large what the establishment had done in Texas for years: provide a home for tory Democrats. At the same time, the President was thereby giving his administration the appearance of bipartisan support, gaining a tough and articulate advocate, and, by no means least, securing Texas for the 1972 election.

Connally admittedly knew little about the Treasury Department, and less about economics. His functions were similar to those he performed in the private sector —offering solid advice, and representing well his client's views before various government bodies. He provided an attractive and forceful personality unhampered by protocol or accountability, bypassing the men surrounding the President and earning their silent enmity. In the Nixon administration, Connally stood out like a brass spittoon in a funeral parlor.

Some journalists criticized his opportunism, his outrageous ego, the obvious pleasure he took in offering facile testimony. His mind was termed hydrofoil; it was said that he had no depth. But some respected newspaper columnists were firmly on Connally's side. James Reston described him as "a really bold man in a field of doubters and pretenders." Joseph Alsop picked Connally as "one of the half-dozen ablest members of the Cabinet in the last fifty years," and Joseph Kraft felt that Connally was "at one with the political and economic realities of American life."

Connally could get things done, he took sides openly and unequivocally. Pragmatism was a woefully inadequate description of his style. He opposed tax cuts on the basis of intuitive "feel," rather than testing the strength of "bare statistics." He advocated low interest rates, not for the benefit of the small borrower but because high credit costs were hurting big business. Contradiction didn't bother him, although it upset some subordinates.

Connally took an obvious pride in terming himself "a sort of bully-boy of the manicured playing fields of international finance." That was a tribute both to latent Texas xenophobia, and to his precipitous opposition to a rise in the price of gold. He was telling the world that the United States had decided to look after itself first, but his delivery of this information was unnecessarily combative.

Smaller nations got their shins kicked first, and resoundingly. A Washington lawyer and career civil servant, who had the opportunity to observe Connally closely, says, "Nowadays you don't just go in and tell your counterpart from another country that you're going to screw him. It's not very diplomatic. Connally's actions came at a time when our balance of payments was off. His position worked then, but later it came back to haunt us."

Connally at Treasury had brought a whiff of the yard to a sequestered institution, and the twang of political expediency left over from the Great Society. In instructing subordinates, he liked to indulge in such down-to-earth expressions as "Go run your traps" (meaning to gather more information). At the same time, however, he wore expensively tailored suits, a formal gray hat with a thin black band, and was usually chauffeured around in his white Mercedes. His fastidiousness was legend. Connally's former aide in Texas, Mike Meyers, told Connally's Texas biographers, Jack Keever and Ann Crawford, "Connally thinks things should be proper, your desk, your conduct. . . . Everything should be proper, should be done properly. You should never make an ass of yourself. . . . Some great men have made asses of themselves, but you are never going to catch John Connally making an ass out of himself."

Control was another paramount virtue. Once a private airplane in which Connally was traveling encountered a severe storm, and seemed destined to crash. The plane's owner, a Texan accustomed to squalls, was terrified. For twenty harrowing minutes Connally sat and read a magazine, before finally turning to his companion and saying, "I don't know about you, but this scares the shit out of me."

Connally's definitive act as Treasury Secretary was his sponsorship of the $250 million federal loan guarantee to Lockheed Aircraft Corporation. Weapons had long occupied a special place in the hearts of Texans. They had been eager and prominent members of military appropriations committees since the Second World War, when the state was a center for military training and manufacture, as well as the scene of widespread scandals involving misuse of federal funds. Johnson fought for military appropriations for Texas during the Eisenhower years, thereby securing establishment support at home.

The weapons industry in Texas boomed with Vietnam. The equity value of corporations based in Texas rose accordingly. In 1964, the state ranked eleventh in defense spending, a year later it ranked eighth. By the last quarter of 1967, Texas had soared to second position—just behind California—with expenditures totalling $1.5 billion. During that same period, spending for government contracts around the country rose 55 percent, yet in Texas they grew 460 percent, with many of the funds going to NASA's Houston Space Center.

Federal subsidies in Texas greatly contributed to the extraordinary growth of conglomerates and holding companies. Public money created a kind of feudal barony in casual fief to Washington, and that barony was a new power center in America. National security was the vague justification—even in outer space—the funding of large, diverse corporations the objective. Nominally conservative Texans saw no conflict here, since that conservatism was based on the cost-plus contracting (cost of production plus an agreed rate of profit) of the Depression, the sole, perverse remnant of the New Deal in Texas. This hybrid so dear to Connally and Nixon favored an ever-increasing role by the federal government in maintaining social order, providing a favorable climate for commerce and money for the giants. Free enterprise was for *small* operations, and supplied a vocal defense against threatened tax reform or anti-trust activity. It was a kind of privileged Socialism that benefited the already wealthy, and filtered down to others in the form of job security and guaranteed incomes.

Connally pursued the Lockheed loan relentlessly, aided by Representative Price Daniel and by Jake Jacobsen. He searched the House Committee on Banking and Currency for those members favorable to the loan, those opposed, and those uncommitted. According to a committee staff member, "Connally did one hell of a lobbying job. If he had to personally go and see the lowest guy on the committee, he went. And he didn't try to be the big administration dog. He knew the committee members didn't know much about the facts, that they didn't really have time to learn, and were mostly concerned about the politics of the loan. That was his bag."

The fact that Lockheed had subcontracts in congressional districts all over America, employing 60,000 people, was not lost upon either Connally or Nixon.

Lockheed received the loan guarantee, and Connally took no chances of having his victory reversed. He refused to allow the Comptroller General of the United States to audit records of the government's proceedings.

Connally's resignation from Treasury came at the height of his influence in Washington. Before returning to his law firm in Houston, where he would reap the fruits of his Washington labor, Connally traveled around the world, ostensibly to explain Nixon's policies to allies and friends. The trip took him to all the major oil-producing nations—including an unscheduled stop in Iran. He was the most influential private citizen in America.

Democrats for Nixon sprang from seeds sown in 1969. Connally and Nixon had entertained common interests for twenty-five years, those interests as varied as strident anti-Communism and oil. A godly connection between the two was Billy Graham. Nixon's real interest in Connally developed when Connally dropped by the White House and announced that he was available for advice—and to solicit contributions, a gesture that was greatly appreciated. He knew where the power would lie in Washington for many years, and saw a role there for himself in swinging national Democrats in the direction of Democrats at home. The new majority seemed real enough at the time, Connally its ideal advocate.

Nixon appointed him to the Advisory Council on Executive Organization. The resentment felt by Agnew and by senior White House aides bypassed by Connally—Ehrlichman would praise Connally, between clenched teeth, for his "great loyalty"—was lost on Nixon. He often telephoned Connally at his law offices in Houston, and Connally had greater access to the President than Cabinet members. After Connally had become Treasury Secretary, Nixon referred to himself as the coach, Connally as the quarterback. When it became public knowledge that Connally would head Democrats for Nixon, he was invited to accompany Nixon and "Bebe" Rebozo to Robert Abplanalp's island in the Bahamas, the highest of courtesies.

Connally announced his support for Nixon shortly after returning from his trip around the world. His friend and associate George Christian suggested the name "Democrats for Nixon," and the idea that the organization should stress opposition among Democrats to McGovern's "isolationism and radicalism." Connally, Christian, and Jacobsen met in Washington to plan their strategy.

Their primary aim was to raise money. This was accomplished by providing names of people to be solicited to the Nixon organization, holding parties at Picosa, and making Connally a highly visible advocate of Nixon and administration policies. Connally was particularly well received in California, where his television broadcast attacking McGovern displayed his talents as a political infighter, and as a ruthless disciple of others more powerful than himself. The broadcast cost more than $100,000, and was probably the most effective single effort of Nixon's 1972 campaign.

Invoking the name of the Democratic party, Connally launched a slashing attack on McGovern that can justly be compared to the style of Senator Joseph McCarthy. He lauded Nixon for his skillful accommodation of Russia and China, and at the same time characterized McGovern as a Communist sympathizer by scornfully quoting McGovern's remark that the Soviets "would regard me as a friend, and would do everything they could to keep my friendship." Connally claimed that McGovern had compared George Washington to Ho Chi Minh, a reference that Connally's aides were never able to substantiate.

He accused McGovern of cowardice in foreign policy

"He is out of touch with the real world," Connally said. He called McGovern's proposal to cut military spending "the most dangerous document ever seriously put forth by a Presidential candidate in this century." He then invoked the names of Wilson, Roosevelt, Truman, Kennedy, and Johnson—with accompanying photographs— as being representative of a tradition basically at odds with McGovern. Many Democrats, Connally declared— without the faintest glimmer of hesitation at such ultimate hypocrisy—"agree with John Kennedy's comment that sometimes party loyalty asks too much."

Connally's conversion to the Republican party was its own unique form of deviation. That he saw himself as the savior of America's Sunbelt against the Eastern liberals is almost axiomatic—the only man in Connally's own expansive view who could successfully oppose Teddy Kennedy. This was to be Connally's final role, and the manifestation of Texan "greatness."

It is the great irony of his career that he has never attained what he has most desired, which is not simply money, or power. Talent and intelligence have been diluted by other instincts; his failing is emotional. None of the rich Texans who graced his Picosa lawn that April evening would follow him into the Republican party (with the exception of Julian Read)—they would not be guilty of such a breach of the code. Party affiliation was not important, belonging was. Connally had proved himself reluctant to blend into the gray nimbus of Texas wealth and influence, had jeopardized his membership for the sake of some vague, disproportionate need that was rooted, some of the guests later suggested, in his past.

Interlude

THE EDGE OF THE COUNTRY

A damp chill hangs over San Diego in September, 1973. The parched hills of Mission Valley provide the backdrop for the Republican State Convention, where Connally is to deliver the main address on Saturday night. It is his official debut in his new party, and a calculation: California and Texas have more in common than oil and grapefruit. Or so Connally seems to believe.

The setting is auspicious. Acres that a few years ago supported only a burger stand, sagebrush, and an occasional flash flood are now fast in concrete, shaped for the maximum attraction of large cars and their inhabitants —rectilinear hospitality that offers the illusion of comfort, the inconvenience of too much space, and the reality of hard cash and fleeting service. (Try to hail a bellboy, rampant on his golf cart.) The motif is Luau Gothic. Cunning walkways lead to boutiques, to restaurants with names suggesting piracy, or to nowhere at all. The pool is edged with Astroturf; the cabana is topped with a gigantic replica of a carved mask, with a gas flame fluttering in the breeze.

Connally comes as supplicant to the country club. It is the beginning of another bad season in the worst year yet for the GOP, and the men wearing madras jackets and lacquered Guccis and women hung with gold pendants fashioned into elephants with jeweled tusks search for the Golden West Room and the assurance of their leaders. They are worried about Watergate, Agnew's impending indictment, the fact that Reagan has failed to dismantle the Democratic party in California. Connally is a welcome diversion, a potential Presidential candidate of brilliance, an ally in time of need who may be trusted with pool privileges.

The room where Connally is to hold a press conference is crowded, the hot television lights throwing shadows of contesting bodies across the door through which he is to pass. The young organizers could all pass for Jeb Magruder in their dark blazers and neatly trimmed hair, their walkie-talkies reverberating with a blend of sports argot and words created by IBM.

Connally enters, tall and resonant of voice, as he confers briefly with George Christian. He wears a blue suit, blue shirt, and blue tie that complement his silver hair, and his eyes are the color of prepared mustard. He looks like a photogenic TWA pilot who has been kicked upstairs into public relations.

Is he a Presidential candidate for 1976?

"I'm not ruling it in, and I'm not ruling it out. . . . I'm not driven to be President of this country."

He pronounces it "cuntri," with a trace of south Texas drawl. The fingertips are manicured, but the lumpish chin belongs to a country boy who has known some hard work and deprivation.

Should Nixon hand over the tapes?

After some thoughtful evasion, "I suppose if *I* were President, there might be times when I would have to record conversations, but I would be extremely reluctant."

Is there any conflict of interest in Connally's involvement in the Russian gas deal?

Connally confronts problems as if he is squinting into the sun. This problem issues from the mouth of an earnest, bearded young man, who is referring to a proposal to bring Siberian gas to America, a deal worth several billion dollars that involves some of Connally's oldest associates, and stands to make millions of dollars in legal fees alone for his big Houston law firm.

"Conflict of interest? . . . Why, if this country needs hydrocarbons, and I can help make them available to Americans, where is the conflict of interest?"

Connally's earnestness can match that of any examiner. His brows shuttle up and down, his mouth forms a tight loop of sincerity that the cameras can best appreciate.

What role does he hope to play in the Republican party?

"I'm just a fellow with ideas and information not available to all."

That is a fair, if modest, appraisal. Within twenty-four hours he will personally advise Nixon not to hand over the tapes under any circumstances, and to launch a counterattack with the appearance of candor and gut outrage. He will state publicly that there are times when a President of the United States would be right in ignoring a decision of the Supreme Court.

Connally is linked to Nixon like a rhinestone yo-yo. He hesitates out there in the political ionosphere, spinning off shafts of refracted light that have very real value in the financial world. And why had he recently left his post as Nixon's special adviser?

"Hell, I didn't leave mad. I couldn't *afford* to stay any longer."

The theory is that he was "mousetrapped" by Nixon. After Connally refused to join those in the Watergate bunker, Nixon simply made the announcement that he

had been recruited as a special adviser, and Connally
had no choice but to hole up in the Mayflower for a time.
Or so the story goes.

To close, Connally offers a gratuity: "The press should
ask hard questions. That's your job. If I was in your
place, I'd ask hard questions, too."

A *Newsweek* reporter says with dogged admiration,
"He plays us like a piano." And a local television reporter adds, "You'd buy a used car from that man. You'd
buy one with no hood and no fenders, pay twelve percent
interest over forty-eight months, and think you'd been
done a service."

A Texan can feel at home in southern California. More
immigrants here come from the Lone Star State than
from any other. They remain nominal Democrats, but
vote Republican. California and Texas are still the biggest recipients of defense spending. Southern Califor-
nians, like Texans, are greatly attached to their property
—the outward sign of some inner grace. They are descendants also of movers across the latter-day frontier
from small towns in the Midwest, the border states, and
the South. Today they wouldn't consider actually living
in a small town, but they have retained the small-
towner's notion that his way of life is the only way. The
rate of economic growth is the key to political life in the
Sunbelt, where cities like Houston and Atlanta have
much more in common with Los Angeles than with
Charleston. The success story is a large part of the myth.

Connally is not an easy man to reach. I had to travel
to San Diego to get permission to interview him—as it
later turned out—in Houston.

"You'll have to fly on out," Christian told me, speaking
of the convention. "The Republicans out there want to
touch John, and to sniff him."

Connally has retired to the Jabberwocky Lounge, to sip
Corton-Charlemagne and talk with party leaders. Then
he and Nellie walk across to dinner, past the pool and the

gas flame that adds a touch of warmth to evening on the edge of America. Watergate or not, there's comfort in two thousand success stories bent on sirloin and baked potatoes in the convention hall, resounding with the distillate rock of the Mike Curb Congregation.

Connally receives a standing ovation when he finally approaches the podium. He points out that this is his first speech as a Republican, and then tells the oldest joke in Texas Democratic politics: "There was this old-timer who decided to go to church one Sunday, and he found that he was the only person there. Well, the preacher let fly with his best sermon anyway. Later, the old-timer told the preacher, 'When I go out in the field with a load of hay, I don't drop the whole load for one cow. . . .' "

It is unabashed Texspeak, a mushy Methodist unction that goes down better with the Uvalde Jaycee-ettes than with bottom-water Republicans. Nothing like reverberations of LBJ to poison the head table. But the audience seems anxious enough to embrace another big, intransigent nimrod, and Connally and Nellie are mobbed on their way out, after he admonishes the gathering not to let Watergate "be our Waterloo."

In the foyer, a conventioneer stands pressed against the wall by the crowd. He wears his identification badge high on a double-knit lapel, and stares at Connally with red-rimmed, agitated eyes. "I didn't go," he says to no one in particular, while diluted bourbon spills from a clear plastic cup over his hand. "This is supposed to be for Republicans."

Although Connally passes close to the man, he does not hear him, for he is busy signing autographs with a gold pen, moving inexorably toward the door.

"Let him labor in the vineyards," the man says, relishing the phrase. "Two, maybe three years. Then we'll see. But nobody's moving in, nobody's taking over *this* party. . . ."

3 ☆ THE SOURCE

Oil and Patriots

The derrick stands elemental and forlorn against the autumn sky, an outpost on the edge of the vast Texas oil field. Roustabouts work in the shadow of steel girders. Except their hard hats, and the sight of bright red mud pumps—the slimness of the rig itself—and the scene suggests the wilder, raucous, and more promising 1920s.

The oilman wheels his Cadillac toward the well. He sports a modest white pompadour, but he drives with the assurance of a much younger man who expects expensive machines to perform. His four-door brown-and-cinnamon Fleetwood lunges through ruts laid down by tractor-trailers hauling drilling pipe, the carriage scraping.

"This well'll cost a hundred thousand," he says, with a throaty drawl that might never have been east of the Fort Worth Club. "And it'll probably be dry."

He is an independent, one of a declining breed whose sole purpose is the finding and producing of oil. Independents are the backbone of the industry in Texas, a business known for its risks and its profits.

"We took a chance on a gas well out past the Permian." He gestures westward with a large, open hand. "Gas wells go deeper. We sank two million in a dry hole, on a tract that cost six hundred thousand to lease. We figured we were on the edge of the play, so we whip-stocked it—drilled off at an angle—and we hit. Now she's producing about twenty-three thousand a day. That's dollars."

The oilman is one of the few survivors of the early boom that so changed the state. His office reflects his tastes—heavy Japanese breakfronts, a stock of Old Worthy Scotch, a sterling-silver hard hat—and bears evidence of his considerable success, including intimate photographs of him with Johnson, Connally, and Nixon. In 1931, the oilman invested his money in leases north of Dad Joiner's famous discovery, and sank a well into the belly of the east Texas field. It produced 18,000 barrels of oil a day, and brought Harry Sinclair himself down from New York with an offer of almost $2 million for the operation. The oilman turned him down, sold out for $2.5 million to someone else, and watched him sell out for $37 million to Standard of Indiana.

"Things are tougher now. Then you could lease, and get the majors to come in with money for drilling. The majors do everything themselves now; there aren't any farm-outs. Oil's harder to find. The big fields have all been discovered. We have to poke around for the little pockets, drill deeper, take bigger risks. And the goddamn paperwork is killing us."

Oilmen consider themselves beleaguered and exceptional. Success depends upon knowledge, guts, and luck, in equal measure. An independent operation resembles a military campaign conducted in a world without allies or frontiers. Geologists and geophysicists chart the hidden terrain, providing the intelligence; land men scout the prospects and contract with the natives. Primary concerns are capital, the availability of supplies, and logistics. Casualties are dry holes, or "bummers"—wells that can't pay expenses. If there is a common enemy, it is government.

The oilman parks among mud-spattered pickups, and we mount steel stairs to the doghouse. The tool pusher, wearing a white shirt—symbol of authority—with a slash of grease down one arm, crosses the platform with a big grin on his face. He and the oilman shout at each other over the roar of the diesel. The roustabouts take no notice as they whip chain around a dangling length of pipe. They are bare-chested, and one has hair hanging six inches below the rim of his hard hat, an expression of individuality that a few years ago would have assured him a fistfight a day until he got it cut. The jump in the price of crude oil brought many young men back into a rough and dirty occupation.

This is just a stop to show a visitor from the East what a wildcat well looks like, on the way to the more serious activity of hunting doves. We drive on to one of the oilman's ranches, to warm up by shooting skeet, and to check on the progress of the football game—a consideration in Texas almost as important as the weather. (The Oakland Raiders lead the Kansas City Chiefs, 6–0.)

The doves are not forthcoming, so we must find them. The Fleetwood speeds across the open range, brush sweeping its polished sides, scattering meadowlarks. I cradle a handsome Browning automatic shotgun, the barrel protruding from the window. The oilman grips his polished stock, wheeling with his free hand.

We skirt watering holes, plunge among cottonwoods, teeter on the very edge of a deep, dry gully. A solitary dove sits on a distant telephone line, watching us with disbelief, and we bear down upon the quarry.

"Shoot 'im."

I comply, and the bird flutters among the rocks.

"Now watch out for *ruttlesnakes*."

The game retrieved, our mobile hunt continues. The

oilman's car is festooned with mud-caked weeds and brush by the time we reach another of his houses, this one set on an artificial lake, and faced with a view of empty hills and flooded willows. We walk down to the water's edge to clean the kill. He stands with his feet widespread, deftly extracting the birds' breasts, and dropping them into the empty ammunition box.

He has forgotten the key to his wing of the house, where the whiskey is kept. We attempt to force the sliding door, but without success. "I feel like knocking it down," he says, without rancor, as we move on to his wife's wing.

The oilman turns off the burglar alarm, and we step into an airy pavilion decorated with Oriental prints and enamel statuary. The atmosphere is curiously formal, like that of some monument erected to leisure out of a sense of duty rather than desire.

"We've never spent a night here," he says, with a short laugh. "Isn't that something?"

He searches the cabinets, but can find nothing stronger than Coke. We sit in hunting clothes on a white brocade couch, in front of the television set. The Raiders now lead the Chiefs by two touchdowns, and the game is almost over.

Driving back to town, his guns still resting on the front seat, the oilman turns off onto a narrow, pocked road. Down the valley can be seen Fort Worth's new office buildings, touched by the last of the sun.

"This used to be the only road out to the west Texas field. I don't know how many times I drove it between here and Wichita Falls, back in the '30s. I always rolled in after midnight. I'd see the lights of the city, and know I was almost home."

That is as close as he comes to reverie. Oilmen are distrustful of too much self-reflection, and of questions that go beyond life's reckonables.

He drops me off in front of the Sheraton, insisting

that I take the doves and eat them for breakfast the next morning.

"Now you write about our problems," he instructs good-naturedly, and is gone.

The receptionist shakes her head at my request, more disbelief than refusal. The bellman only shrugs. I make my way back to the kitchen, where a waiter sits smoking on a stool.

"Cook don't come in till tomorrow." Skeptically he takes the ammunition box and hands it to the girl at the counter, instructing her to write a note to the cook.

"Where'd you get them birds?"

I mention the oilman's name.

"Oh, yeah? Well, then, that'll be all right."

He tells the girl to write the oilman's name on the note. Then he asks, "That the father or the son?"

"The grandfather."

"Oh, yeah?" He turns back to the girl. "You better write 'Mr.' in front of that name."

Oil and Texas, horse and carriage. Spindletop made the two synonymous at the beginning of the century, although oil was discovered in Texas just after the Civil War, up in Nacogdoches County, and a field in Corsicana was developed with Eastern backing in 1894. But it wasn't until 1901 that the tenacity of the one-armed son of a Beaumont gunsmith, Captain Anthony B. Lucas, the advice of his Austrian engineer, and the money of a team of Pittsburgh speculators, Guffey and Galey, brought in the world's most famous well in southeast Texas.

Spindletop's gusher, Lucas No. 1, produced 800,000 barrels of oil during the first ten days, a volume that had been reached at Corsicana only after four years. The new discovery initiated the wildest scramble for a natural resource—with the possible exception of the gold rush—the country has witnessed.

Spindletop was heralded as the symbol of a new age, crucible of the new Texan. Certainly it indicated that the state harbored significant reserves (six months after the first gusher, Beaumont produced 600,000 barrels of oil a day) and opened the Gulf Coast to production. But Spindletop ruined more men than it enriched, came to signify exalted hucksterism, and established in the state what can best be described as the Texas bonanza syndrome. It became known as "Swindletop"—a gilded dipstick gauging Texas's ability to produce millionaires of the future.

When Columbus M. Joiner drifted into Dallas thirty years later, an old man affected by wildcat fever, it was no longer necessary to search for uses for oil. Automobiles had made the difference. Joiner took up leases in the impoverished Sabine River Basin east of the city, an area discredited by geologists because it contained no salt domes or other formations known to trap oil.

Dad Joiner's financing of his Daisy Bradford wells—named for the widow who leased him the land and fed his drilling crews—combined perseverance, hustle, and not a little faith. He sold interest in the wells to anyone who could spare twenty-five dollars, old pipe, dry goods, and labor. He issued his own scrip. When he finally punctured the richest field of all—134,000 acres of prime real estate that still produce today—Joiner drowned in litigation. He sold out for some peace of mind to a man named Haroldson Lafayette Hunt, who would make $100 million on the deal, and died a poor man on a Dallas side street.

Wildcatters who fanned out over the state were the progeny of the early fields. They learned by roughnecking, outfitting, servicing, hustling leases, either for themselves or for the major oil companies that moved into Texas in a big way. Wildcatters risked capital and person alike (if an operator fired his tool pusher, he also had to fight him), often teaming up for protection and to raise funds. An office was the back seat of a car, or just a worn back pocket. They followed the geologists, their instincts, or the prostitutes, who were credited with reliable noses for oil. (Kansas, it is said, suffered a dearth of wildcatters because of that state's poor collection of whores.)

Two of the most famous wildcatters, Clint Murchison and Sid Richardson, were representative of the quirks and excesses of the profession; their heirs exemplify the divergent courses oil money has taken in Texas. Both men grew up in the little east Texas town of Athens. Murchison's father owned the bank, where Clint worked without enthusiasm until he met Richardson, five years older, a trader in cattle and oil leases. They headed west together after the 1921 depression, and eventually turned up in Wichita Falls with $50,000 between them. Clint heard a rumor about a well coming in near the Oklahoma border, pulled Sid out of a card game, and together they sneaked past the guards, getting close enough to smell oil. They bought every lease they could, an investment that increased in value 300 percent the first day.

Clint Murchison returned to east Texas at age forty-two, wealthy enough to retire. Short, articulate, neatly mustached, he inspired confidence, and put his money and that of others back into the ground during the 1930s boom. He found more oil, and gas—which was more embarrassment than a commodity in those days. Exploiting the discovery, he formed the Union Gas Company to supply the cities of Texas.

East Texas was awash in oil in the early 1930s. The price of crude fell to ten cents a barrel, and Governor Ross Sterling called three special sessions of the legislature to find a solution to overproduction and declining profits. Significantly, Sterling had been an oil operator

before becoming governor, and was one of the founders
of Humble Oil. He saw to it that the Railroad Commission was empowered to set production allowables, known
as proration. Proration became the standard means by
which an organized industry, with government help, kept
the price of oil up by limiting production (although, in
the 1930s, many oilmen attacked the government for trying to prevent them from running their wells wide open,
and did so anyway, thus producing "hot" oil). But in the
beginning proration produced the same anarchy, and the
same unlikely fortunes, as did Prohibition. Oilmen became accustomed to creeping under cars to avoid bullets,
and to the sight of brazen Texas Rangers chaining illegal producers and hired guns to telephone poles.

Murchison formed the Liberty Oil Company, choos-
ing a name to symbolize his opposition to proration—
and government in general—with only two hundred dollars of his own money, and the rest borrowed. Some say
he ran hot oil as a matter of principle, although the
profits were not inconsiderable. Over the years, he took
$15 million out of the company for other ventures, and
sold out in 1949 for $6 million.

Money is like manure, said Murchison. Spread it. The
scope of his operations, and the risks involved, forced
him constantly to seek new partners for the foundering
properties he located through investment hounds. He
bought the properties cheap, installed new and autonomous management, sold out at a profit. His companies
included Delhi-Taylor Oil; American Mail Line; Holt,
Rinehart & Winston. (The only advice he gave his publishing house was to bring out an edition of *Folk Medicine*, a book of home remedies, which became a great
best-seller.) By 1959, his consolidated insurance companies, another Texas bonanza industry, had assets of
$140 million. His Dallas bus line, to become Transcon-
tinental, had assets of $23 million. His oil investments
extended from Canada to Venezuela.

The friendship between Murchison and Richardson was the sort that exists between men who have shared large sums of money, hardship, and a skepticism about most human endeavor. They simply wanted to make more money. Most mornings, they talked together by telephone or radiotelephone, regardless of the distance. Their ventures included the operation of the Del Mar Turf Club in southern California on a tax-exempt basis, supposedly to provide funds for a nonprofit organization called Boys, Inc. Some of the money went to Boys, Inc., in the form of rent, but most of it went to the investors. Del Mar provided a haven for politicians and entertainers; it also provided a place for Sid Richardson to drink.

He was a barrel of a man who walked with a curious rolling gait, the result of an early oil-field accident. Richardson was more devoted to cards and to bourbon than was Murchison, more withdrawn in company. Three-hundred-dollar tailor-made suits could not obscure the rough edges. He talked dirty, but wrote letters of remarkable urbanity and wit.

Richardson made his first fortune wildcatting, lost it, made another. That one he also lost, owing to fluctuating oil prices and the Depression. Then he leased land in what became the Keystone field in west Texas, and made several million dollars. "It was luck. I did it by jumping up in the air six feet, and holding myself up by my own bootstraps."

Some say it was not luck. He is believed to have bribed a geologist working for Gulf Oil, a common enough practice, and to have obtained valuable information early enough to get in on the play. Subsequent discoveries put Richardson up among the half-dozen richest men in America.

Both men avoided publicity, often with good reason. Richardson considered the press and politicians contemptible; he ignored the former, and bought a few of the latter. But mostly he enjoyed himself, entertaining aspirants to his fortune who labored in vain. "They're all wanting a landing field," Richardson said of women, "but mine's fogged in."

Richardson and Murchison were early examples of Texans gate-crashing the countinghouses of the East. Murchison, with Richardson's help, joined the Alleghany Corporation in its successful fight for control of the Morgan-Vanderbilt New York Central Railroad in 1957.

The deal between the two men involved $20 million. Richardson initially thought he was in for only $5 million, until Murchison explained that he must double his stake. Richardson readily agreed, but added, as the story goes, "Say, Clint, what was the name of that railroad?"

Murchison's sons John and Clint, Jr., graced the cover of *Time* in 1961, as much a tribute to Texas as to the old man's genes and business acumen. They conveyed a flintiness, a tendency toward thin lips and thin lapels, and an obvious discomfort in the face of publicity. The occasion was the struggle for control of the Alleghany Corporation, a superlative Texan takeover so unexpected on Wall Street that it gained added vibrancy. Oil had nothing to do with the fight except that it provided the means by which the Murchisons won control of Alleghany.

Both Murchisons were still in their thirties, and considered callow by their opponents, although their connections in the East were sound. Both served apprenticeships as directors at Holt, Rinehart & Winston. Clint, Jr., was a product of Lawrenceville, a Texan impressed by the environs of Princeton who moved on to Duke and MIT. John graduated from Hotchkiss, less of a student than his brother. The Air Force provided him an excuse for abandoning Yale before it abandoned him.

Murchison Brothers occupies the twenty-third floor

of the First National Bank Building in downtown Dallas. This is the world headquarters for enterprises including insurance, construction, real estate, finance, sports, energy development, and various other entrepreneurial theaters, the extent of which is unknown beyond the hard nucleus of executives in for life. The halls and boardrooms are appointed with valuable paintings and sculpture by contemporary artists, considered by John as prime investments, and often shuttled between museums.

The atmosphere is subdued, informal, reflecting the assurance of a well-run family business. Here Clint, Jr., owner of the Dallas Cowboys, stood on his head in the foyer to view one of his brother's recent acquisitions, and pronounced it more appealing from that perspective.

Money for them has become more complicated than manure. The Murchisons still favor investments easily converted to cash; their leverage is concerted, delicate, and pervasive. They acquire large assets with little of their own capital—turning $20,000 in cash, say, and an $80,000 promissory note into a construction company worth tens of millions of dollars.

Timing is a key factor, as illustrated by the case of the Cowboys. The team was organized in 1960, before professional football boomed, simply to make money. Profit in the first ten years was almost $2 million, and that after five years of deficit. The franchise cost only $600,-000. After a decade, it was valued at about $12 million —a capital appreciation of 2,000 percent.

Around the time of the purchase of the Cowboys, the Murchisons sold most of their gas and oil properties to the major oil companies. They still control Delhi International Oil Corporation, and have properties in Ecuador and Thailand, as well as a coal-mining company; but oil has become a largely titular resource in the Murchison portfolio.

"We don't do much drilling," says a spokesman.

☆ ☆ ☆

Sid Richardson died an apparently lonely man. His body was flown to his private island in the Gulf for funeral services—as was Billy Graham, the invocator—and buried in his hometown of Athens, an addition that earned the local cemetery a $100,000 donation. But Fort Worth was Richardson's real home, and the repository of his fortune.

The Sid Richardson Foundation, set up in 1947 on the advice of Richardson's friend Amon Carter, a publisher and fellow oilman, received his properties after his death.

All of Richardson's assets and debts were turned over to the foundation. Its primary business is the management of properties, settling debts, and collecting revenue, and most of its meager grants go to Texas hospitals, colleges, churches, and civic organizations. The trustees, including Perry Bass, are involved financially in enterprises where the foundation's money is held.

In *The Big Foundations,* Waldemar A. Nielsen wrote, "The philanthropic record of the Richardson Foundation is a Texas-style exaggeration of the faults of others in its asset group. It has no defined program, no formulated plans for the future, and has not voluntarily issued any public reports."

Richardson's legacy in oil continues to reflect the history of the business in Texas. The family firm fell into a slump following the Korean War, when the Railroad Commission again throttled production and import quotas were imposed to protect domestic producers. The company cut exploration drastically in the late 1950s, when capital investment fled the industry. Then the Railroad Commission stopped proration—a signal to the Arabs that America had no excess production capacity. The jump in the price of oil and the delay of the Alaska pipeline pumped new life into the industry. Exploration tripled, drawing out every available rig and string of pipe, and initiating demands for steel, pumps, and labor that became near chaotic, as well as highly profitable.

The company is run by Richardson's great-nephew. He could be called a third-generation wildcatter, although the description seems slightly unsuitable. Antiseptic white walls predominate at the company's headquarters, where glass panels expose every office to the sweep of carpeted hall. The cubicle of the chief executive doesn't differ much from its neighbor, except that his desk, of spare contemporary design, bears copies of Kant's *Critique of Pure Reason* and Merleau-Ponty's *Phenomenology of Perception*. He is thirty-three years old. He is not predisposed to like journalists, and though he agreed to be interviewed and quoted, he requested that his name not appear in print. He says that when it does, people write to him and say, "Dear Sir: You have plenty of money. I don't have any. Please send me some by return mail."

"I don't like opinions in journalists," he says softly, holding up a popular magazine open to an article about oil. "This writer assumes that profit comes first in the oil business. Profit is important because it is a measure of our performance—how well we serve our customers, how well we use resources. Business does something for mankind, and *that* is how we get our profit."

The suit of English cut, spectacles with thin gold rims, and hair that falls smoothly over three-quarters of each ear suggest an appreciation of fine distinctions not shared by his great-uncle, who "taught me a fantastic lesson in ethics, human nature, horse sense. The old work ethic. Richardson was a Baptist, but he might as well have been a Mormon. If he had had a better education, he might not have been suckered into some of those deals. He would have run a better organization."

The smile seems too ingenuous.

"I can't resolve the demands for political contributions. But if I walk away, I still have employees to pay. Politicians put incredible pressure on business, individuals and labor—a form of extortion. You give, and you keep it a secret so you won't be called a lobbyist.

"You can be an independent oilman if you have the courage, and you don't mind losing. I don't run a big bureaucracy like the majors do, but I can compete with them in exploration. A firm like Exxon has to be rated on performance every month. People judging people. Here I don't judge people. I get a wild idea, and I move fast, without having to go through a lot of committees. I go after oil Exxon would sneeze at."

Andover and Yale shaped sensibilities not essentially Texan, proof of upward mobility of a different sort.

"I love the East; that's where I grew up mentally. I spent years trying to get rid of my accent—I had to be understood. Most of my time was spent in the arts, and in reading philosophy. My friends are all artists, or art historians. I paint, of course.

"Texas lacks in relation to the East what America lacks in relation to Europe. Europe has a beautifully ingrained tradition, so important to perpetuating mankind. They are proud of their monuments, and their history. They preserve as well as look forward. Education pervades all classes. There a man can appreciate a flower arrangement without being considered sissy. Here we just throw money at art because it has status."

The question of alternatives is a disturbing one, even at this exalted level of success.

"Would I do something else if I could? God, yes. But I have a responsibility to see that certain assets are productively employed." His eyes glisten momentarily. "I'm certainly more blessed than cursed. I don't seek any sympathy."

Houston's prestigious Petroleum Club rests, appropriately, atop the Exxon Building. Black chandeliers resembling stylized offshore rigs hang high above the parquet floor, the only adornment other than a vast tapestry representing Texas's geographical strata. The draperies are gray, as are the suits of most of those who eat their strip sirloin and pecan balls with subdued noontime jocularity. There are no women. (Wives of members may lunch in the remote Discovery Room.) The only real color is orange, a hue of distilled sunlight in the jackets of Latin waiters, gliding above a sea of white tablecloths.

The view from forty-three stories up is of other tributes to oil—the two Shell Plazas, the Gulf Building, the big banks that house the law firms that grew up with the industry. Houston has become the oil center of America (belonging to the Petroleum Club is not nearly as important as failing to belong), a stark and vibrant citadel of downstream production: refining, petrochemicals, manufacturing, research, and all the attendant services of the most pervasive and sophisticated industry.

Directly below the Petroleum Club are the headquarters of Exxon Company, U.S.A., the business end of the Exxon stick. In 1972, Standard Oil of New Jersey merged with Humble Oil in Houston to form Exxon, and now the New York offices function only as a holding company. Houston manages exploration, development of oil and gas, marketing crude, refining, and transportation. Houston also oversees the marine division, the system of service stations, coal-mining operations, uranium exploration, real-estate investment, chemical research, and overseas exploration.

The office of the chairman of Exxon, U.S.A., Myron A. ("Mike") Wright, has been reduced to the bare essentials of commerce. A metallic briefcase leans against a desk remarkably uncluttered for that of one of the most powerful executives in the world. There are no mementos here, no stock of twenty-five-year-old Scotch for journalists, just a couch and chairs, and a large, detailed globe representing the planet Earth.

"We have to bridge the energy gap," says Wright, who began his career digging ditches on wildcat wells outside Seminole, Oklahoma, and retains a workmanlike approach to language. "Now this can be done by stepwise decontrol, or stepwise changes in prices, or the tax situation. We've got a self-destruct tax deal." Ten thousand people in Texas work for Exxon, U.S.A.

Houston is also the headquarters for Exxon's division dealing with the Arabs, and with Far Eastern operations. The city provides qualified personnel, technical knowledge, and some of the country's best attorneys in matters of federal regulation. Three of the law firms are among the largest half-dozen in America. These lawyers have contributed greatly to Houston's pre-eminence as an oil center and as a growing force in American foreign policy.

Houstonians are not likely to read about the intricacies of politics and oil in the pages of the Houston *Post* or the Houston *Chronicle*. Any criticism of the industry is considered slightly demented, if not downright subversive. Oil and country are not contenders for the position of greatest good, for they are synonymous. If Houston is the oil center of America, it is *de facto* the most American city.

"New York has a welfare problem," says Wright, of a city where he has lived. "It has a minority problem, a labor problem. . . . Everybody's anonymous in New York. Here the individual has identity. And there's work for everybody who will work."

Wright lives in the River Oaks section, where stylized reproductions of Tudor mansions sit next to those of Monticello. He plays golf with the most influential men in Texas; he sits on the boards of several large corporations, among them Houston's First City National Bank.

Wright did not attend Connally's party for Nixon at Picosa, not because he wasn't well acquainted with the establishment in attendance, and sympathetic, but because he represents, in effect, an autonomous state, and cannot afford so open a display of partisanship.

The question of political affiliation prompts pained amusement: "I'm an independent."

The oil industry, like the press, prospers in time of crisis. Wars are best. So powerful was the industry by the end of World War II that the complexion of Texas politics had changed forever. Representatives slow to embrace the militant new conservatism suffered. Sam Rayburn at first lacked the proper enthusiasm for oil and its advocates, and was seriously challenged in 1944, forfeiting any chance of becoming Roosevelt's running mate because of the need to return to Texas to campaign. A few years later, Senator Tom Connally, symbol of the old cotton and cattle hierarchy in Texas, was shown a collection of cash raised by oilmen for his defeat, and he wisely agreed to step down.

Johnson scrambled to accommodate this source of patronage, or of the most formidable opposition. The New Deal had provided his auspicious start in politics, but later his association with Roosevelt threatened to unseat him. Rayburn told his biographer, Dwight C. Dorough, that oilmen tried "to destroy me. Destroy Lyndon Johnson." That was before Johnson became a loud advocate of military preparedness, in opposition to Truman—a theme pleasant to oil, and to Texas's burgeoning weapons industry. As a member of the House Armed Services Committee, which absorbed the Naval Affairs Committee, Johnson pursued his new cause aggressively. The secretariat of the United States Navy—the largest consumer of oil in the world, and leasee of valuable oil lands —came to resemble an adjunct of the Lone Star State.

One of Johnson's early accomplishments as a senator was the political destruction of Leland Olds, a member of the Federal Power Commission who brought about utility rate reductions in the millions of dollars. Olds was anathema to the oil industry. During confirmation hearings on his renomination for a third term on the FPC in 1949, Johnson—chairman of the subcommittee—implied that Olds was sympathetic to Communism, and led the effective Senate floor fight to defeat the nomination. It was not a simple case of conservatives versus liberals, for Olds had powerful enemies within Interior, but the effects were detrimental to the liberals.

"The whole liberal cause went down the drain when oil became gold," claims Thomas Corcoran, Washington lawyer and Roosevelt's agent-without-portfolio, who was also a friend of Olds's. "The boys from Texas took over, everybody was fighting to get under the cover of the industry."

The tidelands issue galvanized oilmen in 1952. Adlai Stevenson refused to support claims by individual states to the submerged lands off their coasts, stimulating a mass exodus in Texas from the Democratic party. Sid Richardson had earlier flown to SHAPE headquarters in Paris to convince Eisenhower to run for President. He had known Eisenhower for years, and entertained him and Mamie on his private island.

"General, there's no way out," Richardson reportedly told Eisenhower. "You've got to do it. I'll go along with you any way you go, but if you go as a Republican, it's going to be hard."

Not since the Civil War had support for a Republican in Texas been so strong. An unreckonable amount of oil money was made available to Eisenhower, who did not disappoint oilmen on the tidelands issue. These same men contributed heavily to the cause of Senator Joseph McCarthy, among them Clint Murchison, who also supported the campaign to defeat Millard Tydings of Maryland. Politically, Murchison belonged in the company of other oilmen like H. L. Hunt and Hugh Roy Cullen, voices too shrill and egocentric to have much lasting effect.

Richardson had more political aplomb. Eisenhower appointed Richardson's friend and fellow Texan Robert Anderson to be Secretary of the Navy. Anderson had served on the Texas Racing Commission, where he had become acquainted with wealthy oilmen, and became president of the Texas Mid-Continent Oil & Gas Association. Richardson later discussed with Eisenhower the possibility of substituting Anderson for Richard Nixon as his Vice-President in 1956. When Richardson asked Anderson if he would consider running with Eisenhower, Anderson said he must first have enough money in the bank to alleviate any financial worries. Richardson then arranged for royalty interests in oil to be assigned to Anderson by various oil companies with which he was associated, for the sum of one dollar and "other valuable interests." These royalty interests were eventually bought back from Anderson for almost a million dollars—by Richardson's nephew Perry Bass.

Anderson was not chosen as Eisenhower's running mate. Instead, he was made Secretary of the Treasury, and appointed to a Cabinet committee studying oil imports. His case is not unusual, nor is the amount of money involved disproportionate to that in other arrangements whereby officials within the oil industry assume government positions, with jurisdiction over their own interests.

Johnson's liaison man with the oil industry in general was Connally, whose services were so apparent during the debate on the 1956 bill to deregulate natural gas.

As Corcoran says, "The natural-gas bill was just part of the big oil push."

The political interests of Texas oilmen are not limited by party, or state boundaries. The Murchison brothers provide an example. When Richard Nixon left the office of Vice-President in 1961, he bought a lot in a Beverly Hills real-estate development known as Trousdale Estates, a Murchison property. Nixon paid only $35,000 for the lot, an extraordinarily good price. Two years later, he sold the lot for $86,000.

Clint Murchison gave Rose Mary Woods $5,000 in cash for Nixon's campaign in 1968. The donation did not show up on any records filed by Nixon for that year. John Murchison served on the Committee for the Preservation of the White House while Nixon was President, and he and half a dozen other Texans provided $100,000 to refurbish the Red, Green, and Blue Rooms. The Murchisons' generosity did not end there: they donated $50,000 to Nixon's 1972 re-election, in cash.

In early 1974, the Justice Department, the Federal Trade Commission, and the Securities and Exchange Commission began investigating possible anti-trust violations by executives sitting on various oil-company boards simultaneously. John Murchison was one prominent name mentioned. Another was Perry Bass, who contributed $20,000 to Nixon's election. Bass owned three oil companies, but he was also a director of Murchison's Delhi International Oil. Murchison was also a director of Hamilton Brothers Petroleum and of Kirby Industries, a subsidiary of Kirby Petroleum.

A lawyer who worked for the Justice Department commented that while John Mitchell was Attorney General, oil was not "a highly favored subject for litigation."

Oilmen remain among the largest political contributors in recent years. In Texas, oilmen often give money to several candidates in a single race. So pervasive is the industry now that opposition to it is as unlikely among politicians as among businessmen, unless a neat course can be steered between the independents and the majors. For instance, the bill proposed by Senator Lloyd Bentsen to increase payments to the federal government for offshore production could be seen as an effort to counter Bentsen's association with oil, at a time when his aspirations for national office demanded it. Such a law would have cost the majors money, but not the independents, whom Bentsen sought to assist by proposing another bill to make it cheaper for them to get in on the offshore play, and to preserve their share of depletion. At home, the independents are still the biggest campaign contributors, and a more potent force than the bureaucracies of the majors.

Texas produces about 3.5 million barrels of oil a day, or slightly more than a third of the oil produced in the United States. Its percentage of natural-gas production is even larger. The industry is certainly sleeker and more diverse than it was thirty years ago—a versatile thoroughbred, rather than a dray. It has competition from the bonanzas it helped engender.

Sam Rayburn said of oilmen, shortly before his death, when discussing with his biographer industry efforts to unseat him, "They just hate." It was the harsh judgment of a survivor, and a witness to the awesome tide. That oilmen know their enemies is a kinder view, one that reflects the values of an earlier era uncomplicated by big government, unpopular wars, the demands of the poor and the discontented, and the certain knowledge that oil is a source of destruction as well as power.

To be an oilman is to be beset: the sentiment has created a curious unanimity among an army of individualists. "Just leave us alone, and let the free enterprise system work," urges Corbin Robertson, head of Quintana Petroleum. He stands at the window of his office high above Cullen Center, a portion of the legacy of Hugh Roy Cullen, and Houston's equivalent of Rockefeller Center. Robertson is Cullen's son-in-law, and testy. A book displayed in his outer office contains letters from famous businessmen defining freedom. *Freedom—a reward granted those who earn it. . . .*

Until recently there existed no better symbol of oil's united front than the depletion allowance. Depletion was an obvious target for critics of the industry, and representatives of the majors suggested that it be done away with as a large public-relations gesture—one, significantly, that did not really affect their profits, which derive from the downstream industry. Depletion became the majors' red herring to divert attention from other, more lucrative arrangements, like foreign tax credits. For years the independents were silently resentful of the majors' overseas investments—aiding the Arabs and themselves at the expense of production at home, and of some value vaguely American. The suggestion that depletion was expendable amounted to treachery.

A third force has emerged in the industry, with little regard for the old relationships and some contempt for the mythos of oil. The phenomenon is known as the promoter, who raises drilling funds from outside sources. Unscrupulous promoters have gulled such disparate personalities as Walter Wriston and Barbara Walters; reliable ones have found oil for their investors, which they treat as just one more commodity.

"Say you have a million dollars you have to pay taxes on. I fly up to New York in a little Lear jet to get you, and you say, 'Get rid of the million, get me a deduction.' I say, 'O.K., I'll put up the tangibles—the Christmas tree, the hard goods—and you take the intangibles.' I'll charge you a small management fee, about two percent. If you give the money to the government, it's gone. But if you like to roll the bones, and you give the million to me, there's a chance you'll get something back. And a chance you'll get a hell of a lot back.' "

He sits drinking Manhattans briskly in Houston's Press Club, the most anonymous bar in town. He is young, impeccably dressed, and on his way toward becoming a millionaire. The company he assists in running owns ranches, car lots, barges, trucks, feedlots, real estate, a professional ball team, oil and gas production, crude-oil processing facilities, petrochemical feedstocks, and gas stations.

"Half a million dollars is the smallest private placement we take. If you only had a hundred thousand to invest—well, I might do you a little real estate, do a little cattle. But if you don't have an interest in a minimum of ten wells, you're spitting in the wind. . . .

"The oil business is too romantic. Most oilmen are superpatriots. They just think in terms of barrels. And they love to say, 'I am an oilman.' I'm trying to get away from that. I say, 'I'm a businessman.'

"Personally, I don't give a big one about depletion. Getting rid of depletion means getting rid of a lot of small independents who are dumb asses anyway. They don't understand investment and return. They ought to be driving trucks. The business has become too technical. Let them sell their production to bigger independents, or to the majors. I'm not afraid of the majors. They'll try to break it off in me, but I'll break it off in them, too."

Interlude

FLIGHT TO MIDLAND

The Cessna Golden Eagle rises and plunges a mile above the west Texas plain. Lesions in the clouds reveal a sullen, uneventful landscape, and the occasional spidery thrust of a drilling rig. To view the producing wells —brackets of pipe only, and silver-toned storage tanks— we would have to fly lower, and this is not the day for that. The geologist sprawls in the tail section, fighting air sickness. The pilot and co-pilot, sporting razor cuts and platform shoes, mutter to one another. But the plane's owners scan their Fort Worth *Star-Telegram*s unperturbed: the dexterity with a cup of coffee and the ash at the tip of a long green cigar attest to years spent hopping between investments in the worst of weather.

They are George and Kelly Young, independent oilmen in their mid-forties, and an ideal combination of reserve and gregariousness. George wears dark business suits, carries a briefcase, and carefully drives a Jaguar XKE. Kelly prefers blazers and Guccis ("My wife's gonna give me hell for getting these Italian shoes wet"), and the requisite and more comfortable Cadillac.

George is wary in the presence of a strange reporter,

who, for distraction, inspects the new packs of playing cards in their appointed slots on the table, the magazines dealing mostly with airplanes, and the altimeter that verifies the sudden dips, releasing the stomach from the effects of gravity. George spent the evening before with friends, including the geologist, at the new Fort Worth Hilton, not a "twist-off"—a term for the loss of pipe down a well, and for excessive partying—but still an exertion. His expression when I tell him that I did not pledge a fraternity in college reveals that some carefully considered social theory has just been confirmed.

Kelly doesn't care. He feels guilty because he has not spent time up in Washington kicking ass in Congress over the threat to depletion. Talking to a reporter about the problems of the business might help, and hell, he likes to talk anyway. Even at seven in the morning, in the middle of a squall. The evening before, in his lavish new house, he gave me drinks mixed by a bartender in an electric-blue velvet jacket and black tie, and regaled me with stories about Tahiti. "They call it 'boom-boom' out there. I mean, some little girl'll just walk right up to you, and say, 'Hey, you wanna boom-boom?' . . ."

Now rain beats on the windshield with the sound of violently tearing canvas as Kelly leans across—mentholated Benson & Hedges clamped between thick fingers—and shouts, "Take away depletion, and you wipe out eight thousand independents. And the money'll just get pissed away in some welfare line."

The Youngs own a considerable interest in two thousand wells around the United States. They both have degrees in geology from Washington & Lee—Kelly's took a bit longer than the usual four years ("About twice as long. I had football to think about")—for oil is the family business. Their father, Marshall R. Young, began his career as a driver for a major oil company outside Tulsa. His sole advice to Kelly's bride was "Have babies, get royalties."

It is raining in Midland. Kelly breaks out an umbrella, which he holds carefully over my head as we make our way to the car. The road into town leads past seemingly endless lots containing bits of old rigs; purveyors of heavy equipment; various service companies that cater to the oil industry. Midland would have a population of six hundred instead of sixty thousand if it were not for oil, and the reputation for enriching those who can stand the isolation and the sand.

Downtown Midland has the harsh, scrubbed look of new money. "There's the tallest building between Fort Worth and El Paso," says the geologist, now recovered, pointing to a yellow brick structure maybe ten stories high.

The Marshall R. Young Company is housed in a modern cubicle, along with oil operators, seismologists, and lawyers specializing in leases. Maps paper the walls of the boardroom—geographical whorls interspersed with numbers, the names of leaseholders, the symbols of oil and gas wells, and dry holes.

Seated at the table are the company's land man, a geophysicist, and a heavyset independent in a new windbreaker. They are all involved in drilling a deep well south of Lubbock.

"How much oil has the area produced?" asks George, coat off now, and sleeves rolled up.

"About seven and a half million barrels."

"Amoco had leases there," says the land man. "They gave up in an economy drive."

"We don't think it was part of this play."

"It's too subtle for Amoco," decides the independent. "A man responsible to Amoco wouldn't have the guts to drill it."

"We're looking for a Pennsylvania reef," Kelly explains, slapping the map. "A kind of coral lagoon under the ground that traps oil and gas sands. It's the best formation. You go up behind one of these old geologists who hang out in the 007 Club"—and he imitates a shuffling reprobate—"and you'll hear him saying to himself, 'If I could have just found me a *reef* . . .' "

"I've been living off a reef," admits the independent, "since 1957."

The well will cost a quarter of a million dollars. There are no contracts among the investors, for an oilman's success depends largely upon his reputation. The chance of discovering oil on their leases is one in fifty. But then, $100 million worth of oil would be worth the risk and the five years of careful preparation.

"Just doodling," Kelly calls it.

We lunch at their club, where a suit of armor stands in the lobby, exposed to the odor of corned beef and cabbage. The clash of cutlery is an eloquent tribute to Midland's new boom, as members hurry to get back to their offices.

Later, Kelly takes me to meet the head of a large oilfield service outfit, to prove that costs have risen along with the price of crude. Indeed, the man says that prices have doubled, as has his business. His friends are up in Denver, attending a convention. "They're all drinking olive oil, getting ready for tonight. I wish to God I was with them, but I'm too busy."

The deal is completed, with drilling due to begin in three months. The Youngs' pilots have brought the Golden Eagle in to the downtown landing strip, and we all head east, away from the sun.

Kelly feels the need to sum up what might appear to be a random and somewhat manic process. "Oilmen have an insatiable desire to find more oil than they produce. There's some driving force, something more than the gamble."

Scotch and soda in styrofoam cups softens the atmosphere inside the plane. We are now mercifully free of thunderstorms. Fort Worth appears on the horizon like a toy city. It is home for the Youngs, although where they live is relatively unimportant. An oilman's business, like his recreation and most of his friends, is usually elsewhere.

Conversation shifts, as it often does in Texas, to football, and the future of America.

"In another twenty years," says George, "it won't matter what we do."

Kelly agrees.

"I'm afraid," he says, as the Golden Eagle banks dramatically above the runway and the ground rises to meet us, "that the free enterprise system is going down the drain."

4 ☆ A SUNBELT EMPIRE

Brown & Root

"Whereas America has a favorite colloquialism too frequently lavished upon the undeserving. It is the word 'tycoon.' It means Herman Brown, who belonged to no city, but to the great state of Texas, and

"Whereas ... bridges will sprout, highways will multiply, dams will be sculptured from the mountains, industrial plants will stand tall on the horizon because of Herman Brown, and they will be his enduring monuments, and ...

"Whereas Herman Brown's career was an epic to free enterprise ... and

"Whereas Herman Brown started to build roads with the help of two mortgaged mules and some wagons, given him in lieu of a paycheck. His business grew along with the highways. ... As though touched by magic of the sorcerer's apprentice, it became gigantic. Military bases were built, and then, overnight, Brown & Root turned into one of the nation's largest shipbuilding concerns ... and billions of dollars changed hands, and

"Whereas ... the construction company has left the imprint of twentieth century man across the face of the

*earth. In Europe, Asia, South America, Canada, the
desert, the ocean and polar reaches vast changes have
taken place because this giant came out of Texas . . . and*

*"Whereas it is unfortunate that Herman Brown did
not live long enough to see completed what promises to
be the company's 'moon shot.' Science handed him the
assignment Project Mohole, to drill beneath the sea,
through the earth's outer crust, and into the unknown
inner mass of the planet . . . and*

*"Whereas this was a whole man, masculine to the
core. He had a zest for hunting and football and for
politics. . . ."*

—*Resolution offered to the Texas Senate
in 1963 by Senator Criss Cole.*

Sprawled on the outskirts of Houston's business district,
but not part of it, are the headquarters of one of the
world's largest construction companies, Brown & Root.
Although the complex is strikingly modern—a stark,
modular office building backed by an array of prefabricated warehouses—it lacks the drama of the city's new
skyline. Like some quarantined government project, it
appears dour, utilitarian, downright military. Signs
posted high on the steel mesh fence surrounding the
complex warn that television cameras stand guard. All
visitors are required to sign a ledger before their names
are conveyed by telephone to the proper department. No
furniture adorns the concrete foyer, where are displayed
scale models of deep-sea drilling platforms, gas-separa-
tion plants, and atomic reactors built by the company
and shipped around the world.

Executive suites occupy the top floor. Sumptuous in-
house publications rest on the glass coffee table in the
reception area—there will be no coffee—providing the
only information Brown & Root releases concerning its
far-flung empire. So guarded are Brown & Root secrets,

and so assiduous the security, that routine inquiries
by the press or outside agencies produce a kind of
frenzy within the company's public-relations department. (Brown & Root publicists are furtive and certainly underworked, and have been known to deliver
these same in-house publications to the hotels of insis-
tent journalists late at night, to avoid personal contact
with the enemy.)

Anonymity might have been the motif assigned the
interior decorator. It is reflected in the manicured potted
plants, the oil painting of bluebonnets in a rural scene
that appears ripe for development, in the faces of middle-
aged women who move with quick determination among
the many offices. Somewhere near the end of that thick
beige carpet, protected by a handsomely paneled but un-
marked door, and the casual deception of his secretary,
sits George Rufus Brown, who, with his late brother
Herman, shaped one of the most phenomenal business
organizations of mid-century America.

For many, Brown & Root is a perfect symbol of col-
lusion between big government and big business. The
company's rise paralleled that of Lyndon Johnson from
hill-country swain to the most powerful man on earth;
it managed to benefit from every administration from
the New Deal to Nixon's New American Revolution, and
beyond. That Brown & Root could grow fat on a steady
diet of cost-plus government contracts and at the same
time defy organized labor as Socialistic is a tribute to
home-state political pragmatism. (Where money is involved, there can be no hypocrisy.) That Brown & Root
could exploit Vietnam as its own personal bonanza, all
in the name of anti-Communism (for patriotism in the
mouths of consortia, read profits), and now be in league
with the Russians to develop their Siberian gas reserves
with appropriate subsidies provided by the United States
government is indicative of the subtle anarchy that
reigns among the multinationals.

The Brown & Root story is also one of obsessive secrecy, of meticulous accommodation of those in power —the Browns bought a magnificent country estate in Virginia's hunt country, just to be close to Lyndon's Washington—and the pervasive hand of privilege. Influence is personal, always discreet, reflected in the words of Johnson's aide who, when asked to suggest some essentially Texan music to be played at campaign rallies, said with only a trace of a smile, "Why not 'Sweet George R. Brown'?"

Their great-grandfather was a King, a fact succeeding generations could not get over. He came from Alabama to Milam County in the early nineteenth century, and served as the first chief justice of the Supreme Court of the Republic of Texas. His son Rufus King was the first judge of Lee County, which he helped establish, and named after his general in the Civil War. The family seemed to lose its interest in the law. Herman and George Brown's father ran a dry-goods store in Belmont, and raised seven children accustomed to hard work.

Herman drove a grocery wagon for thirty-five dollars a month, saving enough to enter the University of Texas, which didn't suit the style of a young man experienced beyond his years. Stocky and remarkably confident, Herman was hired by the Bell County engineering department to carry a measuring rod and inspect building materials. It is fitting that his first employment away from home was with a public agency.

He began to haul dirt for a road contractor, and became a foreman before he was old enough to vote. Herman never objected to the hard work, or the fighting, and took some consolation in cards and whiskey. He lived in a tent, patient and more trusting than he would later be. His boss went bankrupt, owing him nine months' back pay, and Herman took the man's baggage instead: eighteen mules, four fresno scrapers, a pair of plows, six wagons, and the tent. He finished the job, and married the offspring of a prosperous family.

The parents of Margaret Root did not appreciate Herman's prospects, or the fact that he moved his new bride into a tent. He grew a mustache to lend himself age, and landed his own contract to build a road in Williamson County. He transcended a sea of black mud, and hungry mules, and later that year formed his construction company in partnership with his brother-in-law Dan Root. New roads and bridges were the best job security, since Model-Ts proliferated, and the Federal Road Act loomed. The Texas Highway Commission was created, and staffed with men like Herman who had a real interest in the subject. The newly formed Associated General Contractors bore a striking resemblance to the Texas Highway Commission. In 1955, Texas *Parade* carried the headline: "TEXAS HIGHWAY SYSTEM AND ORGANIZATION OF CONTRACTORS THAT BUILT IT HAVE GROWN UP TOGETHER." An inadvertent revelation.

Herman's brother George was less driven. He deserved Rice Institute, left it only for the Marines in 1918, attended UT for a time, and finally obtained a mining engineer's degree from the Colorado School of Mines. George went to work for Anaconda Copper, but was injured in a cave-in. He returned to Texas, where Herman set him to dynamiting the floor of the San Gabriel River for the construction of a bridge, which neither of them knew much about. George stayed with the company, and in 1926 set up a branch office in Houston.

Herman's connections were good all over Texas. Success was easier if one knew—and was capable of impressing—the right people. Quality of work was important, but so was prior knowledge of projects to be bid upon, and the materials involved. It was even better if a contractor had some say in the choice of those materials. Bribing commissioners before bidding was often artless, whereas largesse dispensed in the wake of a successful bid produced gratitude, information, and occasionally influence on future projects. It was all part of growing up together. Most important was the cost overrun—the doubling and tripling and quadrupling of the cost of construction after work began—a venerable practice that would extend from those early gravel trails right up through that vast portal to the moon.

The death of Dan Root in 1929 left the brothers in charge of a rapidly expanding business. They retained the name Root, but from that time on the action was strictly Brown and Brown. (When George was asked what job he did in the company he replied, "What Herman doesn't do.") They had friends in every courthouse and city hall, and for eight years depended upon local government for jobs. But the big federal contracts coming out of Washington eluded them.

Then Herman had the good sense to hire the intelligent and versatile Austin attorney Alvin J. Wirtz to represent Brown & Root. Wirtz was widely known in Texas, and became the guardian of the nascent establishment that grew beneath the tent of the New Deal. He was brought to Washington as Harold Ickes's Undersecretary of Interior at Johnson's suggestion, and was instrumental in abetting Texas's new bonanza mentality. By helping Johnson get into office, and stay there, Wirtz contributed to the foundations of Texas power in the Capitol. It was Wirtz who urged Richard Kleberg to take Johnson to Washington as his congressional secretary in the first place; it was Wirtz who would later hire Connally on the rebound from Washington.

Like many Texans close to power in the late '30s, Wirtz was considered a liberal at home, his Austin firm a hotbed of radicals. Actually, he knew where the benefits of big government touched the state most profoundly, and had little enthusiasm for ideology. (Make a compromise between the social concern of a Sam Rayburn, and the *Realpolitik* of an Alvin Wirtz, and you will have a Lyndon Johnson.) Wirtz was in favor of big federal projects—dams, rural electrification, irrigation, roads— that would bring some prosperity to the people, and fortunes to a select few. He was a loyal Democrat, not at all the same thing as a liberal.

Wirtz's position on the Lower Colorado River Authority, and his connections in Washington, helped Brown & Root secure their first federal contract in 1937, which was the company's watershed year. The initial contract for construction on the Marshall Ford (Mansfield) Dam on the Colorado above Austin was only $5 million, but the figure soon mounted to $27 million. Wirtz had urged his local congressman, James P. Buchanan, chairman of the House Appropriations Committee, to award Brown & Root the contract, and the raise.

That the name Brown became synonymous with "conservatism" in Texas is one of the New Deal's supreme ironies. Roosevelt and his policies were unpopular among the cotton, cattle, and railroad fortunes, and among the trusts, which viewed the emergent Texas entrepreneur through red-tinted glasses. The old money failed to realize that its competition lay in the public coffers. The Browns understood the slope of the new land, and the fact that anyone who let philosophy stand in the way of profit was a fool.

Another connection between the Browns and Johnson was Ed Clark, who looked after the interests of Brown & Root in the state legislature. Clark had acted as Johnson's campaign manager in 1937, after Johnson served as director of the National Youth Administration in Texas. And Wirtz was chairman of the state advisory board of the NYA, which dispensed $32 million worth of opportunity in Texas, enabling Johnson to build a political organization of sorts. Johnson's support of

Roosevelt's plan to pack the Supreme Court almost cost him the election, but it won him gratitude from the President, and the flood of benefits for friends and constituents.

During his first two years in office, Johnson and his advisers saw that $70 million worth of federal money found its way into his congressional district. Wirtz hovered close by, advising, accompanying the young Lyndon into Roosevelt's office to secure funds for the Pedernales Electric Cooperative, the largest Rural Electrification Administration cooperative in the nation. Brown & Root, Wirtz's client and Johnson's supporter, was the most obvious beneficiary. The firm began to collect REA, Works Progress Administration, and Public Works Administration contracts for dams and power stations along the Highland Lakes, the Colorado River, and the Pedernales. More construction jobs became available through the Texas Rural Electric, a statewide association of power cooperatives, represented by the protean Wirtz.

Johnson's first link with big oil was also provided by Brown & Root. The Browns formed Texas Eastern Transmission Corporation, and in 1947 acquired the Big Inch and Little Inch pipelines from the federal government for $143 million, and had one converted for the transmission of natural gas to the lucrative Eastern market. But that followed the Second World War, and Johnson's advocacy of military preparedness that helped secure Brown & Root its biggest contract yet, right down home in Corpus Christi.

In 1940, Roosevelt told his Secretary of the Navy, Frank Knox, that Lyndon Johnson should be consulted in the matter of a naval air station to be constructed— at an eventual cost of $100 million, three times the estimated amount. Brown & Root received a third of that contract, beginning a long and profitable association between the company and the Navy that would involve projects in the Pacific, Spain, and Vietnam. The most profitable deal, and the one that put Brown & Root up among the top contracting firms in the nation, involved shipbuilding contracts secured from the Navy by Johnson. The Brown Shipbuilding Company put $6 million into a yard in the Houston ship channel that by 1944 had built $357 million worth of subchasers and destroyer escorts, employing 25,000 workers at the height of the war.

When Johnson ran for the Senate against "Pappy" O'Daniel, he set up his campaign headquarters in Austin's Brown Building. Johnson had the ready use of an airplane, and was able to purchase seemingly unlimited radio spots and newspaper ads, and to plaster Texas with billboards showing himself shaking hands with FDR. A $25,000 limit on campaign expenditures had been set by federal law, but Johnson spent half a million on the campaign—a tremendous amount at the time, and most of it contributed by Brown & Root. Johnson narrowly lost the election, but the Browns did not lose their investment.

The Internal Revenue Service undertook an investigation of Brown & Root's campaign activities. The company had deducted campaign contributions as business expenses, attorneys' fees, or company bonuses. The Victoria Gravel Company, a Brown & Root subsidiary, served as a conduit of funds into Johnson's organization, which were dispensed by company lawyers to pay for the radio spots, printing, and other expenses. The IRS further discovered that Brown & Root awarded extraordinary bonuses to company executives in the spring, rather than just before Christmas, so the money could be paid at the beginning of the campaign, to which the executives were heavy contributors.

After the election, Brown & Root complained that harassment by the IRS was hindering their construction efforts for the war. The investigation limped along for another year, in spite of Brown & Root's appeal to patriotism. Then Wirtz acted with characteristic effectiveness, taking Johnson with him into the office of President Roosevelt and requesting relief for his clients. Roosevelt requested a full report of the investigation from the IRS office in Dallas. A new agent was dispatched to that city, and the liability of Brown & Root was promptly assessed at more than a million dollars, with a penalty for fraud of another $532,000. The company, for reasons that never became clear, was asked to pay only a total of $327,000, which it did with alacrity. And the investigation was officially closed.

Just how much Brown & Root contributed to Johnson was never disclosed. Nor were the details of the settlement and investigation by the IRS. The contested tax returns, and other pertinent records, were all stored in a Quonset hut in south Dallas. It mysteriously caught fire in 1953, and burned to the ground, destroying the material completely.

The lesson learned was one of stealth. Campaign contributions by Brown & Root executives and employees, and the use of company planes, were once again major factors in Johnson's race in 1948, and his narrow victory over Coke Stevenson. Johnson's dubious case was presented to the State Democratic Executive Committee by a lawyer in Wirtz's firm, Charles Francis, who had earlier been instrumental in the Browns' obtaining of the Big Inch and Little Inch pipelines. Francis was a stockholder in Texas Eastern Transmission. He presented Johnson's case again in federal court, where the district judge found evidence of "fraud in the manipulation and counting of votes."

The case went to the Supreme Court. Again, it was Francis who took his argument personally to Hugo Black, accompanied by Abe Fortas, later to become a Justice himself. (The Texas end of the controversy was handled by Wirtz, and by Ed Clark, whose law partner ran what had become the repository of Johnson's fortune, the Brazos-Tenth Street Company.) Black heard the case in his chambers, and ruled in Johnson's favor, thereby killing the investigation.

Johnson's theme of military preparedness pleased the Brown brothers. Senator Johnson told Congress in 1948 that the Air Force must be strengthened: "No matter what else we have of offensive or defensive weapons, without superior air power America is a bound and throttled giant, impotent and easy prey to any yellow dwarf with a pocketknife."

The war had wrecked the industries of the European countries, and Brown & Root was able to go abroad with ease. Much of their construction would provide bases for future wars, such as the installations built by the company on Guam—a $130 million contract—that became logistical bases for Vietnam. During the next five years, $100 million more went to Brown & Root for additional construction on other islands in the Pacific, and in Alaska and Canada.

In Europe, Brown & Root teamed up with another contractor to build nine NATO air bases in France, at a cost of $200 million. In league with Raymond International and Walsh Construction, Brown & Root shared in a $357 million cost-plus contract for Navy bases in Spain. Part of that contract was eventually converted from cost-plus to fixed price, but the partners, BRW, claimed almost $7 million in "excess of reasonable estimates." The General Accounting Office, Brown & Root's nemesis, pointed out that this figure included almost $4 million for expenses at the companies' home offices. "We found no evidence," the GAO report stated, "and BRW has presented none, to show that the home offices of the individual joint ventures performed any significant services for which they had not been otherwise adequately reimbursed." Another overcharge involved half a million dollars paid as bonuses to American workers, intended by the government to be paid out of the companies' profits but claimed as costs.

The Navy readily paid what BRW asked, but the GAO charges forced the top brass into a show of concern. The Navy's solution was to award BRW additional contracts, and then claim the government had retrieved its money through administrative costs assumed by the companies. The Navy was accused of padding the accounts by duplicate accounting of jobs already finished, overestimating the amount "recovered" by $2 million. The GAO labeled the errors made by the Navy "obvious," but the Navy insisted that the contractors were under no obligation "to effect any refund." During the time of the controversy over the bases in Spain, the Secretary of the Navy was John Connally.

The Browns' influence was great in Texas, and it also extended to Washington. By the early 1950s, Herman helped block legislation in Congress he considered obnoxious. His heavy backing contributed greatly to the success of the Taft-Hartley Act, and in Texas he could affect passage of almost any bill through the legislature. The Browns' influence was not based solely upon money; it was rather the judicious and vigorous application of money, in conjunction with an active interest in politics. Herman and George not only had powerful friends and several fortunes, but they were also willing to spend their own time and effort seeing that candidates were elected, bills passed, and the state of Texas kept safe for free enterprise.

Both brothers were members of Houston's 8-F Crowd, prominent businessmen who met in Herman's suite at the Lamar Hotel to play cards, drink, and talk—mostly about politics. Other members included Jesse Jones, former Secretary of Commerce, publisher of the Houston *Chronicle*, and Mr. Houston himself; Judge James

Elkins, lawyer and banker; William A. Smith, railroad tycoon; James Abercrombie, oilman and lawyer; and Leopold Meyer, a merchandiser of great wealth. Gus Wortham, another member, rented the suite next door to 8-F, where the group met when the Browns were not present.

All these men were millionaires, self-made, and of similar opinions. During the 1940s and 1950s, they exercised a concerted influence in Texas that was unparalleled. Not only did they raise a great deal of money for candidates, but the endorsement of the 8-F Crowd meant that a candidate had the general approval of the business community, was the establishment's anointed. Also, the collective number of employees working for those men in Herman's suite represented a bloc of votes that was substantial, and potential for further contributions. They did not hesitate to pick up the telephone and solicit support from other influential men. They reveled in partisan politics, in a state where there was no other kind.

They also had a good time, meeting in the afternoons after work and often staying late. They traveled together, attending horse races in southern California, New Orleans, Saratoga. Herman, Wortham, and Judge Elkins always rented the same apartment at the Kentucky Derby, where every year they remained from Thursday until Sunday.

Those afternoons in Suite 8-F were often raucous affairs. "Our families sometimes got a little impatient when we didn't get home to dinner," Wortham fondly remembers. "There were a lot of serious things about the 8-F Crowd, too. We talked about public affairs, exchanged ideas. . . . Herman was an excellent conversationalist, when he wanted to talk. He was extremely positive in his views, he never doubted that he was right."

One member of the 8-F Crowd who did not go home

late to dinner was George Brown. In the beginning he was overshadowed by Herman, and yet George was smoother, not gregarious, yet ultimately receptive. He seemed to anticipate the changing face of wealth in Texas, and would be able to make the transition from hard-bitten, self-made man to corporate entity much more easily than would his older brother. There was something austere about George—he seemed to lack genuine enthusiasm for the prolonged company of other men—some intimation of second-generation money.

The standard procedure for rich men seeking influence in the state legislature was to contribute to lobbying organizations such as the Texas Manufacturers Association, the Texas Medical Association, the Mid-Continent Oil & Gas Association, or the Texas Good Roads Association. Austin's hospitality suites, free meals, and entertainment are familiar to all state legislators. But Herman Brown was the only individual who maintained his own personal lobbying force in the capitol. Ed Clark and Frank "Posh" Oltorf, a cherubic man with a permanent grin, kept close watch on the legislature when it was in session, and Wirtz himself often showed up in support of key Brown bills.

Legislation that Herman found most repulsive was that identified with labor—minimum wages, grievance clauses, unemployment insurance, the very recognition of unions. He was powerful enough to obtain an injunction in state court denying organized labor the right to picket any Brown & Root construction sites, or even to distribute printed literature. He is given credit for the passage of the most favored of laws by contractors, which made it illegal for an employer or an employee to enter into a contract requiring membership or lack of membership in any organization as a condition of work. (After a Brown & Root car was damaged by picketers at a construction site, Herman saw to it that anyone willfully damaging a motor vehicle could be sentenced to ten years in prison.) Such laws were the culmination of the Browns' running battle with organized labor during the 1940s; they were often represented in court by Wirtz and Connally. The Browns never used union labor when it could be avoided, which was most of the time—and managed to shed the stigma of New Deal liberalism in the process.

Herman could be vindictive. One of Texas's most popular radio broadcasters and an employee of Connally's KVET, Stuart Long, was an independent force in Austin, and would become an institution among the state's journalists. He was considered a liberal, reason enough to be thought a threat to Brown and his friends at a time of growing contention between organized labor and Brown & Root. Long did an exposé of a high-ranking state official who accepted $100,000 from a big oil company to settle a lawsuit, and that earned Long the further enmity of Brown and other oilmen. Ed Clark, Brown's lobbyist and an officer in Brown's Austin bank, pressed for Long's dismissal from KVET. When Long's wife, Emma, opposed Brown on local political issues, Long was summarily fired. (Long founded his own news service in the capitol, and became such a favored source for out-of-state reporters searching for skeletons in Lone Star closets that he now charges a twenty dollars an hour consulting fee.)

Herman Brown's direct intervention in political affairs was something of a watershed; previously, wealthy men usually remained aloof from the sordid realities. Such men depended upon company lawyers to represent their interests, but that was changing. Connally would be the first governor to place the rich on state boards, giving them a primary role in running the state.

Employees of Brown & Root were—and still are—expected to support company-approved candidates. Races for Congress, the state legislature, the Houston school board, and the mayor's office are treated with equal seriousness. Employees contribute, as well as vote. For years, Brown & Root bought a block of tickets to the annual safety show in Houston and passed them out to employees. The company's political arms, such as the Conservative Action Club, conduct mass mailings on behalf of favored candidates.

Indoctrination sessions are held before each election. A young attorney who went to work for Brown & Root straight out of law school describes the process: "We are all called into staff meetings before elections, and handed a list of candidates for whom we are to vote. Their opponents' names are not on the list. The approved candidates' virtues are described, but there is no discussion of the issues involved, or what the approved candidates represent. Then we are given time off to attend political rallies of the approved candidates, with buses provided by the company.

"I had fairly long hair when I started work, and was told to have it cut. I also had to regularly attend pep talks by company officials. The general theme is that business knows best how to regulate itself, that organized labor is evil. They tell us that what's good for Brown & Root is good for America."

In 1935, the assets of Brown & Root were a mere $658,-000. This figure doubled over the next two years, after the first flush of New Deal contracts. Wartime construction brought company assets quickly up to $5.5 million, a figure that did not include Brown Shipbuilding, the biggest earner, and not reflecting other, hidden assets. Prior to the big cost-plus contract in Spain, Brown & Root's assets in 1954 were $27.5 million, and the profit was $13 million.

Not long after Herman Brown's death in 1962 George sold Brown & Root to the Halliburton Company, the world's largest oil and gas service company, for a reputed $37 million, but there remained a question of who controlled whom. George acquired Halliburton stock in the swap; Brown & Root continued to operate independently. In 1965, the company did $639 million worth of business, a third of it outside the United States. Four years later, it had become the nation's largest construction firm, with a volume of $1.77 billion, and a record of massive and diverse projects completed in Thailand, Haiti, Mexico, Australia, Puerto Rico, Italy, the North Sea, Peru, Venezuela, and the Persian Gulf.

The name Brown had become associated with the most ambitious and profitable development projects, and with insurance, banking, and oil. George moved with Episcopalian grace among the private corridors of the most powerful, from Houston's First City National Bank to directorships of such corporations as Trans World Airlines, Armco Steel, and the organization that, other than Brown & Root, seemed most appreciative of his talents, International Telephone & Telegraph.

The Brown Foundation, set up in 1951 as the haven for the estates of Herman and his wife, was reported to have become a substantial contributor to organizations connected with the Central Intelligence Agency. One of these, the American Friends of the Middle East, received $50,000 from the Brown Foundation in 1960. Shortly thereafter, Brown & Root won a contract for construction of an oil pipeline in Saudi Arabia from the Arabian-American Oil Company. The Brown Foundation made another $50,000 contribution in 1962, and two years later gave AFME an impressive $150,000.

"Brown's interests were also peripherally involved in other CIA funding operations," wrote David Welsh in an article that appeared in *Ramparts* magazine in 1967. ITT was an obvious example, but there were operations closer to home. A director of Texas Eastern Transmission was the founder of the mysterious, tax-exempt San Jacinto Fund, which received large anonymous contributions, and dispersed the money among various organizations considered worthy. These included the National Students Association, later disclosed as a major front for domestic CIA activity. The AFME received a million dollars from the San Jacinto Fund between 1960 and 1962. The fund's headquarters were in Houston's San Jacinto Building, downstairs from the Brown Foundation headquarters, and the offices of several companies owned by Brown & Root.

The Brown Foundation didn't maintain offices separate from Brown & Root until forced to do so by the Tax Reform Act of 1969. The foundation embodied the obsessive secrecy of the Brown family, who shared the board with company executives. Although the foundation disposed of $30 million in unpublicized grants, it was primarily a tax-saving device involved in brinkmanship between financial gain and the appearance of developing worthwhile programs. It found itself involved in state scandals, such as the creation of the Lyndon B. Johnson State Park on land directly across the road from Johnson's ranch, while Johnson was still President. The land was condemned by a public agency, but the money raised among secret, private contributors. The Brown Foundation donated $50,000, an inconsiderable amount by Brown standards. (While Connally was governor, Brown & Root gave the governor's office a large passenger airplane because, according to George, the company just didn't need it anymore.)

Brown & Root continued to obtain the most lucrative government contracts with Johnson on the doorstep of the White House. When NASA needed a new space center, Texans were mighty glad Johnson happened to be such an exalted figure. Although billions had already been spent on initial installations for space shots in Florida, and twenty American cities were clamoring to be chosen as the recipient of one of the biggest slices of federal largesse since the New Deal, the final selection was a swampy plain outside Houston. That surprised few who reflected upon the fact that Texas Congressman Albert Thomas was chairman of the Appropriations Subcommittee controlling NASA's budget, and that Thomas was a loyal friend of George Brown's. Both Brown and Thomas were Rice alumni, and George had donated $500,000 to the school to create the Albert Thomas Chair of Political Science.

It was a charitable Humble Oil that donated land through Rice for the Space Center—1,000 acres out of some 50,000 owned by the company in the area, which sky-rocketed in value after construction began. Humble's real-estate subsidiary did millions of dollars in new business, including an industrial park built on the ship channel, recreational facilities, and a vast housing project. (Johnson's friend and associate Jack Valenti, a former Humble employee, was granted the advertising contract.) And Rice received a space-science department— appropriately subsidized by the federal government.

Everybody profited, but none like Brown & Root. In a book entitled *Decisive Years for Houston*, Marvin Hurley of the Chamber of Commerce proudly writes, "Early in June, 1961 . . . I heard rumors of some type of new installation for the nation's space effort, and made calls at the office of Vice President Johnson and upon Congressman Albert Thomas and Bob Casey. . . . The inspection team conducted its investigation a few weeks later. . . . George R. Brown was especially effective in working out site arrangements with Congressman Thomas."

Brown & Root was chosen as the primary contractor at the $250 million Space Center. The company also received a maintenance contract with the Northrop Corporation for another $10 million a year. Brown & Root undertook most of the road and industrial construction adjacent to the center, built the million-dollar "spaceland airpark," became the principal contractor for Humble's development at Baytown, and on the $100 million project developing Nassau Bay.

Project Mohole was not so neat a piece of work. The bizarre project to drill through the earth's outer crust—the "Mohorovičić discontinuity"—into its interior was hailed as a momentous venture that would provide valuable scientific data. But it proved to be one of the most blatant cases of political favoritism, and of as much interest to oil companies as to scientists. The hole was to be drilled at an estimated cost of $20 million. This estimate rose 800 percent before the contractor, Brown & Root, was denied further funds from the government. The company's aim, however, was at least partially realized: the development of new technology at public expense for the drilling of deep-water oil wells.

Brown & Root was one of five companies bidding for the Mohole contract, awarded by the National Science Foundation. The competitors were oil companies, and the leader in an evaluation by experts of the companies' capabilities was Socony-Mobil. Brown & Root placed last in that evaluation, and their estimated price was almost double that of the lowest bidder. Yet Brown & Root received the contract.

Johnson was President of the United States; Congressman Albert Thomas controlled appropriations for the project. The role of the NSF in such maneuvering seems uncharacteristic until one considers that Johnson had just appointed the president of Humble Oil—Brown's friend—to the NSF board. To avert criticism, the project's overseers announced that it would provide oil companies "unfair competitive advantage" if any received the contract. But the name Brown was a large force in oil, and not just through Texas Eastern Transmission, or the smaller oil subsidiaries. Within months of receiving the contract for Project Mohole, Brown & Root would merge with Halliburton, the prime oil-well service company. The technology developed on Mohole would put Halliburton/Brown & Root years ahead of the nearest competition.

Mohole's test run cost $1.5 million, and over the next four years $125 million more was added to the estimate. Brown & Root was guaranteed a $1.7 million profit, whether or not the project failed. (Details of the contract award were never released because, said the NSF, such information wasn't "in the public interest.")

The costs kept rising. In 1966, Brown & Root asked for an additional $20 million, and the House Appropriations Committee finally drew the line on what had become known as "Project Rathole." Johnson personally appealed to Congress not to kill the project, and his view might have prevailed if it hadn't become known that George and members of the Brown family had donated $23,000 to Johnson's President's Club the week before. George termed the charges of influence "ridiculous," and added ingenuously, "We do things in a family way."

Defending Brown & Root's role in the affair, George added, "Mohole is little more than a drop in the Brown & Root bucket."

Johnson's liberal accomplishments while he was President remain a central issue in contemporary politics, and a kind of wonder. His concern for the poor and the minorities was his greatest liability among his principal backers. Just as LBJ had to counter his early association with Roosevelt and his policies by loudly advocating military preparedness, he found it necessary to perform some act of atonement after he espoused civil rights. Vietnam was that act.

The construction contract in Vietnam was the largest of its kind ever awarded. Such accelerated military projects are ordinarily undertaken by the military itself, but in this case a mammoth consortium was employed to transform South Vietnam into a staging area for the conflict. Four companies were involved, the other three being Morrison-Knudson, Brown & Root's partner in various dam-building projects back home; Raymond International, Brown & Root's partner in Spain; and J. A. Jones Construction, also previously involved with Brown & Root at home. They were known as RMK-BRJ, and it felt like old-home week to the principals involved.

The price of construction in Vietnam was to be $1.2 billion, the Defense Department announced in 1962. The crash program began, and during the mid-1960s there appeared airfields, barracks, and roads. The consortium built Danang and Cam Ranh Bay, two of the finest ports in Asia, which cost $150 million apiece; a new United States Embassy; a $25 million extension of the Pentagon; Tan Son Nhut Airport; and the headquarters and military jail at Long Binh.

There seemed to be nothing that RMK-BRJ couldn't accomplish, and the military loved them. Lavish trailers housing the contractors and engineers bordered the beaches, plugged with heavy air-conditioners. Their occupants were known by the Vietnamese as "the horrible ones," who often drank heavily, abused the local people, and rode Hondas up the steps of Buddhist temples. A quarter of the work force these Americans supervised was Vietcong, but that did not unduly bother their employers, as long as the work was done, and the stolen material could be charged to the government. There were innumerable charges that workers were treated as slaves. Peak employment was reached in 1965, with some Americans receiving $2,000 a month, and some Vietnamese as little as eight cents an hour.

In September, 1966, the Navy was threatened with a major scandal in management. Two former employees of RMK-BRJ—they had been "surplused," a euphemism for laid off—claimed that out of $830 million paid for construction by the government, only $590 million had actually been completed. The $240 million loss was the result of "poor planning and waste."

True to form, the Navy defended the consortium. The Naval Facilities Engineering Command, manager of the construction program, responded: "We have done a fantastic feat, and are proud of our effort." Part of that feat was the creation of a leviathan capable of $40 million worth of construction a month. Next to the Vietnamese armed forces, RMK-BRJ was the largest employer in Vietnam. The construction project began to wind down coincidentally with the revelation of massive waste. "Surplusing" of large numbers of Vietnamese workers again threatened the country's economy.

The Navy's defense became more suspect when it was discovered that for the first two years of RMK-BRJ's activity in South Vietnam, the consortium was audited by only one man. That number was doubled before the accelerated program began in 1966, and later half a dozen Air Force officers were added to the staff. But that was still woefully insufficient, and the General Accounting Office moved in again. The GAO discovered that only a seventh of the cost reimbursements had been checked, at a time when construction was humming along at more than $5 million worth per month.

In the meantime, Texas was enjoying its own end of the Vietnam bonanza. Two and a half billion dollars flowed into the state's defense industry in 1966 alone. Chemical companies sold more than $10 million worth of defoliants; there was rubber and petrochemicals, and an order for $186 million worth of aircraft fuel was placed with Texans that December.

RMK-BRJ reacted loudly to criticism. They were in Vietnam, the consortium claimed, "mainly for patriotic reasons." However, Brown & Root's revenues for 1966 were 57 percent higher than the previous year, before the crash program began. Raymond International enjoyed its highest six months' earnings for more than ten years in 1966. (The previous year the company actually showed a deficit.)

In 1967, the GAO reported that millions of dollars' worth of materials and supplies had been dumped in temporary open storage areas, and issued without controls directly from those temporary areas. It was impossible to determine what had been used on authorized projects, what had been appropriated by military units without authorization, and what had been stolen and resold. It was unofficial policy with RMK-BRJ to maintain a considerable element of unaccountability, so the Navy would have to automatically issue wavers. A Navy procurement officer set the figure representing material unaccounted for at $45 million. The GAO's estimate was $120 million.

Senator Abraham Ribicoff, after visiting Vietnam, told the Senate he found "serious questions regarding the performance of certain American construction firms." The enormous loss brought about other stirrings of congressional discontent, and so RMK-BRJ decided to act. Miraculously, between May and November the consortium by its own accounting managed to shrink the figure for lost, wasted, and stolen material by $115 million.

As Ribicoff later stated, "I find it incredible that the RMK-BRJ joint venture could reduce the total figures . . . particularly after the GAO had indicated such a lack of accountability controls. . . . In my view, the information given us was completely unconvincing."

Vietnam was not the only instance in which the reliability of American contractors was brought into doubt. Brown & Root and Morrison-Knudson received a $42 million contract to build a road through Peru's jungles and across the Andes, connecting the Pacific coast with the lush Amazon Basin. Such a road had been a Peruvian dream for a decade. Money for the project was put up by the Agency for International Development and the Export-Import Bank. After the funds were turned over to the government of Peru, however, these agencies remained aloof from the project. The stipulation was that Peru must retain American contractors, and that details of construction were then a private matter between the contractors and the Peruvians.

American officials in Lima acted in concert with the American developers. Enthusiastic reports about the benefits of a superhighway were prepared for government officials. Brown & Root's plan was elaborate, and oddly unreal, showing an idealized highway spanning the Andes and yet somehow remaining almost flat. The highway was to cost four times that of a more modest road that would follow the natural contours of the land, but the Americans rejected such an old-fashioned approach.

The initial bids were impossibly high, and some cosmetic economizing had to be done. It was decided that the highway's asphalt covering would simply be eliminated, for no one seemed concerned about erosion. The basic plan, calling for such measures as blasting cuts in the mountains two hundred feet deep, remained unchanged. Brown & Root was chosen as the contractor overseeing the actual construction work, performed by Brown & Root's partner Morrison-Knudson. It is difficult to imagine a more advantageous arrangement for contractors operating abroad. In 1965, Morrison-Knudson shipped the necessary equipment 2,500 miles up the Amazon, and work began on the highway.

Two years later, an American engineer monitoring the project for the Agency for International Development found that the equipment operators on the job were few and poorly trained, and that the accident rate was "abnormally high." Worse, the road grades were in many places either too low or too high. "The supervisory personnel working now on the job," the engineer reported, "have had most of their experience on dam and missile sites, which is not quite the same as road construction, particularly in the Andes and the jungle."

Then auditors for AID discovered that a top official of Brown & Root had used labor and materials from the road project to build his own house, and to help furnish it had charged some expenses to the government. He was fired, but fled Peru before he could be prosecuted.

Meanwhile, landslides began to cover the road. The cost to Morrison-Knudson of clearing away the debris was more than $2 million. Improper dynamiting, and the building of access roads dangerously close to the tops of major cuts led to the landslides, and Brown & Root's supervising engineer refused to authorize payment by the Peruvian government to Morrison-Knudson to correct their own mistakes.

The engineer would have cause to regret this display of integrity. A meeting was called between high officials of Brown & Root and Morrison-Knudson, and the engineer's decision was later reversed. He was fired, and unofficially blackballed in the construction industry, so that by 1972 he had applied unsuccessfully to more than thirty construction firms for a job. The Peruvian government commented upon the fact that Brown & Root and Morrison-Knudson were not exactly adversaries, were in fact associates of long standing, and the reversal of the engineer's ruling was suspect.

The Peruvians sued, confiscated some equipment, and the funds from America dried up. The road was never completed, and the controversy raised serious questions about the activities of Brown & Root abroad. The GAO later released a report stating that Brown & Root had in designing the road not "performed surveys nor taken adequate core borings" in areas where deep cuts were made. Drainage facilities had also been improperly placed under the road, causing some stretches to subside.

It was at this time that Treasury Secretary John Connally suggested that we "get tough" with South America because, he said, "we don't have any friends left down there anyway."

Interlude

FAST FOOD

The last commuters urge their cars toward distant pleasures. Those of us who remain downtown after business hours must all be strangers, faced with the prospect of an evening alone in Dallas.

An imitation gas lamp beckons from the hub of a gilded wagon wheel. Although the restaurant is only blocks from Neiman-Marcus and two of the biggest banks in Texas, it is almost empty. The few customers are salesmen from Amarillo or St. Louis, or even New York, who have strolled over from the Sheraton to take their pick of the plush red booths, and expensive processed food.

My choice is the Burger Deluxe. During the short wait before its arrival, I leaf through the Neiman-Marcus catalogue, a collection of glossy color panels where exotic objects lurk in opulent gloom. An earlier visit to the store itself failed to produce an interview with Stanley Marcus, arbiter of taste in Texas and something of a legend: he was appropriately in Paris.

There's worse entertainment than the Neiman-Marcus Christmas catalogue. It is Marcus's way "of setting the mood for the excitement to come, and to help you begin your shopping . . . it reflects the Neiman-Marcus determination to edit [*sic*] the world's markets for the finest . . . forward-oriented fashions and furs, the fun of toys, and superb epicurean gifts. . . ."

Such a modest introduction. Who unfamiliar with the institution of Neiman-Marcus would shortly expect to be offered a nickel-plated brass penguin filled with antarctic ice "custom chipped and hand-carried from an authentic south polar iceberg"? At $3,450, it must be pure whimsy. But what about the two carved wooden horse heads, "dated in the 18th century," for $7,500? They do not resemble horses I have seen in Texas, or anywhere else, having lost their ears somewhere between India and Dallas.

Further setting the mood for excitement to come is the World Time Computer that for $4,750 provides "at the touch of a button" the correct time anywhere in the world. These are serious gifts, and they get more serious. The Fabergé egg, "traditional gift of Imperial Russia, in translucent and iridescent enamel on gold, set in a gold tripod stand," costs $25,000. And the 106-carat opal, supposedly described by Pliny—"You shall see the living fire of the ruby, the glorious purple of the amethyst, the green sea of the emerald . . ."—goes for $150,000.

My Burger Deluxe arrives, meat blowing bubbles in the hot grease of its own decomposition, languid on half a seeded bun. Ribbons of carrot garnish a plate otherwise empty of color, and banked with fries pale and thin as minnows skimmed in a cave.

I take solace in the catalogue, and its photographs of pampered, frail men and women who lack the milk-fed heartiness of Texans. They, and the people who work in various Neiman-Marcus stores, seem to have been hired because they look decidedly un-Texan. For instance, the couple modeling the His and Her Hoverbugs, gliding gaily from their vibrant green lawn to the surface of their lake, and back again, are apparently members of a Virginia hunt set.

And the couple on a veranda in what must be the Algarve appear downright foreign. He's "the One-Up Man . . . wants clothes to accentuate his appearance, not hide it. . . ." Which includes the oil on his hair, and his brow, perhaps the effects of drinking gin in the Portuguese sun. He grips the empty glass, while a woman lounges at his side. She wears a pink shirt "with the where-with-all to wear with all," and insect-like sunglasses. Both she and her companion stare at something on the beach that does not please them.

Is there a lesson in these alien faces, as there is in much of that precious copy? The catalogue can be pedantic. Neiman-Marcus dresses have "a neat, correct shape seen everywhere." The length of a fifty-dollar pair of kid gloves "is correct for current wider sleeves." Marcus has made a fortune showing rich Texans what they are not.

He has some competition. Sakowitz in Houston offers piano lessons by Peter Duchin for $3,750, swimming lessons by Mark Spitz for $115,000, lessons in making odds by Jimmy the Greek for $565,000. There's broncobusting by Larry Mahan, skiing by Killy, conversation by Capote. The whole package is available for just under a million dollars.

While considering these things, I notice a rat standing on the stairs, not ten feet away. He is a large rat, and he is staring at the remains of my Burger Deluxe, his nose thrust between the bars of the railing, his black eyes uncomprehending and unafraid. No one else notices. The man on the far side of the stairs is bent over his second shrimp cocktail; the waitress, one hip against the relish counter, is lost in dreams.

Before I can raise the alarm, the rat turns, leaps onto

the carpet at the foot of the stairs, and disappears beneath the seat of an empty booth, leaving the tassels swinging.

"Did you enjoy your dinner?" asks the cashier as I come forward to pay the bill. She has sculptured blond hair, and a proprietary smile.

I lie, and add, "Except for the rat."

Her smile does not falter. "We've tried everything we can to get rid of that rat—traps, poison. Just nothing works."

Her equanimity is unsettling, as is the mention of poison. I think of the seeds on my Burger Deluxe.

"You know something?" And a note of mischief enters her voice. "That rat's kind of cute, the way it plays there on the stairs like a kitten." She leans toward me, over the mints. "The other night two couples came in, and they sat in that booth where that rat likes to go. Before long that rat came out to go up there and play on the steps like he likes to do. Well, those girls saw him . . ."

It occurs to me then that no one will believe this story. Indeed, I am having some difficulty myself, and will later wake up in my hotel room doubting the entire experience, in spite of the digestive murmurs.

". . . and they let out a scream like you never heard. I'm telling you, that rat jumped two feet in the air." Her smile is replaced by lips tight with disapproval. "Those girls like to scared that rat to *death*."

Weeks later, far from Dallas, I again opened my Neiman-Marcus Christmas catalogue, and came across the most unique gift of all: "The N-Bar-M Mouse Ranch is a mousetrap any mouse would love. We created it as the possible fulfillment of your childhood dream, and a paradise for mice . . . complete with mesa, cacti, upper and lower pastures, corral, feed barn, watering tanks, feed bins, plenty of fencing, and a windmill. . . . Imagine the thrill of sitting around the campfire (or fireplace), singing songs of the prairie under the full moon . . . (or lamp), with your own herd lowing softly (squeaking gently?) . . . Picture the thrill of rodeo time . . . The N-Bar-M Ranch is a controlled and utopian environment created in clear acrylic . . . you will receive silver plated round-up tweezers and personalized branding iron (using a special indelible ink so you won't traumatize your herd) . . . $3,500."

And it's tax-free.

5 ☆ THE HUNTS

Silver, Intrigue, and a Wooden Indian

The death of H. L. Hunt, one of the world's richest men, in late 1974 surprised many Americans, who assumed he had long since met the fate of dollar oil and "Facts Forum." That Hunt went to his office in Dallas daily to the end, riding in a wheelchair and sometimes carrying his lunch in the notorious paper bag, seemed quaint and a little sad. If he had any peers left among his countrymen, they were limited to Howard Hughes and J. Paul Getty, fellow oilmen and galaxian entrepreneurs separated from their nearest competitors by more than barricades of cash: they took the great risks. And even Getty once admitted, "The corporations in which I own shares are rich enterprises, but I am not wealthy. They hold the property, they control me. In terms of extraordinary, independent wealth, there is only one man— H. L. Hunt."

The name is synonymous with inordinate wealth, personal idiosyncrasy, and political obsolescence. The excesses of the anti-Communist propaganda broadcast for years over "Life Line," Hunt's heavily endowed and widely transmitted radio program that also advertised his Gastro Magic health foods, influenced millions of listeners glued to their Motorolas in the kitchens and milk sheds of the heartland. Hunt was the quintessential self-made man, fond of battered old cars, whole-grain snacks, and crawling on all fours for exercise. His qualities were those that made men rich in the grandest manner of his era in Texas. Perseverance, luck, shrewdness, ruthlessness, frugality, and some charm are traits that rarely transfer to heirs in that ineffable mix known as a tycoon. Indeed, in the death of Haroldson Lafayette Hunt we seemed to have lost some elemental chunk of America.

Or did we? The day before Hunt died, it was widely reported that two of his sons, Nelson Bunker Hunt and William Herbert Hunt, were busy trying to acquire the nation's largest grower of beet sugar, the Great Western United Corporation, in which they had a sizable investment. Their offer to buy almost a million additional shares of common stock at $27.50 a share understandably upset Great Western's officers, who appeared powerless to prevent a takeover. Actually, the deal was nickel-and-dime for the Hunts. Controlling a major supply of sugar at current prices represented just one cubbyhole in the vast roll-top desk of contemporary Huntdom, sandwiched between a $13 billion lawsuit filed against Mobil Oil Corporation and, say, their big splash in the world's silver market.

Bunker and Herbert Hunt took control of the family businesses in 1969. With their younger brother, Lamar, they personify the best of the latter-day wildcatters at play in the most lucrative fields, including commodities, real estate, professional sports, oil production and marketing. Second-generation oil money has often been frittered away on art museums, water gardens, or foundations, but the Hunt fortune remains untainted by excessive culture, charity, or enduring monuments, which do not even earn interest.

The Hunt Oil Company is that roll-top desk, housed at the top of the First National Bank Building in Dallas. The company's weekly income has been estimated at upward of a million dollars, but some insist that figure is woefully inadequate. The modest reception area on the twenty-ninth floor offers a view of the city's ragged collision with the country, and no amenities. On the wall hangs a framed reproduction of the official Hunt crest— a leopard seated stiffly below an ax. "The surname Hunt appears to be occupational in origin," the text explains, "and is believed to be associated with the English meaning: 'One who hunted game.'" On the table stands a collection of paperback books written by H. L. Hunt himself—*Why Not Speak, Right of Center, Right of Average, Weekly Strength, Fabians Fight Freedom*— windy, urgent tracts advocating "constructive" politics, Hunt's hybrid conservatism.

Inquiries about Hunt Oil produce a publicist in an iridescent green suit and ventilated shoes. He regards the visitor with severest disapproval while reciting the accepted litany: "The Hunts' activities are varied, and not just based in oil. Mr. Hunt had a keen interest in cosmetics and drugs, the remedies of nature, real estate, and cattle. The Hunts own Indian Springs, near El Paso. I believe they have nine springs down there, most of them hot. . . ."

He offers copies of Hunt's books, and the elevator.

Hunt Oil is still a creation of its founder, best understood in his terms. The sons inherited their father's business élan, without the polemics and the proselytizer's zeal that only get in the way of making more money. Today the company represents a billion-dollar anomaly embodying the fustiest traditions of American capitalism and the most brazen ploys of modern international finance. The extent of its holdings, the hidden nature of its operations and the men who head them, and its influence upon prices and policy approach the fantastic.

☆ ☆ ☆

"My early background helped me to appreciate the value and benefits of Freedom, and to understand that Karl Marx's communistic dream poses the worst threat to Truth and Freedom, as well as to our Republic." So begins Hunt's autobiographical *Early Days*, which is unhampered by modesty. "I was one of the youthful prodigies . . . who learned to read about as early as they could walk. In my second year, I commenced reading the St. Louis *Globe-Democrat*."

He was the youngest of eight children, born near Ramsey, Illinois, in 1890, and raised in a rural setting. "I quickly discovered that recognition for achievements had to be earned through constructive accomplishments and industriousness," he wrote in *Hunt Heritage*. His mother's family "were Huguenots from France." She read her youngest son the Bible in Greek, Latin, German, and French, and then translated into English, realizing there were some limits to his prodigiousness. On his father's side, "The Hunts have long been among the most constructive of the early settlers in this country. Robert Hunt . . . was chaplain for the expedition under Captain John Smith." Haroldson Lafayette worked as a clerk in his father's bank before going West at age sixteen "to grow up with the country."

A photograph taken at that time reveals a firm-jawed young man with flaxen hair parted in the middle, and eyes radiant with idealism. That gaze later became as much a part of Hunt's identity as his square-tipped bowties, and the white tonsure with fluffs above the ears— an evangel who saw himself as part of the historical process. Even antiquity posed no problem in his association with great figures. He wrote that he, Cleopatra, and Alexander the Great equally appreciated the healing properties of an exotic plant, *Aloe vera*, which Hunt decided to market. ("Cleopatra won the love of Caesar," he explains, with an insider's panache, "and later, of Marc Antony, almost destroying the Roman Empire.")

He topped sugar beets in Colorado, drove sheep outside Salt Lake City, wrestled with mules on a roadbuilding team in southern California. A trip to Reno for a position on a semiprofessional baseball team saved him from the San Francisco earthquake. He and his brother farmed in the Texas Panhandle, where Hunt learned to parboil chicken, a recipe he dutifully sets forth in *Hunt Heritage*. "The skillet must be iron. . . . Aluminum and many other metals are unhealthy."

He speculated in cotton in the Mississippi Delta, and went broke in the depression following the First World War. His earliest brush with oil came in El Dorado, Arkansas, where it is said he won his first well in a game of five-card stud. Whether or not the story is true, Hunt did not limit himself to wildcatting. He learned the oil business, from drilling to brokering leases, and established his reputation as a fastidious young man on the make. "My credit," he wrote, "was unlimited up to the small operating expenditures required, as I engaged extensively in small business transactions and always succeeded in paying my bills." In the West Smackover, Arkansas, field he sold his interest in forty wells for $600,000, and built steadily upon that score.

Hunt's involvement in the famous east Texas oil boom is interpreted in a typically expansive manner: "A telephone call I received one day turned out to be one of the truly momentous events, not only of my life but in world history." A friend told him about Dad Joiner's wildcat wells, and soon Hunt was on the scene offering to buy Joiner out. Joiner told him, "Boy, you would be buying a pig in a poke," an unlikely description of the world's richest field. Hunt bought 4,000 adjoining acres, and finally obtained Joiner's holdings.

He continued exploration in the United States and

Canada, and moved after the Second World War. There were some setbacks—millions wasted on exploration in Pakistan—but the Hunts' big ventures were successful, including one of the century's greatest oil discoveries in Libya.

"If you know how much money you have," he reportedly later said, "you aren't very wealthy."

His favorite President was Calvin Coolidge. "He summed it all up when he said: 'The business of America is business.'" Much of his conservatism derived from his more vivid early years, when he worked hard for small wages. He contributed heavily to right-wing causes, and during the '50s exerted some influence in national affairs. His "Facts Forum" was a fifteen-minute radio program conducted by the former FBI agent Dan Smoot. "Life Line" came to be carried by four hundred radio stations, and received the tax exemption given to religious organizations. These programs were prepared in Washington, D.C., by a staff of two dozen, and advocated causes other than anti-Communism, including the right of American citizens to bear arms and the need to make General Douglas MacArthur President of the United States in 1952. (Hunt's speech at the dedication of a wax figure of MacArthur at the Texas State Fairgrounds is printed in *Why Not Speak*.)

His politics were set forth in his utopian novel, *Alpaca*, in which a citizen's voting power is determined by his wealth. Hunt had the book translated into several languages, and shipped by bulk to developing nations he thought needed advice. He attacked Socialism, taxes in general, federal regulation, and any opponents of the oil depletion allowance. Paradoxical as only an oilman can be, Hunt was both an isolationist and a heavy investor abroad. He shared Hugh Roy Cullen's view that our joining of the United Nations in 1945 proved America was "decaying politically—so fast that it is very doubtful that we can continue as a democracy." Both men ardently backed the Bricker amendment to limit the President's treaty-making powers.

Hunt and Cullen helped finance For America, a political action group that claimed "international leadership has captured both parties" in America, and was pushing us into Socialism. In 1956, For America backed Senators Bricker and James Eastland. Hunt and his associates interpreted unrest among the nation's poor farmers and laborers as a sign of the insidious influence of Communism, rather than of changing times. He helped usher in the modern era, and yet he resented it. Hunt had distributed thousands of copies of Senator William Jenner's committee report, Interlocking Subversion in Government Departments, which claimed Communists had penetrated the foundations of American government.

"Facts Forum" provided funds for McCarthy's investigations into alleged subversion. The programs were broadcast live, an "All-American . . . non-partisan, educational" effort to bring America back to "the land of the free and the home of the brave." Hunt's constructionists made up one side of this nonpartisan struggle, the other being comprised of Communists, New Dealers, and "Fifth Amendment leftists." There was no longer any place in America for "the wholly indefinite and uncertain Middle-of-the-Road thinking"—a reference to Eisenhower—which was "the stronghold of entrenched apathy."

After the assassination of President Kennedy in Dallas, Hunt became every liberal's favorite cardboard cutout reactionary. The "Life Line" broadcast in Dallas and other areas on the day of Kennedy's visit predicted that Americans would soon not be able to own guns and rise up against their oppressors, whether the oppressors came from Moscow or Washington. His son Nelson Bunker was a sponsor of an inflammatory full-page anti-Kennedy advertisement in the *Morning News,* and was later advised by the FBI to take a trip from Dallas for his own safety. When Jack Ruby was taken into custody after fatally wounding Lee Harvey Oswald, he was found to have two "Life Line" scripts in his pocket. A few days earlier, Ruby had visited the office of Lamar Hunt, but not even the most tenuous link between the Hunts and Kennedy's death was ever established.

Hunt was considered an eccentric in his last years, a judgment that amused him. He wrote a weekly newspaper column, "Hunt for Truth," and took to the Baptists and yogurt, pecans, dates, raisins, and bouillon, on his second wife's advice. He continued to ride to work in an old car, parking blocks away to avoid parking fees. "I like to think that my head is in a cloud of constructive dreams here in my 29th floor office in Dallas," he wrote, "but that my feet are still on the ground back in Carson Township in Fayette County, Illinois."

Following a car accident that injured his back, Hunt became an advocate of yoga and other exercises, and kept vibrating machines in his home in the White Rock Lake district of Dallas—a reproduction of George Washington's Mount Vernon, only larger. One of his favorite exercises involved movement on hands and knees. "Creeping," said Hunt, "is probably the second-best exercise in the world. Next to swimming, it's perfect."

Hunt long overshadowed his children. He was known for alternately spoiling and denouncing them, and allowing his favor to shift from one to the other, along with his money. The spending of that money was no real factor, as long as the spending was done with style and some promise. (According to one popular story in Texas, when Lamar Hunt lost a million dollars in his first year of dabbling in professional football, H.L. dryly remarked that at that rate he'd go broke in a hundred years.) Hunt's oldest son, named after his father, became a partial invalid while still in his twenties, and Herbert was looked to for a while as H.L.'s potential successor. He attended Washington & Lee, and obtained a degree in geology—*de rigueur* for the heirs of oilmen.

As a vice-president of Hunt Oil, Herbert also dealt with another of the Hunts' major producers, Placid Oil Company. A Dallas attorney who once worked for the Hunts said that Herbert made the mistake of giving advice to Placid executives without first clearing this with his father, who discovered his son's unseemly show of independence while talking to Placid's president on the telephone. H.L. casually informed the president that Herbert was no longer a Hunt Oil vice-president. Herbert was sitting in his father's office at the time, according to the attorney, but had been given no advance warning of this decision.

Herbert later headed Hunt Properties, which developed real-estate properties around Dallas, including Dallas North, whose 4,000 acres were sold at prices ranging from $10,000 to $40,000 an acre. Hunt Properties undertook a high-rise office complex in Atlanta, residential development in Florida, industrial property in California. The Hunts probably own as much real estate in America as any private entity. During their diversification in the 1960s, the Hunts bought up much of the land available around Dallas, and in other parts of the state.

H.L. hired some of the craftiest and most aggressive land agents, who could talk the galluses off the marginal farmers and ranchers. He often accompanied them on Saturdays, and would have his agent point out a farmer in a small town who was reluctant to sell his farm. H. L. Hunt would then approach the man, offer him a good price for his land, and warn him that if he refused, the offer would not be repeated. The word got around that the first offer was also the last.

Hunt wanted his sons to stick to oil. Lamar, given a few million dollars to play with, began drilling oil wells as tax write-offs, but those wells kept coming in. He may have managed to lose a million dollars his first year investing in professional football, but has made a great deal more since in sports. Lamar bought the Dallas Texans, and then—un-Texan-like—moved them to Kansas City. He purchased a soccer team, the Tornadoes; a baseball team, the Dallas Spurs; and World Championship Tennis, an immensely lucrative endeavor.

There is something essentially Texan about the ability to make great sums of money out of adolescent preoccupations with play. Lamar also bought the *Cotton Blossom*, the Mississippi River wheeler used in the film *Show Boat*, to be part of Worlds of Fun, the "Disneyland of the Plains" in Kansas City, which last year lured more than a million paying guests. He even offered to buy Alcatraz Island from the federal government, to be transformed into what Lamar considered a testament to American enterprise, in a perfectly logical location—a space museum in the middle of San Francisco Bay.

Lamar is in many ways a typical youngest child, easygoing and affable. He is the only member of the family to recognize the value of public relations and promotion. To build support for his football team, he hired a number of attractive young women in Dallas, dressed them as cowgirls, and sent them out in a fleet of Renaults to sell tickets. So taken was he by the abilities of the cowgirl who sold the most tickets that he married her. Lamar decided to buy a new car only after he founded the American Football League, and was "enshrined" by the AFL. He learned to take advice. When he acted as host at a luncheon that cost $150 and left only a dollar tip, he allowed an aide to persuade him to leave more.

Lamar Hunt's office in the First National Bank Building resembles the bedroom of a teen-ager whose indulgent parents share his dedication to sports. It is cluttered with sports equipment, books on sports, balls of various types signed by professional athletes. A full-size silver football rests on his desk, and beside it stands a life-size wooden Indian, a symbol of his ownership of the Kansas City Chiefs.

"Different interests make the world go round," he says of his family's diversity, between drags on a Dr. Pepper. He wears a maroon tie covered with blue race horses, a pair of black-rimmed spectacles, and an expression of benign indifference. "Dad always had the philosophy to help his children. He would have liked us to stay with the oil business, but he never said we couldn't do something. I hope I can be as broad-minded, although sometimes you have to knock a knot on a kid's head."

The question of wealth seems to surprise him. "What am I worth? I wouldn't have the least idea. I just know where the problems are, how to put a value, for instance, on pro soccer. If I had spent as much time on the Chiefs, or on tennis, I would have made more money."

H. L. Hunt's personal and professional traits seemed most evident in Bunker. Perhaps for this reason he suffered a kind of ostracism in the family business as a young man, was slower to develop than Herbert and Lamar, and yet would become the most apparently successful.

"He's shy, and daring, just like his old man," said the Dallas attorney who worked for the Hunts. "Bunker always took the highflyer. He was willing to risk a lot of money on the chance of making a whole hell of a lot more."

Bunker was one of the first oilmen to realize the value of the huge Sarir oil field in Libya, and he entered into a fifty-fifty partnership with British Petroleum to develop the port facilities at Marsa Hariga. His father commented contemptuously to associates that he himself could find more oil with a road map than Bunker and King Idris could with a platoon of geologists. Other

Texas oilmen said openly that Bunker's move was foolish, considering the political instability of the area, and
the unproven reserves. But Bunker confided to an associate that if he was allowed to operate in Libya for a
few weeks, he would get back his investment.

The port was ceremoniously opened in 1967 with the
slaughtering of a dozen sheep, a salute fired by the
tanker *British Confidence*, and the presentation of a gold
key worth $5,000 by Bunker to the King. *Time* printed a
photograph of a short, plump American businessman,
wearing a gray suit more appropriate to Dallas than the
desert, and his grin, bent slightly at the waist as he
offered to the bearded Idris the ornate box containing
the key.

Marsa Hariga was soon flowing with oil—100,000
barrels a day—making BP Bunker Hunt the fifth-largest
major producer in Libya.

Bunker betrayed an interest in things other than oil—
and a style alien to the Hunts. He bought real estate,
of course, but he also bought ranches. Seven and a half
million dollars went for the Little Big Horn Ranch,
which he immediately stocked with 9,000 head of prime
beef. He bought 4 million acres in Australia. In 1971, he
held the world's largest sale of Charolais cattle on his
Circle T Ranch at Roanoke, Texas, where 1,700 purebred
cows sold for between $5,000 and $20,000 a head.

Two years after presenting the gold key to Idris,
Bunker and his wife, Caroline, entertained five hundred
guests at Claridge's in London, after flying Woody Herman's band over in his private jet. He had developed an
interest in race horses. Bunker's Dahlia became the first
filly to win the King George and Queen Elizabeth Stakes
at Ascot, where the Bunker Hunts are regular atten-
dants. The same filly won the Washington, D.C., International at Laurel. He bought Pretendre for $450,000,
transferred him to America, where Pretendre sired
Canonero II, who won the Kentucky Derby in 1971. He

has a stable of more than two hundred thoroughbred race horses.

H. L. Hunt apparently approved of Bunker's oil ventures, and Bunker and Herbert took operational control of Hunt Oil the same year as the party at Claridge's. ("The old man always liked Bunker personally," says the same Dallas attorney. "When Bunker had an appendectomy, H. L. Hunt went to the hospital and insisted that Bunker's nurse give him some Gastro Magic, his remedy for stomach acid.") Bunker's aversion to publicity grew with his notoriety. There was the $5 million lawsuit against Mobil Oil and Pan American Energy for allegedly using Bunker's and Herbert's studies of potential coal development in North Dakota, where they had extensive investments. There was also BP Bunker Hunt's suit against Coastal States Gas Producing Company for allegedly meddling in their Libyan oil field after BP's interest had been nationalized, a suit filed in courts in such diverse places as Texas, Italy, and Brazil.

Bunker soon developed a need for an effective liaison in Washington, for two distinct reasons. One was the threatened nationalization of his own interests in Libya —not a reaction against him, whom the Arabs seemed to like, or his business methods, but in retaliation for United States policy toward Israel. The other reason was a family squabble of true Texan dimensions.

A struggle for control of the Hunt fortune shaped up between Hunt's sons and two daughters by his first marriage, and the four children of his second marriage. H.L.'s first wife, Lyda Bunker Hunt, died of cancer in 1957, and he married her companion two years later, a young secretary from Shreveport named Ruth Ray. Hunt adopted her children of a previous marriage, but Ruth Ray Hunt was later quoted in the Houston *Chronicle* as saying that Hunt was her children's real father.

The focal point of the struggle was H. L. Hunt's personal aide, a lawyer and former FBI agent named Paul

M. Rothermel, Jr., who for years acted as a combination adviser, bodyguard, and satchel man. He traveled with Hunt, and became so trusted that Hunt gave Rothermel an official letter authorizing him to make any sort of transaction in Hunt's name. Rothermel reportedly suggested to Hunt that he leave 51 percent of his holdings to the children of his second wife, a suggestion not calculated to win favor with the first succession of children, who, Rothermel said, were "well taken care of in trust funds. However, the other four children . . . had only about three million dollars all told in trust funds."

Rothermel's telephone was tapped, and federal indictments were handed down against two private detectives after Houston police captured a man changing a reel of tape on a recorder near the Rothermels' home. The police had answered a call from Rothermel's wife, who noticed a red car repeatedly parked near the house; they pursued the fleeing suspect, and captured him and $40,000 worth of bugging equipment. Police described the man and an associate as "inept." They were granted immunity, and their testimony led to subsequent indictments of Bunker and Herbert Hunt.

The Hunts filed a million-dollar lawsuit in state court against Rothermel and two former Hunt employees, accusing them of taking kickbacks from food suppliers, arranging fraudulent deals, and generally conspiring to take advantage of their high positions in the family affairs. Rothermel's wife filed a $1.5 million suit against the Hunts, claiming they had tapped her phone and listened to conversations she had with friends—and with patients under her psychiatric care. Depositions in the various suits were taken. A judge ordered the records sealed, with the comment "A lot of dirty laundry came out."

Attorneys for the defendants in the Hunts' suit claimed the former employees had been coerced as "pawns in the struggle for succession to the Hunt for-

tune." The defendants, their attorneys said, "have been
H. L. Hunt's closely associated subordinates," and "at
his instance, or at the instance of members of his family
authorized by him, they have engaged in many confiden-
tial and clandestine transactions for him with other
persons such as holders and seekers of public office,
labor leaders, actual or potential competitors, influential
job holders in commercial contracts, professional sports
figures, and non-business social persons."

Rothermel let it be known that he planned to write a
book about his fifteen years in Hunt's service. "What
was brought out was just the top of the iceberg. How
the old man operated is fantastic. No one could ever
believe it. He'd call me in, and say, 'Here is five thousand
dollars. I want you to deliver it to Mr. X.' And I would
count it, and there would only be four thousand. I was
one of the few who could holler at him, and I'd tell him,
'You only gave me four thousand—where's the other
thousand?' And he'd tell me, 'You make up the difference.' . . . I just couldn't take it anymore. I couldn't
work for a man playing God."

Bunker Hunt somberly presented himself for arraignment in March, 1973. He was released on $10,000 un-
secured bond, and allowed to keep his passport because,
his attorney said, he had "extensive interests abroad
that require his personal attention from time to time."
He and Herbert, also indicted, hired as an attorney a
specialist in wiretapping cases, Philip J. Hirschkop, a
seemingly unlikely choice who had defended such clients
as Rennie Davis, H. Rap Brown, and Norman Mailer.

"I like them," Hirschkop said at the time. "They're
nice people. We sit around and kid each other about our
conflicting ideologies, but there's no problem."

Bunker Hunt maintained a close relationship with the
Nixon administration. One connection was John Connally, who became an associate of Hunt's—according to
a story buried in the Dallas *Morning News* in July, 1973

—after Connally's son and Hunt's nephew met as members of the National Guard in Texas, and went into business together. Bunker eventually put Connally on a retainer to look after his interests in Washington, reportedly $75,000 a year for ten years.

A month after Connally's Picosa party, Bunker appeared on the Mississippi ranch of an old friend, Senator James O. Eastland, who also happened to be chairman of the Senate Judiciary Committee. Also present was U.S. Attorney General Richard Kleindienst. According to an article by Earl Golz that appeared in the *Morning News* a year later, a proposal for a deal was funneled through Kleindienst to John Mitchell, and at least part of the deal was said to involve campaign contributions. When the indictments were handed down a year later, Hunt's attorneys loudly denounced the Justice Department. "There was an agreement not to prosecute if the Hunts performed certain actions," said one attorney. "They performed those actions, but there was an indictment anyway."

Another possibility for reciprocity lay in the Hunts' widespread contacts in the Arab world. They were approached by FBI agents, and asked to provide the names of El Fatah members operating in the United States. Since El Fatah, the Palestinian terrorist organization, had the open support of Libya's new ruler, Colonel Muammar Qaddafi, the Hunts could ill afford to be associated with a movement against El Fatah. The theft of a briefcase from the Dallas Arab Information Center, belonging to a Dr. Seife Wadi, was reported at the time. Before Wadi left Dallas for Libya, he was seen several times at the Hunt offices. Speculation had it that the burglary of the Arab Information Center was arranged by the FBI as a cover for Wadi, who had already provided the Hunts with the information the FBI sought.

Three trial dates were set and postponed in the wiretapping case against the Hunts. (A Lubbock judge once dismissed the charges on grounds that telephone conversations couldn't be used as evidence, but that was appealed by the U.S. Attorney's office.) A federal grand jury in Dallas began to look into the allegations that the Hunts may have attempted to have the original indictments quashed through contacts in the Nixon administration.

The Hunts were finally brought to trial in the summer of 1975. They contended that the Justice Department had been hounding them since 1966 because Bunker had refused a CIA request to allow the agency to infiltrate his Libyan oil operations. A twelve-member jury in Lubbock acquitted them, and Bunker admitted that the Hunt fortune had made that acquittal possible. Ordinary people, he said, would have been forced to make a deal, or plead no defense. He added that it takes great wealth to fight government prosecutors "when they are out to get you." The case cost the Hunts $1 million, and they contended to the end that they didn't know wiretapping was illegal.

Bunker Hunt's problems in the Middle East were considerably different, and involved a great deal of money. In June, 1973, Qaddafi announced over Libyan radio that Hunt's oil interests were being nationalized as "an act of sovereignty." A spokesman for Bunker estimated that he had lost 5.5 billion barrels of oil, or about $23 billion. Bunker had been the center of controversy involving Qaddafi and the other oil companies in Libya—Oasis, Amoseas, and Armand Hammer's Occidental—and was singled out the preceding fall when the Libyan government demanded more than 50 percent of his production. Bunker refused, hoping that Connally's intervention in Washington and Tripoli might help alleviate matters.

Negotiations were carried on in a fitful manner, with Bunker backed by a "coordinating team" representing the five major American oil companies—Exxon, Mobil, Gulf, Texaco, and Standard of California—impressive compatriots who had a very real interest in preventing nationalization of Bunker Hunt. Whatever action was taken against him would eventually fall upon the majors. Qaddafi's nationalization of British Petroleum two years before was admittedly undertaken in retaliation for Britain's complicity in Iran's occupation of three Arab islands in the Persian Gulf. Economic vengeance had become official policy in Libya.

"We tell America in a loud voice today," Qaddafi said in June, 1973, the third anniversary of the ouster of U.S. forces from Wheelus Air Force Base near Tripoli, at a rally also attended by Egypt's Anwar Sadat, "that she needs a sharp slap in the face from the Arabs. The United States is threatening us with spy planes and naval ships. The time has come for the Arabs to take up the challenge of the United States, and to pose a serious threat to American interests in the area."

Connally's retainer notwithstanding, the United States government did not move to help Hunt. Connally was asked to become Nixon's official "unpaid adviser," and it may have been that any effort by the administration on Hunt's behalf would have appeared too blatant. Whatever the reason for the lack of action, it soon became clear that the Hunt interests had expected government intervention.

Bunker's chief assistant, Ed Guinn, also a lawyer, said publicly that the State Department was "a big joke. They could go in there and slap a boycott against Colonel Qaddafi's regime, and even blockade Tobruk harbor, but they won't. They are much too timid for that. They are more concerned about what somebody in Bombay or some other such place might say than they are in protecting the American people's business interests abroad."

Bunker Hunt filed one of the largest anti-trust suits in history against Mobil Oil, claiming that Mobil had reneged on an agreement to help Bunker make up his losses in Libya, and demanded the $13 billion in damages. Mobil was the first of the fifteen producers supposedly offering a "united front" against Arab demands. Bunker Hunt claimed breach of contract, and also asserted that Mobil had entered into collusion with other oil companies, including Texaco, Gulf, Standard of California, Royal Dutch Shell, Atlantic Richfield, and Occidental, in an effort to get Bunker Hunt to take the brunt of Arab displeasure at American foreign policy.

"They used Hunt as a guinea pig," said Hirschkop, "a sacrificial lamb."

Mobil replied that it found "a report of a suit against us by Nelson Bunker Hunt as simply incredible."

Hunt's lawyers claimed he was not part of other strategies used by the majors, including taxes, royalty interest, participation, and posted prices—the prices on which taxes are paid, but not the actual price of the barrels of oil, which is higher. This allowed major producers to subtract more money from the U.S. income-tax payments, and act to keep out competition in the Middle East. This breakup of the "united front" actually marked the beginning of the end of the era of cheap oil. The Organization of Petroleum Exporting Countries raised the price of oil in June, and again in October, the day before the embargo began. The nationalization of Bunker Hunt's interests was the first major step in a radical change in the policy of oil in the Middle East.

Bunker Hunt was not hurt financially in real terms, as his and Herbert's activities in the commodities market indicated.

In early 1974, the price of silver rose to record highs during seven consecutive sessions in the European bullion markets, where trading was heavy. Reports persisted that speculation was rampant in the Middle East, and that an American was accumulating massive amounts of silver. On February 12, the price of an ounce of silver touched $6. In London's financial district, it was assumed that oil-producing countries were using their newly gained foreign exchange in the commodities market. But the flow of silver to America was difficult to understand.

The name repeatedly mentioned by brokers was that of Bunker Hunt, who in fact held 30 million ounces of silver—or almost $200 million worth at those prices.

"One can never analyze something one doesn't understand," admitted Guy Field, head of the bullion department for Samuel Montagu & Company, London's largest bullion dealer. "The dominant factor . . . is the fact that investors have lost confidence in the accepted forms of investment." He said there was much speculative activity in the Middle East, mostly short term. "The shorts are in trouble," Field added.

A trade short in the silver business is someone who sells futures against inventory as a form of insurance against the loss of stock value. Speculative shorts are those who agree to sell a commodity they don't own, in the hope that they can obtain it at a lower price when they have to deliver. Their risk is that the price of silver might go up.

It did go up, at least partly because of Bunker's activities. He had obtained small packets of 5,000 and 10,000 ounces when the recession price of silver sank to $1.20 an ounce back in 1970, through the Dallas office of Bache & Company. The price then soared more than 100 percent. His first massive purchase, made in conjunction with Herbert, of 20 million ounces was delivered in December, 1973, just before the price peaked, yielding a profit, if cashed in, of $65 million.

Bunker bought silver contracts and, instead of trading the contracts in a conventional manner, allowed them to run out, taking possession of the silver. Much of it was left in various bank vaults around the world, where he assumed the storage costs. Millions of dollars' worth of silver was stored in warehouses around Dallas.

The brokers along Commerce Street in Dallas came up with what they call a "horseback estimate" of the world's silver supply for London's *Financial Times*. They estimated annual world production at about 250 million ounces, and annual consumption—mostly electronics and photography—at about 450 million ounces. Stocks in the United States and Britain amounted to some 120 million ounces. Private bullion and meltable coin supplies amounted to another 350 million ounces; secondary sources—flatware, old coins, jewelry from India—could have brought the total to 500 million ounces in the world at the time.

Bunker continued to buy, and collect. His holdings were last estimated at about 50 million ounces—or 10 percent of the calculated world supply—more than all the Arabs had. Some suggested that Bunker planned to trade silver for oil—two ounces for a barrel—thus protecting his investment while converting some of his capital. Paper profits ran to $250 million.

In April, 1974, on his way to Ascot, Hunt stopped in New York, and for the first time visited the floor of the New York Commodities Exchange. The traders sat at their desks and stared. Bunker later said of the experience, "I thought to myself, There's a lot of sharp-looking fellows in this room." He offered the briefest explanation of his activities to *Barron's*. "Just about anything you buy, rather than paper, is better. You're bound to come out ahead, in the long pull. If you don't like gold, use silver. Or diamonds, or copper, but something. Any damn fool can run a printing press."

Associates say that Hunt is even more shy—and more circumspect—than his father was. "I've worked here almost thirty years," says a woman who is an administrative assistant in Hunt Oil. "I've watched the boys grow up. When Bunker and I pass in the hall, we exchange smiles. But then he always looks at the floor."

Bunker may lack his father's vocal "constructionism," but their politics are quite similar. H. L. Hunt was an ardent backer of George Wallace, and once sent him several thousand copies of his books to be sold to raise campaign funds. The Hunts strongly supported Wallace for President in 1968. Mrs. Nelson Bunker Hunt was one of thirty-three very wealthy contributors at a luncheon given for Wallace that year in Dallas, when Wallace was pushed even further to the right. The John Birch Society took over the Wallace drive in Texas (Robert Welch, leader of the Birchers, was a frequent guest at Bunker's house on Lakeside Drive), when fifteen members of the state executive committee who were Birchers took control of the American Party, throwing out five other members labeled troublemakers because they had qualms. Two million dollars was raised for Wallace in Dallas alone.

H. L. Hunt did not play favorites among his children in his will, but he did leave all his stock in the Hunt Oil Company to his second wife. The extent of those holdings was undisclosed. Hunt stipulated that challengers of the will would forfeit their rights to benefits, but that is unlikely to prevent an intense internal struggle. No minority shareholders were ever allowed in the Hunt enterprises, because no dissenting opinions were tolerated. Now those dissenting opinions seem to be locked in. The monolithic nature of Huntdom precludes any buffer zone of upwardly mobile executives. Employees have always known there was no chance of becoming a member of the inner circle, and so there has been no corporate stair-stepping, no office politics. The most powerful entity in Huntdom is the nucleus of family lawyers. They may be able to prevent a bloodbath on the twenty-ninth floor of the First National Bank Building in Dallas, or they may prefer to allow a violent disintegration to take place.

Meanwhile, it is business as usual.

One week after the funeral of H. L. Hunt, two full pages in both *The New York Times* and the *Wall Street Journal* were purchased by Bunker and Herbert to advertise an extension of their offer to buy 910,000 shares of Great Western. Simultaneously, federal district Judge Gerhard Gesell ordered the Hunts—and their brother-in-law oilman Randall A. Kreiling—to stop filing allegedly false statements with the Securities and Exchange Commission about their reasons for purchasing large blocks of stock.

The agency charged that papers filed by the Hunt group with the SEC failed to state that they intended to eliminate divisive factions from Great Western's board by buying enough shares to give the Hunt group decisive influence. The complaint also alleged that the Hunt group began discussing large purchases of shares months before, and played on various factions on the board, which resulted in management problems and depressed stock prices in relation to other sugar producers.

The Hunt group neither admitted nor denied the charges, which did not affect the tender offer. It was generally recognized that Great Western represented an anomaly, with total assets of more than $250 million, and revenues for the three-month period ending August 31, 1974, of $123 million. "A beleaguered company," as an attorney for Great Western put it, "that is prospering."

That beleaguerment was firmly rooted in Dallas. Not incidentally, funds used in the purchase of Great Western stock, when the takeover was complete, came from a loan secured by warehouse receipts for silver bullion.

A telephone inquiry put through to the office of Bunker

Hunt gets no further than a secretary with the restraint of a kindly aunt. "Mr. Hunt appreciates your interest," she says, "but he doesn't wish to be interviewed."

And she adds, without being prompted, "He's a very nice man."

Interlude

A QUESTION OF MAIDS

The Sheraton Motor Inn sits on the outskirts of El Paso, in rolling sandy hills where modern shopping centers bloom among the creosote bush, and thrust the neon symbols of American consumption high into the desert air. A decade ago, visitors would probably have slept and dined at the old Paso del Norte, a rambling hotel downtown, less than a mile from Mexico, where the habitués doze beneath the Tiffany glass dome in the lobby, Stetsons on their laps. In another era, they all dealt cash in the cattle swaps upstairs; today the money is strictly in imported Mexican beef.

The cattle business has faded, and so has the Paso del Norte. Feedlots and mechanization have taken the romance out of what remains of the cowboy trade, a passing most lamented by the cowboys themselves: "Even the roundups are different. Used to be when we castrated the young bulls, we'd throw those things right into a hot skillet on the fire where the irons were heated. We'd eat them as we went along. Now most of the branding is done electrically. You can't cook mountain oysters on an electric branding iron!"

El Paso: the name suggests transience and new prospects. For more than four centuries, travelers have
crossed the original Pass of the North, a groove worn
by the Rio Grande—now the line of the Mexican-American border—between the barren Franklin Mountains,
the theoretical tail end of the Rockies, and the Juárez
Mountains, which launch the southward sweep of the
Sierra Madre. Cabeza de Vaca, survivor of an abortive
attempt by conquistadors to conquer Florida, forded the
Rio Grande here in the 1530s, starving and bound for
the Pacific on foot. Stories of gold and silver to be found
in the interior of what is now the Southwestern United
States brought Coronado and other explorers up from
the south, and the Pass became the link between the
Spanish realm in Mexico City and the settlements in
New Mexico.

The inhabitants of the Pass—Manso and Suma In-
dians tending sheep and goats—were joined by the
Spanish soldiers, traders, and missionaries. The first
norteamericanos—trappers of beaver living in what was
then a swamp bordering a deep, fast-flowing river—
didn't arrive until the 1820s. They and the itinerant
cowboys who drifted into the area lived under the Mexican government until the Gadsden Purchase in 1853.

El Paso differed from other notorious Western towns,
like Dodge City, Tombstone, and Cheyenne, because it
was more isolated and remained hazardous longer than
the rest, a rendezvous for gunfighters, gamblers, and
outlaws drawn by the building of the railroad.

El Paso retains the harsh physical contrasts of a frontier community. The manifestations of industry—copper
and oil refineries, an eight-hundred-foot smelter stack
that often fouls the air, and an eight-lane interstate
highway that plows right into town—represent a triumph over environment and isolation. The frontiersman's
characteristics prevail: candor, friendliness, sensitivity
to criticism, a willingness to uproot and move on. For

many, El Paso is the happy end of a road that began in Pennsylvania or Michigan. Many say, "We just came out to visit Sun Country, and we stayed."

More than two dozen retired United States Army generals live in El Paso. Fort Bliss, the Army's air defense center and gateway to the massive White Sands Missile Range, exercises the single greatest economic influence on the city. Established before the Civil War, Fort Bliss served as a base for General Pershing's invasion of Mexico, and is reminiscent of a nineteenth-century pukka garrison, with rows of officers' homes graced with Spanish colonial façades, and two muzzle-loading cannons outside headquarters that point south.

El Paso and the city it faces across the Rio Grande, Juárez, make up an interdependent community of almost a million people. During the cattle and mining boom of the 1890s, they were known as "the Monte Carlo of the United States." But in 1904 the bipartisan Citizens Reform League drove the whores and the dealers south across the river, and since then El Pasoans have resented the reputation of their city as the gateway to Juárez's night life.

The Juárez main drag is lined with shops displaying cheap booze, leather jackets, endless gaudy "handicrafts" —burros made of tied straw, miniature conquistadors' swords, a bullfight painted in bright oils on black velvet. Walk-up strip clubs emit the blare and skitter of cornets; small men promise myriad diversions, all within five minutes of downtown El Paso. Juárez prostitutes keep to the side streets, the saloons along Pig Alley, and the brothels—a major tourist attraction for more than half a century. But the allure of Juárez is not simply carnal. The city still provides a sympathetic environment where the suspension of late-twentieth-century disbelief is still possible, at least for an evening. It has a wonderful *fin-de-siècle* seediness, part Toulouse-Lautrec, part

John Connally,
as Secretary of the Treasury
(November, 1971).

H. L. Hunt.

UPI

Left to right: Sid Richardson,
Dwight D. Eisenhower,
Amon Carter, Sr.

DALLAS MORNING NEWS

Nelson Bunker Hunt.

Herman Brown.

*Lamar Hunt (right),
at a press conference
announcing the firing of
Kansas City Chiefs coach
Hank Stram
(December, 1974).*

Clint Murchison, Sr.

John D. Murchison (left) and Clint Murchison, Jr., in 1961.

President John F. Kennedy, speaking in Fort Worth on the morning of November 22, 1963. Standing behind him (left to right): unidentified Secret Service man, Senator Ralph Yarborough, Governor John Connally, Vice-President Lyndon Johnson.

*Frances (Sissy) Farenthold votes in the runoff for the
1972 Democratic nomination for governor.*

Upper left: *H. Ross Perot, in front of a drawing of a POW (December, 1972).*

Lower left: *President and Mrs. Nixon visit Mr. and Mrs.
Connally at the latter's ranch (September 22, 1972).*

Senator and Mrs. Lloyd Bentsen, as he announces his candidacy for the presidency (February, 1975).

Damon Runyan, where an Anglo with a little cash can play out most Mittyisms, and no questions asked.

A dozen musicians wearing embroidered sombreros and spangled trousers surround a couple from the University of Texas at El Paso ("Utep") in a cavernous bar, engulfing them in soulful, melodious poetry about love and death. The male student loosens his tie, throws back his head, and releases a high gasping shriek. The mariachis all nod in accord, strumming wildly but with averted eyes, for they are watching a Perry Mason rerun on the television set behind the bar.

The Industrial Village, also in Mexico, is an enclave of American manufacturers—RCA, General Electric, Sylvania, General Hospital—who are allowed to import materials into Mexico duty-free. There they assemble the final products and ship them back to the United States, where a duty is paid on the difference in value of the material and the finished product. The minimum wage paid to the Mexican workers is about three dollars a day.

In Juárez, according to unofficial sources, one worker in three has no job. Unemployment in Mexico has driven thousands of near-destitute people up to the border. Most of the footprints in the bed of the Rio Grande point north. From U.S. 80, skirting the river on El Paso's western limit, Mexico appears close enough to touch, a diorama of desert hills planted with mesquite and the shacks of the *paracaidistas*—squatters who seem to drop from the sky and lay claim to the roadless frontier.

I sit with two members of MACHOS (Mexican-American Committee on Honor, Opportunity, and Service), one of El Paso's many Chicano organizations, in a rented car on the American side of the Rio Grande. They wish to demonstrate the ease with which the international border can be violated, and have brought me to the riverbank so I can try it myself. It is early afternoon, and the spot is in plain view of the highway.

One Chicano says, with typical Mexican politeness, "Maybe they shoot you," referring to the U.S. Border Patrol, but his companion insists that wetbacks are no longer fired upon.

I descend the bank, take off my shoes, flounder across twenty yards of mud flat and through a stream of cloudy water no more than eight inches deep, into a clump of cottonwoods rooted in Mexico. The crossing takes perhaps a minute; the return trip seems longer. As I top the bank of the Rio Grande, shoes tucked under one arm, my feet smeared with mud, I cause some interest among passing motorists, but no one stops to investigate.

During the ride back to town, one of the Chicanos smiles and says, "They wouldn't have shot you, because you weren't running."

On Monday mornings, the arching Paso del Norte bridge is aswarm with pedestrians. Commuters jam the walkway, pressing toward the customs and immigration officials with quiet urgency: students in starched white shirts and blouses, bound for parochial schools in El Paso, laborers in straw hats, women clutching purses and gazing impassively in the direction of the El Paso National Bank Building. A million alien crossings are recorded here each month. Thousands of Mexicans in the area hold "green cards," a hangover from the old *bracero* program, that entitle the holder to work and live in the United States, though most prefer to live cheaply in Juárez and commute.

And there are the official "shoppers," holders of a permit known locally as the *mica,* who are allowed into this country on a temporary basis, to browse for the prized commodities—canned goods, clothes, and appliances. No one knows how many *micas* are issued in any one month; no record is kept of the time of entry of the shoppers. It is eminently possible for a Mexican to cross the Paso del Norte bridge on a *mica*, catch a bus or a cattle train north, and spend the rest of his life in Dallas, Detroit, or Chicago.

The men who patrol the El Paso sector—360 miles of unfenced international boundary—have their work cut out. Most detentions of illegal immigrants are made within the El Paso city limits, where plane and bus terminals, and highways leading out, are watched. Smugglers bring aliens across in vans and drive them to the big cities of the north. Some illegal aliens cross and recross the border as a matter of course, occasionally toting a bundle of dried cannabis or a television set, depending upon the direction of travel.

Most legal aliens work in El Paso's garment industry, stitching Farah trousers, or in producing the famous handmade Tony Lama cowboy boots. For sixty years Lama's has produced dress boots in hides as various as cow, anteater, and shark. Lama boots are a tribute to Mexican craftsmanship; they include what are no doubt the world's most expensive boots—the El Reys, encrusted with jewels and gold leaf, and valued at $10,000 by Lloyds of London. The first pair of El Reys was stolen while on display. The second pair was bought by a filling-station operator in Wyoming, who keeps them in his office and charges motorists twenty-five cents apiece to look at them.

The Amalgamated Clothing Workers of America (AFL-CIO) would like to see the border sealed to cut off the flow of cheap labor into El Paso. But fewer than 10 percent of the garment workers belong to the ACWA. Most El Pasoans are apprehensive about what border-closing would impose on social services—welfare, schools, hospitals, public housing—if some twenty thousand relatively poor families of green-card holders were forced to give up the economic advantages of commuting to work in El Paso from homes in Juárez and move across to the United States. The barrio in South El Paso—a square mile of yardless, one- and two-story dwellings with a tradition of tuberculosis and varying degrees of poverty—is already greatly overcrowded.

Late afternoon in Kern Place, a residential area in the Franklin foothills with winding streets and broad, manicured lawns, combines sunshine, tranquillity, and air so clear that one confronts the view without benefit of depth perception. A supper buffet in a ranch-style house of pinkish granite proves more formal than the invitation implied, and guests arriving in casual dress suck in their cheeks at the sight of long gowns, and coats and ties.

The only Mexican present is the bartender, who comes in late, without explanation, and begins to fill orders. "Typical," says the host, a well-brushed Yale graduate and successful businessman. The gathering has the unmistakable aura of transplanted Deep Southernness: the decorum and self-assurance of, say, Savannah's *haut monde* wintering in Cuernavaca, sipping margaritas— or Cutty Sark—rather than mint juleps, barely touched by the sound of platters of beef being laid out by the other Mexicans who have appeared—the maids.

A Junior League member quips, "Behind every successful man in El Paso, there's a good maid."

It is common for the well-groomed women present to encounter a Mexican farm girl unexpectedly at the front door. Usually she has entered the United States illegally, and carries only a paper sack containing a toothbrush, a rosary, and a snapshot of a child left behind in Chihuahua. She will be paid as a maid about twenty-five dollars a week, part of an arrangement that includes working six full days and sharing a small room with a water heater.

It is not unusual for a well-to-do family to employ three such maids. They are a considerable factor, directly and indirectly, in the city's economy. The more than two hundred women's organizations flourish with an inexhaustible supply of cleaners, cooks, and baby-sitters. (A few of the beneficiaries worry about the fact that their children grow up speaking nothing but Spanish.) And luncheons, year-round riding, golf, tennis, and entertaining all require new clothes, and investment in other amenities of unrestricted social intercourse.

No one knows how many maids work in El Paso. The Junior League suggests, "We couldn't manage with less than fifty thousand."

6 ☆ THE KING AND GOLDEN BOY

Power by Proxy

I love my friends, and hate my enemies.
—Frank Erwin

He sits stolidly before a window in the Headliners Club, overlooking the oaks and the capitol lawn, and Austin's gilded dome. One large hand holds a glass of Cutty Sark and ice, his favorite drink, while the other plucks at the popcorn he has scattered over the table from a basket dutifully fetched by a black waiter in a white jacket. Other than the two of us, the Headliners contains no guests. It is Saturday afternoon, and no football game to look forward to—a kind of purgatory in Texas. He radiates a controlled impatience: a florid, blunt, squarish man with steel-gray hair who seems capable of chairing a board meeting or peddling snake oil up in the Panhandle.

"The status quo will hold for another four years," he says, referring to the state's power structure that he, as one of Connally's chief political lieutenants, helped cement, and still serves. "After that, who knows?"

As regents' regent of the University of Texas, Frank Erwin virtually ran the school for a dozen years, in much the same manner that Connally ran the state. UT has become most responsive to the needs of business and industry. Its considerable influence and holdings have been concentrated in a few hands; it has gained the reputation of a distinguished academic institution afflicted by politicians, in a permanent condition of administrative upheaval, and subject to the caprice of powerful Yahoos.

None of which bothers Chairman Frank. The establishment could have no more effective and loyal member, yet he is too impetuous—too expansively indiscriminate —to be embraced without reservation by the Browns and the Connallys. He was Lyndon Johnson's pal, a corporation lawyer in Austin active in Democratic politics, with a reputation for discerning other men's limitations and then stating them. His gruff, jarring voice, often laced with obscenities, assumed a shrill resonance in extreme situations; he laughed at others, and at himself. He watched Connally operate in the '50s, and decided he was the man to save the Democratic party from mongrelization.

"The Democrats in Texas were in bad shape. The affluent people—the country-club set—had stopped participating in the party. It just wasn't socially acceptable. Even the children of Democrats were ridiculed in private school. I was afraid the party was being taken over by the minorities, labor, and the liberals. Connally was seen as the man who could bring back the party that had run Texas since the Civil War."

Erwin was a Phi Beta Kappa, and he operated well in closed sessions of a few influential men. But, unlike the others around Connally at the beginning of his political career, Erwin also had an affection for people—not poor people, maybe, but almost anybody else. He liked talking, drinking, arguing. He and Connally thrashed out many a political expediency. The story persists that the two of them once walked out of a restaurant across from the old Driskill Hotel and left a paper bag containing thousands of dollars in contributions on the floor, before rushing back to retrieve it, their argument temporarily forgotten.

Erwin attended the strategy session at Dolph Briscoe's Catarina Ranch in 1961 to outline Connally's campaign with Strauss, Bentsen, and the others. It was Erwin who, at 3 A.M., told Eugene Locke that his plan to focus Connally's campaign on state shopping centers was "dumb." He concentrated instead on organizing support for Connally at county conventions, and the state convention in El Paso. For a time, Erwin ran the state campaign headquarters.

"We were backed by the big newspapers and television stations, the independent oilmen, the highway contractors, insurance companies, banks, savings and loan companies. Then we had the power brokers—men like John Peace, who could deliver twenty thousand Mexican-American votes around San Antonio. Or Mayor Martin of Laredo, a poor town, where he could deliver twenty thousand votes just like that. Hell, those voters didn't even think about the candidate, they were totally Martin's. And there was ole Doc Newhouse down in McAllen. We had 'em all. Some could furnish the money, some could furnish work. You put the money men together with the power brokers, and you've got yourself one hell of an organization."

Erwin appealed in a more basic way than others among Connally's men. He was a good partying companion, a storyteller with an earthiness unknown to Strauss, Bentsen, and Locke; he could manipulate lesser men with an egalitarian directness, and reveled in what others considered to be "shit work." After Connally was elected, it was Erwin who opened an office in the Driskill and prepared for the smooth assumption of power, his spidery handwriting covering memos and invoices and seating charts. It was Erwin who insisted upon a victory dinner before the inauguration, specifying black ties— "We weren't going to play down to the public"—and entertainment imported from the West Coast. He was Texas's unofficial Chief of Protocol, and no detail got past him.

Erwin had always been a powerful persuader in his clients' behalf, and Connally made him state Democratic chairman, national committeeman from Texas, and UT regent. He became known as the emperor of the university, a roughhouser in the corridors of the mind, whose job it was to spot the weaknesses of the habitués. Driving a Cadillac of white and burnt-orange, the university colors, he became a willing target for dissenting students and faculty; with his spectacles glinting happily in the harsh lights of freewheeling press conferences, he drew fire that might otherwise have been aimed directly at the university, and the men behind it.

Erwin loved the university for its social life—the cocktail parties and football games and fraternity balls. He will probably wear his heavy Kappa Sig ring to his grave. He supervised every aspect of the university, from hiring and firing of professors to the selection of just the *right* shade of orange. The burgeoning university system was well worth close supervision, since UT owned $700 million in bonds and common stock of private utilities, oil and gas wells, interests in banks, drugs, cosmetics, and many other commodities. Patronage was a gold mine, jealously guarded. When a $90,000 architectural contract for Texas Western College at El Paso was awarded to a firm owned by a Republican, Erwin saw to it that the contract was rescinded.

"Since architectural contracts are not let on a competitive bid basis," Erwin wrote to a critical regent, "they simply constitute valuable gifts that are awarded by the state government. . . . While he [Connally] would

be opposed to awarding contracts to incompetent architects, he is also opposed to awarding contracts to compe-
tent architects who have not been friendly to him and
his Administration."

The regent resigned, and Erwin's control of the board
was assured. He then casually informed the university
comptroller that he would no longer be supervising the
nomination of architects, the school construction programs, or the university bank accounts. Thus Erwin
was able to maintain control over such projects as the
Johnson Library, the medical school in Houston, and the
building of headquarters for the entire university system. Both he and Connally saw the system as subservient
to the industrial demands of the state, and as a bonanza.
Increased enrollment meant a larger university fund
for economic stimulation and contracts; more students
trained in specific tasks provided fodder for a booming
economy. The advantage of perching atop a humming
money machine was not just that you and your friends
were provided with innumerable opportunities at the
moment, but you were also afforded a select view of the
future.

Erwin became a symbol of authoritarianism to many
students and faculty; his style matched his policies. The
two-tone Cadillac, the orange blazers of raw silk, even
the richly paneled door to his office in the Brown Building reflected a flaunted, irreverent dominance. The door
supported no explanation of his position, no title or
qualification, just the single name "ERWIN," in heavy
gold letters three inches tall, lighted by two spots
countersunk in the ceiling of the corridor.

He loved to act as host at the regents' parties held in
the art building before the big football games, dispensing
jokes and hospitality and a sense of bountiful complacency. Physical growth of the university and a winning
team produced euphoria. Erwin was inevitably surrounded by young men, Kappa Sigs and their lovely

pedigreed dates, and solicitous of the power present—
House Speaker Ben Barnes, Governor Connally, sometimes Lyndon Johnson himself. Those were the proudest
moments: enrollment rising, the sun bright on the new
football field, the company of the right people.

Erwin's entertaining extended to the Forty Acres
Club, where he held forth with adolescent frivolity and
a rough charm. "It is difficult to dislike the man on a
personal basis," wrote a reporter on the *Daily Texan*,
only to have his story censored. "He knows how to drink,
how to make people laugh. He is skilled at irreverent
riposte, holding the center court without driving his
companions from the gallery. . . . He's bigger physically
than all his guests, and he dominates the badinage, field-
ing questions with expletives and sardonic humor, brook-
ing no serious arguments."

There was another side, a brooding sentimentality
that became apparent in the late hours at the Forty
Acres, when it stood empty except for Erwin and those
same young men. Their dates were expected to drink and
keep quiet. Some said that the prolonged illness and
death of Erwin's wife from cancer had left him in need
of constant companionship. The Cutty Sark was an ever-
present reminder of conviviality, and slow drinkers
sometimes found themselves fenced in by four or five
glasses of whiskey and slowly melting ice. Erwin always
paid. Laconic conversation centered upon university
politics, the names of administrators and faculty who
had met with disfavor mumbled like those of departed
souls. And they were.

Erwin received a midnight reappointment as regent
before Connally left the Governor's Mansion; he remained Connally's political extension. In 1968, Erwin
flew to the Chicago convention to help convince the
credentials committee not to repudiate the war in Vietnam. But Erwin didn't hesitate to criticize Connally's
mistakes, which he continues to do with characteristic

candor: "What's the name of that black who was assassinated in Nashville? Martin Luther King—well, that statement he made suggesting that King got what he deserved was dumb."

The faculty senate voted to suspend classes in 1970 as a protest against the invasion of Cambodia, but Erwin convinced the regents otherwise. After all, the war was a Texas issue. He welcomed open confrontation with dissident students, and began to hound their organizations. He personally checked the bank accounts of several, including the Students for a Democratic Society, and found what he considered to be evidence of subversion: "Outside elements were supporting the demonstrators. We found out that SDS had one hundred dollars in an Austin bank just to buy *bullhorns!*"

He dominated the regents' meetings, treated dissenters with obvious contempt. Gradually, Erwin took over the responsibilities of the chancellor, and if the maligned president of the University at Austin, Norman Hackerman. Hackerman resigned in 1970, and was followed by Chancellor Harry H. Ransom, an earthy administrator who recognized sound credentials and couldn't abide Erwin's maneuvering. When the noted classicist Dr. William Arrowsmith had come to UT in 1968, Ransom met him at the airport and pleasantly inquired, "Do you believe in laying your cards on the table, Dr. Arrowsmith?" When Arrowsmith said he did, Ransom told him, "Well, I'm going to lay my cards on the table. We got shit for a classics department here, but we're rich."

Arrowsmith stayed, only to run afoul of Erwin two years later in a riotous controversy over Erwin's firing of the dean of the College of Arts and Sciences, Dr. John Silber, now president of Boston University. Silber made the mistake of advocating a more limited enrollment of qualified students at UT. Although Erwin respected him more for his political ability than for his philosophy,

Erwin invited Silber to resign when the faculty committee began to consider him for the post of permanent
president. "John, you're the most intelligent, articulate,
and hard-working man at this university. Because of
these qualities, you make some people in the higher
echelons nervous." That was part of an affable dismissal
that Silber received on a Friday; he was given the weekend to clear out his desk.

During the resultant controversy, faculty members
attacked Erwin and other administration figures in the
newspapers, threatening mass resignations. Erwin countered by declaring that any such resignations would be
promptly accepted. One of the professors who finally
did resign was Arrowsmith, not only a respected classicist but also a recognized critic of higher education in
America. "Your administration," Arrowsmith wrote to
Erwin's chancellor, Charles LeMaistre, ". . . is interested
only in mediocrities and nonentities who can be counted
on to carry out the megalomaniac wishes of Chairman
Erwin."

Erwin personally visited the editorial offices of the
Dallas *Morning News,* the Houston *Post* and the Houston *Chronicle,* and carefully outlined his position to willing audiences. He claimed Arrowsmith was paid an
exorbitantly large salary; he accused Silber of helping
a friend attain a free year in Paris at the expense of the
university. The unstated charge was that dissident professors were dealing with taxpayers' money in a muddle-
headed manner, and that UT was in danger of falling
into the hands of theorists.

Erwin won the dispute and he greatly enjoyed it. Late
one night in the Forty Acres, he confided to the assembled faithful, "Arrowsmith thought he was going to
score on me. He got down to my ten-yard line, and
thought he had it made. But then I started making my
moves, and suddenly he found himself calling defensive
plays."

Anti-intellectualism is probably UT's most enduring tradition. The university has constantly felt the heavy hand of overzealous politicians. In 1930, the legislature carried out its purge of suspected Communists in Austin's halls of academe. In 1944, the board of regents fired the university president, Homer P. Rainey, because he wouldn't deal harshly with suspected "subversives," one of whom had had the temerity to read sections of Dos Passos's *U.S.A.* to his class.

Governor "Pappy" O'Daniel was happy to follow the instructions of his backers—chiefly the president of Humble Oil—with regard to the university training specialists, and to limiting research to natural resources exploitable in Texas. Intellectual "unrest" was discouraged. Connally continued the tradition, adding the element of rapid, massive expansion.

One of the most ambitious plans was for the campus at San Antonio. As early as 1961, a bill was introduced that would have created a school there independent of the UT regents, but it and a similar bill were allowed to die. Four years later, Governor Connally sent a special message to the legislature calling for a four-year college at San Antonio, and such a bill was passed. Arguments for an independent facility were discouraged, since the support of the regents—all appointed by Connally—was needed. The bill required that the site chosen for the school include at least 250 acres of donated land—a guarantee that the school would be built outside the city.

Offers of free land began to flow in. When Bexar County suggested 200 acres south of the city—the opposite side from that already decided upon by the regents —the requirement was raised to 350 donated acres. The regents then chose a parcel of 600 acres north of San Antonio, put together by a group that included two men with whom Connally went into business soon after leaving the governor's office. They were Charles Kuper, whose father-in-law Connally appointed to the Parks and Wildlife Commission, and Alfred Negley, whom Connally had named to the Texas Alcoholic Beverage Commission, and who was the son-in-law of George Rufus Brown. Two months before the regents announced their decision to accept the offer, Kuper and Negley bought options on large parcels of land surrounding the property.

A cozy relationship also existed between these men and John Peace, a regent and San Antonio attorney, who served as Connally's Bexar County campaign manager, handing him the handsome majority there that Erwin spoke of. Peace and Connally knew one another in college, and both worked their way up through state politics. Negley, as a member of the Brown family, was a long-time friend of Peace and Connally, and was a Connally political coordinator during the campaigns of the '60s.

The financial ties surrounding the San Antonio extension proved fascinating. One institution backing Negley and Kuper, and owning a large tract of land adjacent to the chosen school site, was Houston's Gibraltar Savings Association, of which Connally served as a director. Houston Imperial Corporation, of which Connally was also a director after his term as governor expired, was a subsidiary of Gibraltar, and also bought land adjacent to the site. Involved, too, was the First City National Bank, of which Connally was a director.

Ronnie Dugger writes in *Our Invaded Universities* that at a time when Negley and Kuper were buying up options, and two months before the regents' announced decision, "Connally was (1) in business with both of them . . . (2) a director of the corporate owner of the construction mammoth whose chairman was Negley's father-in-law; (3) a co-director, with that same construction firm's president, of the savings association that would soon appear as a financier of the development of Kuper-Negley acquisitions and as a property control-

ler in the UTSA area . . . and (4) tied closely to the
Elkins bank that was a trustee of other land in the
UTSA area."

In 1972, the university earned $25 million in oil and
gas royalties, and bonuses, and $11 million in stock
dividends. It had become a major investor in Texas.
Connally's appointees to the coordinating of the Texas
University and College system reported that "higher
education is the largest industry, private or public, in
Texas today."

Erwin's reaction to questions concerning Connally's
involvement with Negley and Kuper is typical. "They
just formed a corporation to buy an old plane, a Lodestar.
. . . It only cost forty thousand dollars—no big deal."
His disdain for the accusation of impropriety—any
accusation—and his imperial sense of humor were illustrated in Austin after the publication of Dugger's
book. While a celebration of sorts was held for the
author inside Sholz's, Erwin sat outside in his Cadillac,
offering to attach his own signature to any fresh copy
of the book.

The turmoil of 1970 at UT, and the criticism that
arose from it, had little effect among the regents. In
1974, they struck again, through the chancellor, Le-
Maistre, and summarily dismissed the fifth president in
six years, Stephen H. Spurr. Spurr was not considered
forceful enough; he also pushed for increased faculty
salaries, and some minority recruitment at the university. But apparently his greatest fault was a failure to
gain admission for a young friend of Erwin's into the
law school.

No reason was given for Spurr's dismissal. The regents voted unanimously, except for Mrs. Lyndon B.
Johnson, who abstained. The new president, remarked
a veteran professor at UT, would need all the political
skill of a fifteenth-century Italian: "That's all the
Medicis were, Houston bankers."

Erwin would not even bother to dispute that assessment. Still seated at the Headliners Club, still confident of the right of power in Texas, Erwin says of his friend Connally, now among other things a banker, and a Republican: "I love John. I'd do most anything he asked me, legal or illegal. If he has a weakness, it's his love of money. I don't think John can get enough money."

Political turmoil at UT continues.

Brownwood is a farm town near the dead center of Texas. Travelers headed for Brownwood tend to speed, not necessarily because they are anxious to arrive, but because the conformity of the land tempts them to get beyond it, although that effort is futile. Brownwood itself is a collection of farm-equipment and service outfits; government buildings, schools, and churches built during the Depression; and prefabricated, single-story office complexes, where the action today is in construction, cattle, peanuts. Proof of Brownwood's worth is the location there of a Holiday Inn, where a powerful-looking waitress tells guests asking for milk instead of "non-dairy creamer" for their coffee, "I just work here, good-buddy."

Her counterpart on the public payroll is a Stetsoned policeman who spends hours in the weeds beside the highway, tending sophisticated radar equipment. Speeders are promptly taken to the jail, where they are allowed to plead guilty by telephone to the judge, who sits at home in front of a television set. At such times the traveler is fortunate if he can mention to the judge that he has business in town with the pride of Brownwood, a handsome young businessman with hair like burnished brass Brillo, named Ben Barnes.

Brownwood seems an unlikely haven for the former speaker of the Texas House, the former lieutenant governor who received more votes in a single election than

any candidate in the state's history, and the man publicly proclaimed by Lyndon Johnson to be a future
President of the United States. Yet this is where Barnes
makes his money and plots his comeback, operating out
of a large but utilitarian office in the Herman Bennett
Company headquarters, his green ranch wagon parked
in the lot, his needs tended by secretaries apparently
dedicated to a chief executive just now at the age when
most men enter politics for the first time.

Barnes is speaking long-distance with the president
of Skippy Peanut Butter.

"Are you familiar with the water situation in Comanche County?" Barnes asks him, his heavy chin thrust
forward, those blue eyes deadpan. "Well, half the county
is irrigated. Comanche's the chief peanut producer in
the world, and I'm from Comanche County. I know peanuts. . . . We're trying to bring the peanut industry back
down South. Now I want to thank you for visitin' with
me this morning, and I hope to see you the next time
I'm in New York."

He was Texas's—the nation's—comer, recipient of the
mantle of "greatness," the establishment's whitest hope.
"Ben Barnes is the future," Johnson told Austin dinner
guests gathered in Barnes's honor in 1970. "At thirty-
two years of age, he's the youngest lieutenant governor
Texas has ever produced." Johnson went on to point out
that Presidents Jefferson, Jackson, the Roosevelts, and
Kennedy all held important positions at age thirty-two,
and added, "Each of them wound up leading this country. You and I know that Ben Barnes is going to lead
it, too."

"LBJ did me a big disservice, really," says Barnes,
and there is some pain in the memory. "*Time* ran my
photo. Boy, Tower and all of 'em wanted my scalp. The
Nixon people came down here after me in 1970, to dis-
credit me. . . . I was a victim of my own effectiveness."

He appears even younger than he is; his self-assurance

is almost beguiling. He dresses modishly, the word "super" is a favorite superlative. His leg still jerks excitedly in conversation like that of an outsized high-school football star, which he was. He embodies the same polite aggressiveness that distinguished him in his hometown of De Leon ("Dee-lie-on") : an honor student voted Most Friendly who married the class valedictorian voted Best Groomed, an all-American match that ended in an uncontested divorce when he had become the hottest political property, and he married again. "He would organize a club to do something," says Barnes's father—a peanut farmer and oil-pipeline worker—speaking of his son as a child. "He would always wind up being the leader."

His meteoric rise was extraordinary even by Texas standards. Today the Sharpstown scandal is in his eyes just an aberration, an unforeseeable and abrupt end to a string of successes that began when he graduated from UT. In 1960, the state representative from his district had decided not to run again, and Barnes made the race against advice and reason, and against a well-known Brownwood businessman. Using some borrowed money (and his and his wife's shoe leather), he knocked on every door—a big, fresh-faced twenty-two-year-old people couldn't easily forget. The housewives elected him by an astounding five-to-one margin.

Barnes became a conservative from a conservative district. Ideology did not interest him, advancement did, and he found time to campaign for the Kennedy-Johnson ticket that same year. His political judgment was quick, and remarkably sound for so young a man. He had a way of flattering older people without demeaning himself; he reminded many of what they might have been. And he was willing to take chances. One was his support of a tough, conservative representative, Byron Tunnell, who wanted to be House speaker, and then was. The other chance was Barnes's espousal of the candidate for governor who was initially known by only 4 percent of the populace, John Connally.

Barnes seemed destined for the embrace of Connally and his backers. Young, bright, and aggressive, he also knew a lot about the government of Texas—a distinct advantage in Connally's remote and largely affluent camp. Barnes was invited to attend the planning session at Briscoe's ranch, in the role of obliging prodigy. He held down corners of Eugene Locke's maps, enduring the discussion of shopping-center campaign strategy. Barnes caught Erwin's eye, and that of Robert Strauss, who later told Connally, "John, that dumb-looking red-headed boy was the astutest politician in this room."

It was a heady moment for Barnes, and his gratitude was real. He was the first to officially congratulate Connally after he announced his candidacy, and he gave a long and lavish introduction for Connally when he came to speak in Brownwood, his first campaign appearance. "After the luncheon," Barnes recalls, "Connally and I went out and got into his car with a couple of naval aides. They didn't know cotton-pickin' beans about politics, so I gave them a list of contacts. Those were the first names that went into Connally's campaign file."

Barnes's reasons for backing Connally are best understood in terms of the political climate of the time. Connally was associated with the Kennedy administration, which promised a new, invigorated America. Young men saw in themselves a vision of a more vital future, and unlimited opportunity if they were on the right side of the political fence. The answer for pragmatic young conservatives was to bill themselves as "progressives," in favor of education, and sufficient water for farmers. Progressivism allowed promising statesmen to share the excitement of apparent political regeneration when they had little sympathy for the liberal bias in Washington. Today, "progressive" remains a code word in Texas signifying that a candidate may make unsettling noises about, say, pollution, but poses no real threat to the status quo.

Connally and Barnes became progressives together. Barnes campaigned hard for him, and for Tunnell's speakership, and shared in the victories of the two most powerful men in the capitol. Then he began to serve as a conduit between the Governor and the Speaker, and between those two and other members of the House. He traveled with Connally, learned to read his moods. If Connally used the words "In my judgment," he knew Connally's mind could be changed. But if he said, "My instincts tell me," then further appeal was useless. Erwin became fond of the representative from De Leon, and helped him in all matters, including financial. Later it would be Barnes's aides who clustered about Erwin in the Forty Acres, enjoying his bounty, and his abuse of the enemies of order in Texas.

Barnes was named chairman of the Rules Committee —who could object to such an appealing young man asserting himself in the interests of the people's recognized leaders?—and became an unofficial whip, bringing his colleagues round on key issues. The House was the conservative side of the legislature, and sometimes Tunnell balked at the Governor's progressivism, his spending. It was then that Barnes distinguished himself.

The Texas Manufacturers Association awarded Barnes a 90–95 percent favorable rating based on a sample of twenty votes in the House: he was more than clean. At an appreciation dinner for Barnes in Brownwood late in 1963, Connally returned the favor earlier extended to him and spoke in praise of Barnes from the hospital, where he was recovering from his bullet wounds. President Johnson wired his congratulations.

Barnes was already seen as the establishment's answer to the changing face of Texas politics, able to appeal to minorities, the young, and the liberal in a way Connally never could. Connally's ploy was to usurp liberal issues by using such generalizations as "excellence in education," "pollution control," "industrial safety," and "liberalized welfare benefits" to describe programs of little substance. But Barnes treated the liberals with the same facile charm he used on mossbacks. Unaccustomed to such civility, the liberals were only too willing to believe him.

Barnes had come to model himself on Connally, wearing expensive suits and shoes, picking up tabs at the Forty Acres—but still carrying the Governor's bags. His next move was obviously to the speakership, and although Barnes campaigned hard for Tunnell in 1964, he was already planning how to succeed him. The idea emerged to collect signatures of legislators who would pledge their votes to Barnes in the event that Tunnell chose not to run for the speakership next time round. It was a revolutionary idea, and the means of a coup.

The man who takes credit for the idea of the signed, conditional pledges is state Comptroller Bob Bullock, then a lobbyist for the Texas Automobile Dealers Association, a gravel-voiced operator, and a cynical wit. Bullock admits he had only his own interests at heart when he suggested to Barnes that he begin collecting pledges, and offered to placate Tunnell, who was Bullock's close friend. Bullock claims to have typed out the first pledge card, then handed it to Barnes, who "jumped up like a little puppy and ran out of the office, and goddamn, he was back in a few minutes. He had phoned Bob Landis's law office here in town, and he had it signed."

Barnes built up his collection of pledges. Then Connally was given the opportunity to remove Tunnell as speaker when a seat on the Railroad Commission became available just four days before the 1965 legislative session began. Barnes says he received advance warning from Tunnell himself that the speaker's position was becoming available. He certainly received it from Erwin, who helped set up a clandestine operation in a Driskill

Hotel suite equipped with a bank of telephones. Here Connally, Erwin, Barnes, Bullock, and others—including Gus Mutscher, the representative from Brenham, who would have an unforeseen effect on Barnes's blossoming career—locked themselves in under assumed names, and spent thirty-six hours, off and on, lining up support for Barnes. By the time Barnes formally announced his candidacy, the operation was well under way and his election virtually assured.

The abrupt, calculated, secret manner by which the victory was engineered signified a new and more sophisticated muscle in state politics. It also meant, as state Representative Bob Eckhardt put it, "perpetual control of the House by the lobby." But Barnes was in, the legend initiated. His grooming for national audiences began with his attending conferences outside the state for political leaders, some of the invitations secured by President Johnson. Barnes was elected vice-chairman of the National Council of State Governments in 1966, and threatened a public fight if the council failed to endorse Johnson's policy in Vietnam.

Barnes in the House acted in concert with the Governor. He avidly backed the bill—and campaigned for the proposed constitutional amendment—to grant four-year terms to state officials. Such a law would have put Connally in a perfect position to run in 1970 against his enemy Senator Ralph Yarborough, relieving him of the necessity of seeking an unprecedented fourth term as governor. In support of such a move, Barnes told a group in Austin the amendment should pass. "After Lyndon Johnson leaves the White House," Barnes said, "Texas is going to be in sad shape in Washington." However, the amendment was defeated, almost out of habit.

Barnes's only problem now was money. His backers found this situation both embarrassing and a potential threat: men of power should also be men of means. Suddenly he found it easy—effortless, in fact—to borrow money, and to be the recipient of the best financial advice from Erwin and others. He acquired, for instance, a $145,000 interest in two Texas radio stations simply by affixing his signature to two notes, along with those of other investors. "I had nothing to do with the financing of either station," he said later, with a hint of righteous indignation. "They had already put the package together before I came into it."

There was, however, an element of *déjà vu* in the arrangement for those remembering the rise of Lyndon Johnson. An even stronger similarity was the relationship between Barnes and his Brownwood angel, Herman Bennett, who made Barnes a partner in his construction company because, Barnes said, Bennett was "a nice fellow" who "just bet on a young man." That bit of Lone Star ingenuousness requires some explanation. Bennett also made a $100,000 interest-free loan to Barnes, and involved him in several financial deals. These included a cut of the Holiday Inn franchises in Texas, and other real-estate investments, including an apartment complex.

And Barnes showed himself willing to help his friend, without risking his political position. They flew to Minneapolis together to convince executives of Minnesota Mining & Manufacturing to expand its plant in Brownwood, with Bennett Construction to do the work. The resulting expansion doubled the size of Barnes's and Bennett's Brownwood operation. The 3M plant in Brownwood was for the manufacture of reflective sheeting, and in 1967 the state legislature passed a bill written by 3M lobbyists requiring Texas license plates to be made with this type of sheeting.

Barnes also acquired, on a yearly salary of less than $5,000, two farms for the growing of peanuts, and an interest in a Bolivian tin mine. It was all in the best tradition of public service in Texas, but a phenomenon known as the Ben Barnes Club did cause some raised eyebrows among the unredeemed moralists. The "club," established in his home district, consisted of members willing to contribute money for Barnes's activities. What would have been called a slush fund in any other state was described by a club founder as "an exercise in basic good government," an assessment newspaper editorialists apparently agreed with. Approximately $20,000 a year was provided, Barnes said in his own defense, to allow him to meet his many speaking engagements— and to mail out Christmas cards.

During Barnes's speakership, the capitol was a lively and—many agreed—randy place. State politics suddenly acquired style, and promise. Barnes traveled to Hollywood to take instruction at a movie studio to improve his dramatic presence, and to add an aura of responsibility to his perennial sunniness. His hair was restyled, as was that of his constant bodyguard; there was grace in the corridors of Austin, at least compared to what had been.

"For one brief, shining moment," says Barnes, "I think there was a Camelot in Austin—a pride. There was some style even in the Connally-Yarborough split. Even my critics would say my leadership was interesting. But then Connally quit, Rayburn died, LBJ came home, and Preston Smith was elected governor. Things changed."

It was a coming of age, and a rougher one than Barnes could know. He was advised by Connally and others to run for lieutenant governor, and provided with enough money to outspend his opponents by ten dollars to one. He flew to all parts of the state, filled every television screen with the new Barnes persona: youth-*cum*-responsibility. He enjoyed some liberal support because of his backing of proposals for minimum wages and improved anti-pollution laws, was heralded as the man capable of doing the impossible—uniting the left and the right in Texas.

Barnes carried every county in the state. He was one

of the youngest, most popular, best-financed political figures in America; his horizons really seemed limitless. As leader of the Senate, Barnes could comfortably back the minimum-wage bill as a "progressive," and at the same time steer Erwin's renomination as regent through a stormy debate. He attended Erwin's celebration party, along with Johnson, as the victor, "the future."

But that all changed, the result of a seedy scandal known as Sharpstown, and the final stage of Barnes's political development. The scandal would probably never have occurred if not for the efforts of a federal agency particularly interested in a Texas bank failure. The Securities and Exchange Commission announced an investigation of what it termed a multimillion-dollar case of fraud, following the largest payment ever made for insured deposits by the Federal Deposit Insurance Corporation. The investigation led back two years to a bill passed by the Texas legislature that made almost $400,-000 for some of the state's leading politicians, among them Governor Smith and Barnes's House supporter Speaker Gus Mutscher. No direct connection was ever established between Barnes and the confessed swindler, Frank Sharp—described by one state legislator as "just an old country boy in a shiny black suit with one arm longer than the other," who also promoted bank shares and real estate. However, it became known that another of Sharp's banks had loaned Barnes $60,000.

Sharp pleaded guilty, received a three-year suspended sentence and a $5,000 fine, and became a witness for the government. He implicated politicians other than Smith and Mutscher, including the chairman of the state Democratic party, Elmer Baum, and the chief of the Justice Department's criminal division, Will Wilson, who was asked to resign. Mutscher and two of his aides were indicted for conspiracy to accept a bribe, and charged with taking secured loans from Sharp to buy stock in his National Bankers Life Insurance Company. These stocks brought large profits after the price was driven up by manipulation. The stock was said to be a form of bribery, because the legislature had been asked to pass bills removing the Sharpstown State Bank from federal control and examination.

The defendants were found guilty by a jury in Abilene, and given five-year probated sentences. The judge made the melodramatic declaration that "If we can't convict a high public official on the evidence we've got here, then we might as well turn our state capitol over to the moneychangers." The only real punishment was the loss of public office and influence.

The irony of Sharpstown is that it involved none of the powerful, unseen forces in Texas. Rather, it represented an upthrust from the lower echelon of promoters, nurtured by the general climate of rapacity. Sharpstown dragged down several second-rate politicians—but in the process it also destroyed the carefully wrought power base of the establishment, symbolized by Ben Barnes. He was investigated by several federal and state agencies, but nothing linking Barnes with Sharp was ever discovered. When he ran for governor in the next election, he placed a poor third in the Democratic primary, and the establishment deserted him en masse.

"It's very strange," he says, "that people couldn't separate me from the others. They couldn't understand how Preston Smith and Mutscher might know somebody I didn't know. Everybody got painted with the same brush. I still never have met Frank Sharp."

He feels his biggest mistake was not running against Yarborough in 1970, when Bentsen would have stepped aside and Barnes would have remained the golden boy.

"Personally, I don't have any political plans. But every time I speak to a business group, my wife closes her eyes and tells me I sound like a candidate. Of course, I still participate on the local level, as a delegate to the state convention...."

His eyes grow bright, his feet begin to shuffle, as if he is already running.

"There's no reason why Texas can't have excellence. We can have remedial education, and a good water program. We can solve pollution, the problems of the cities; we *can* have a high quality of urban life. Why, the Dallas-Fort Worth Airport is the finest facility in the country. Texas can be Number One—the leader—and that's not Texas vanity. . . . On the national level, we've got no viable programs to solve the energy crisis. And what's Congress doing about it? . . . Attacks on the depletion allowance? Pure demagoguery. . . . If the United States can't form a coalition with other nations —why, then we just can't handle inflation. . . . Internationalism . . . We need a leader we can respect! . . ."

Interlude

EXILES

If democracy can break out in Texas,
no place is safe.
　　　　—Frances Tarlton Farenthold

Her house sits uncomfortably close to River Oaks, in a
block of neat bungalows marshaled among the redolent,
tropical growth of suburban Houston. The lawn is tamed
crab grass, the house functional and vaguely Moorish
in design, with the swimming pool just fitting in the
narrow corridor between sliding glass panels and the
neighbor's back fence. Inside, the clutter of kitchen and
workroom reflects the presence of grown children raised
in the casual ambience of the Gulf Coast. This contrasts
sharply with the elegance of the dining and sitting
rooms, decorated with heavy drapes and brocaded furniture, a table where old and precious art objects—miniature portraits, enamel snuffboxes, exquisitely wrought
figurines—are displayed beneath glass, and the walls are
hung with eighteenth- and nineteenth-century oils, including a highly valued landscape by Corot.

She sits at the kitchen table in jeans and a T-shirt, preparing artichokes for a dinner party. Her assault with a pair of scissors seems more characteristic of a tough public defender than of a deferential, dark-haired Southerner resolutely short of matronhood. Sissy Farenthold is both. And she speaks of her last defeat by Dolph Briscoe in the 1974 gubernatorial race with the disdain of a realist in Texas all too recently proclaimed the standard-bearer of the liberals and the righteous.

"Where are the 'liberals'?" she asks rhetorically. "Among the minorities? Among labor? I didn't have union support this time. Briscoe made inroads into the black leadership, into the Mexican-Americans. . . . What is a liberal?"

For most Texans, Sissy is the definition incarnate. Catholic, opinionated, female, she led the notorious reform group in the Texas House, known as the "Dirty Thirty," that helped bring down Mutscher and Barnes. As a candidate for governor in 1972—that magic year for outsiders—she scornfully denounced "the tyranny of private interests" in Texas. She advocated a corporate-profits tax, increased welfare benefits, a lowering of the penalty for possession of marijuana from a felony to a misdemeanor, the removal of the all-white, showy Texas Rangers from sections heavily populated by Mexican-Americans, and called the man duly chosen by the establishment as its representative in the Governor's Mansion "a bowl of pudding."

"Even then I wanted to remove myself from the liberals. But I was called a 'self-insurgent.' "

She is not speaking of philosophy, but of a group in Texas that amounts to a class. Her association with that group is augmented by the days she spent at the Hockaday private school in Dallas, and at Vassar, and the reputation of her well-to-do Corpus Christi family, the Tarltons. Her grandmother was an early public-school teacher—a task of *noblesse oblige* rather than sheer necessity—her father, a legislator and law professor. A library at the University of Texas bears his name. His daughter was one of three women among eight hundred law students at UT. After working in his law offices, Sissy became the director of legal aid for Nueces County, defender of the poor. There she learned firsthand the limits of public assistance, and of the men elected to public office.

"What politicians do," she says, and it is an indication of her appeal, "is take people's hopes and make policy."

She campaigned hard for a seat in the Texas House, although there wasn't one woman among the hundred and fifty legislators, and she dreaded confronting large groups of people in her own behalf. Her husband encouraged her to run, in part as an antidote to the shock caused by the drowning of one of their children.

"Before I ran that race, I thought it would be ten years before a woman could win in Texas."

Winning was a personal revelation, and an inspiration. Her independence would become an issue right up until 1974 when she decided to run again for governor, against most advice. She personally disapproved of abortion, but defended the right of women to make their own decision, a position that lost her sympathy among some church groups that might have supported her. When embraced by the feminists, she said publicly that "there are many more important issues than my gender."

Some called it plain stubbornness, a characteristic of Texas's most famous contemporary liberal, Ralph Yarborough. Sissy was the only one in the Texas House to vote against a proposal commending President Johnson, because she opposed his policies in Vietnam. Tenacity and some truculence were required to hold together the "Dirty Thirty" during the 1971–72 legislative session, when that unlikely coalition of liberals, blacks, Chicanos, and a few zealous Republicans pushed for the creation of a bicameral committee to investigate Sharpstown.

Sissy tends to deprecate her own role, calling it that of "den mother." But the continual questioning forced the press to take a harder look at what might have been just another scandal in Texas.

The 1972 elections were glorious times for liberals in Texas, and for the generally disaffiliated and disillusioned. The big money shifted to Briscoe early in the race, because it soon became apparent that Barnes was in trouble. Not that Briscoe was part of the old order. He was known to the establishment as a genial host whose best friends were the sellers of automobiles, rich by any standard, and amenable to keeping things in Texas pretty much as they were. He seemed safe and reclusive, and proved to be so.

But no one expected Sissy to come so close. She placed second behind Briscoe in the primary, and there was no time for establishment tears over the demise of Barnes. Not only was she a strong contender, she had also become a stanchion to the reformers, a rallying point for voters as disparate as radical professors and Wallaceites. The fact that she was the only anti-establishment candidate gave new impetus to the movement that began with the "Dirty Thirty."

Underfinanced but not understaffed, she flew back and forth across the state in a chartered plane, riding the reform sentiment, sparking mostly the young, the white, and the liberal. However, she was also attended to by middle-aged couples, the blacks, and Chicanos. At more than one rally, white men were seen wearing stickers that read "Male Chauvinist Pig for Sissy." She told them the governor's office was not for sale that year, was proud of the fact that she was not a "safe" candidate. Briscoe safely avoided confrontation with her, and the discussion of issues of consequence. He played upon her ardor, and her womanness. She was, Briscoe said, emotional, irresponsible, "permissive"; she couldn't properly comprehend certain rural problems because of her training at Hockaday and Vassar, problems like the screw-worm, and water shortages.

That was enough. Sissy lost in the runoff election with 45 percent of the vote, in retrospect an astounding achievement. She had received support from labor, and from organizations with members of the minority, and they were all disappointed that she failed to attain some real power. But the liberals hailed her defeat as a victory, since Barnes was out, and that election as some kind of milestone. A similar revolution had been proclaimed a decade before, when the avowedly liberal Don Yarborough came close to defeating Connally in his first gubernatorial race—a contest of unknowns. In fact, 1972 was a year of mild political catharsis in an essentially conservative state, and wouldn't soon be repeated. It was a grand time for the participants, but not without some grand delusions.

Sissy's liberal credentials were enhanced by her election as the first chairman of the National Women's Political Caucus within months of her defeat. She was seen as one of the most promising women candidates for unspecified public office in America, challenger of the Texas establishment, harbinger of the future. Accepting the chairmanship at the convention in Houston, Sissy called the women's movement "a revolution without arms," and added her note of independence: "Sisterhood does not mean the end of brotherhood."

Soon she was attacking George McGovern for retreating from the standards used to pick delegates to the 1972 Democratic National Convention. She wrote McGovern an open letter advising that it was crucial that the Democratic party not overreact to defeat, and thereby return to policies that would "exclude women, minorities, youth, and the rank-and-file working people." For some Texans, that put Sissy to the left of McGovern—the Democrat most despised among them since Kennedy —and made her seem even more stubborn.

Most observers thought she should pass up the 1974 gubernatorial race in Texas. The state had recovered quickly from its atypical dalliance in reform politics; Watergate provided great distraction from the inequities at home; and Briscoe was firmly entrenched at the Governor's Mansion, having made no mistakes, with his campaign organization wallowing in money.

"But I had to run again," says Sissy. "I've never loitered with the political past."

Her most ardent supporters did little else. She was seen as the successor in the tradition—best represented by Ralph Yarborough—of personal, crusading politics against the obvious evils of corruption and influence. The split between the Connally and the Yarborough factions of the Democrats in Texas had never been anything but vastly lopsided in favor of the party's right wing. It was as much a chemical as an ideological split, an antipathy symbolized by the heads of the two factions, the mutual loathing between pure ambition and uncompromising high-mindedness. Yarborough had made a few concessions to the establishment—he supported the depletion allowance—but he was never considered anything but an anomaly, to be disposed of at the earliest opportunity.

He had led the liberals since 1952. The seventh son of a big east Texas farming family, he grew up with a feel for the finer points of populist issues. His grandfather organized the first Confederate infantry company from Texas, and became its captain. Yarborough himself was as much Southern as he was Texan, a romantic like Connally, but one who found some inspiration in ideas, rather than the acquisition of power and property. He attended Sam Houston State Teachers College, and began to drift in the grand American manner: a year at West Point, two years teaching in a one-room east Texas schoolhouse, a working trip to Europe aboard a cattle boat, further study in France and Germany, more labor

back home in the oil and wheat fields. He graduated
from UT law school in 1927 with highest honors.

Politics became real when he was named assistant
attorney general under Governor James Allred, the last
of Texas's liberal governors. Yarborough lost his first
four political races—one for attorney general and three
for governor—before he was elected to the Senate in
1957. He and Johnson fell out over federal appointments
in Texas, but only for a time was LBJ able to keep him
off the Appropriations Committee. There, and as chairman of the Labor and Public Welfare Committee, Yarborough was able to really achieve liberal objectives,
such as the minimum-wage expansion bill in 1966, and
the Occupational Safety and Health Act.

Although Johnson disliked Yarborough, and considered him an old enemy, he valued the appearance of
party unity back home. He discouraged Lloyd Bentsen
and Representative Joe Kilgore from running against
Yarborough when he first came up for re-election. Any
hopes of settlement of the Connally-Yarborough feud,
however, dissolved with the assassination of Kennedy in
Dallas. Bentsen defeated Yarborough on the coattails of
law-and-order in 1970, a vote described by Maury Maverick, Jr., as "anti-nigger, anti-Mexican, anti-youth, and
sock-it-to-'em in Vietnam."

Some of Yarborough's previous backers—most notice-
ably white workers—had deserted him, and did not return for his comeback attempt two years later. Barefoot
Sanders—a strong candidate with such a name—defeated him with a more centrist position but then lost
to Tower. Even some liberals thought Yarborough got
what he deserved. One claimed that in the past, whenever a liberal in Texas considered running, "he naturally
called Our Leader in Washington and asked for his advice. And Ralph's response was invariably, 'Oh, no,
don't do that. That might hurt me.' "

The old crusades had lost much of their meaning for

labor and the minorities in an increasingly urban state. Taxing the big corporations meant less to them than getting in on the play themselves, and enjoying a share of the federal contracts. Ralph's policies had a moldy touch; Sissy suffered the taint. Those liberals who urged her to run, or who trotted along with her, were moved by the memory of past struggles. Her campaign was an act of political nostalgia.

Briscoe was the docile incumbent, unbeatable even when Texas was faced with several more years of his shadow. Briscoe's greatest contribution may have been to prove that the governor's office functioned equally well unoccupied. The general mood of complacency affected Lieutenant Governor Bill Hobby, Attorney General John Hill, and House Speaker Price Daniel, Jr., all of whom decided to sit tight in a year of national frenzy, when no movement was discernible in the Mansion.

There were other offices for which Sissy could have fought—state treasurer, railroad commissioner, even congresswoman. But she wanted the position of obvious influence. "I play high with politics," she had said two years before. "Why be a safe candidate?"

She announced her candidacy hours before the deadline, adding drama to the catastrophe. Briscoe had already promised that if no strong liberal candidate ran against him in the primary, he would favor the inclusion of more liberal delegates to the state Democratic conventions, and to the party's mid-term convention in Kansas City. But bad blood among the liberals was no deterrent to Sissy. She still had the appeal of human warmth and sincerity; what she lacked in 1974 was an apparent villain for an opponent.

She praised the property tax as a means of raising money for education. She attacked Briscoe and Hill for appealing a federal court decision favoring redistricting, which would bring so many new faces into state politics. But even those who would have profited most from redistricting voted against her. Watergate still distracted them. Texas felt that its scandals were past, that the rest of the United States was just catching up. There were more important things to think about—like stability.

Briscoe won the primary with 70 percent of the vote, and instantly became part of the concentrated push for Bentsen's Presidential bid. He was in the best position to strengthen his grip on the Texas delegation before the 1976 Democratic Convention; Sissy was in political eclipse, and perhaps worse.

"And now," she says, "I'm going back to what I did before, which is being a lawyer."

Politics seems to have lost its allure in the Farenthold household. During Sissy's dinner party for which the artichokes were so carefully prepared, conversation centers on life's amenities, without mention of candidates, campaigns, issues. The guests include the Farentholds' daughter Emilie, two young men from among Houston's flourishing interior-decorating industry, and their friend, who has provided the steaks, sent to him by his mother from a ranch in west Texas. George Farenthold, a stocky, amiable Belgian count and south Texas businessman, discourses knowledgeably on the wines of France, North Africa, and California, and upon his favorite entree, roast venison with chestnut sauce.

Later, when dinner is finished, I offer to help carry the dishes into the kitchen.

"Oh, no," says Sissy, filling the silence with alarm. "The women will clear."

7 ☆ DEALING IN DALLAS

Perot's Half-Billion

> *Any man born in the United States is*
> *twice-blessed. And he is thrice-blessed*
> *if born in Texas.*
> — *H. Ross Perot*

The initial stands for Henry. It was added after the name Perot came to stand for the American bonanza of systems analysis. Even with the addition, the handle lacks the weight to match Perot's extraordinary parlaying of a thousand-dollar investment into assets of some $700 million in seven years, or his personal crusade conducted among the airfields of the world to splendidly return American prisoners of war from Vietnam. The gesture was so parvenu and expansive, revealed so unshakable a faith in the power of money, that Perot became for a time the darling Texan. Then he singlehandedly attempted to reinvest the seers of Wall Street and reverse the recession of the '70s, only to be undone by the money men themselves.

"We would have appreciated a little breathing room

while we rebuilt du Pont," he says, in response to a set of written questions that have been carefully perused by aides. "It would probably be unrealistic to expect it, just as it would be unrealistic for a wounded deer in the forest to expect a reprieve from the other animals until it was able to run again."

His lapels are slightly wider, as are his ties, but he still occasionally wears those same stiff collars with tabs that fasten beneath the hard knot of the tie. The closely cropped hair makes his ears appear too large, lending him the raw, ready aspect of a GI on his first leave, proud of his country and his uniform. His office, housed in Electronic Data Systems' own towering complex in suburban Dallas—the huge letters, "EDS," hang from the roof as if by grappling hooks—reflects a fondness for military paraphernalia, and for slogans. "What exists today was once only imagined," reads a plaque displayed among watercolors of naval vessels. A golden replica of an eagle, wings spread in apparent agony, perches above the assertion "Eagles don't flock."

Perot may be America's only transcendental businessman; he is certainly the most successful. As a young salesman for IBM, he displayed an unseemly enthusiasm in a company that disapproves of excess. Not that he didn't fit in at IBM. In most ways, Perot seemed specially developed for the world of systems analysis, a hybrid uncluttered by philosophical considerations. Reality consisted of perceiving a problem as a component in a larger equation, stating it in the argot that reduced language to relentless generalities ("input," "feedback," "overview"), and solving it as profitably as possible. He definitely looked the part.

Then in 1962 Perot sold his yearly quota of computers by mid-January. He was left to contemplation, a practice frowned upon by his superiors, and for good reason. While thumbing through a magazine, Perot came upon Thoreau's famous quotation, "The mass of men lead lives

of quiet desperation," an assertion that proved incen-
diary within the pearl-gray corridors of IBM. He quit,
borrowed money from whomever he could to incorporate
EDS, while he was still only thirty-two years old, and
within a few years was one of the richest men in Texas.

"Having lunch with Ross down at Kiwanis," recalls
an editor for the *Morning News,* "you wouldn't have
thought he was any different. He was an average guy. I
mean, what happened is kind of incredible."

His father was a Texarkana cotton broker and horse-
trader. He took Ross along on most business ventures,
teaching him the finer points of commerce. "Buying cotton from a man once had very little value unless you
developed a personal relationship with him," Perot later
recalled. "Otherwise, he wouldn't come back to you next
year." His father was also Ross's best friend. He grew
up with a sense of propriety, and a natural respect for
authority and the tenets of free enterprise. He sold
Christmas cards door-to-door, delivered the Texarkana
Gazette along a route that included the homes of many
black families.

He wanted to be a sailor, and entered the United
States Naval Academy in 1949. A writer for the 1953
Annapolis yearbook said that what Perot "lacked in
physical size, he more than adequately replaced by his
capacity to make friends and influence people." Already
he was involved in "information systems." Aboard an
aircraft carrier, he met a representative from IBM, a
close observer of the military as a field of recruitment,
and consequently knew where to go if he decided to leave
the Navy. He did so because "the promotion system and
the seniority system and the waiting-in-line concept
were just sort of incompatible with my desire to be
measured and judged by what I could produce."

After Perot formed EDS, he placed his wife, his

mother, and his sister on the board, since they had sufficient confidence in the company to be appointed. The
bankers he approached all thought the idea of buying
computer time wholesale and selling it retail was so bad
that they wouldn't lend him money. Perot flew to Hawaii
on his own investment, with a yellow legal pad upon
which to formulate his ideas about EDS. He wrote that
the company should be "the most respected e.d.p. [elec-
tronic data processing] service firm in the United States."
It should also be the largest, "provided that size does
not adversely affect the quality of the work being done."
There would exist "complete intolerance toward company politics."

His first client was Collins Radio. Earnings began to
grow; Perot held on to most of the corporation himself.
He was the essential man in the right place at the right
time. The public was receptive—breathless—for new
stock issues, and computers were the way of the future,
a measure of a company's sophistication and prospects.
Businessmen who had never heard of print-outs suddenly couldn't live without them. And very few knew
how to plug into the voracious new consumer.

In the beginning, EDS had two employees—Perot and
his secretary. Within a few years there were three hundred employees, nineteen of them full-time recruiters.
The computer boom had lifted Perot and EDS higher
than he had ever imagined; his expectations grew with
earnings. EDS acted as a customer's data-processing department, furnished the computer, programmed and
operated it, taught the customer how to make use of the
information produced. At times there were more demands than computer time, and an endless line of executives anxious to sign Perot's book-length contracts for
five years' worth of software.

To work for EDS was to ride the rim of American
business technology, in a city growing famous for bright,
analytical minds plugged into the computer bonanza.

They were drawn to EDS by the meteor's bright tail—EDS went public with stock worth a hundred and eighteen times earnings—and the prospects. A man could rise by his own accounts, in an atmosphere free of politics. The only thing that could get a salesman fired faster than office power plays was to associate with a woman other than his wife. EDS men may have entertained their own moments of quiet desperation, but they did not even *talk* about those attractions that lay outside the bounds of what the boss's moralism permitted. Besides, too much sex vitiated ambition.

The most faithful had been allowed to purchase shares before EDS went public, for twenty cents apiece. More than forty of these investors became millionaires, and many more had stock holdings in five years worth hundreds of thousands of dollars. When EDS went public, Perot owned about 80 percent of the company, and was worth $300 million.

"People were convinced that we had some secret," he says. "They thought we had all this programmed on a computer in some way."

Offices opened in every major city; there were soon 2,500 employees, with a median age of thirty. Perot took pains to be fair, hiring some members of minority groups, loaning money to Negro businessmen. But the Dallas establishment waited in vain for Perot to come forward, in the traditional manner of men of great wealth, to seek a position on the Board of Education or the Citizens Council, or to take some active part in running the city. The rich young men, including Jimmy Ling and Sam Wyly, did not share the old views of the prerogatives and responsibilities of wealth, and their horizons weren't limited to the suburbs of Dallas.

"The nation is faced with problems," Perot said more than once, in his expansive, sincere manner. "We have the money, and money is just like oil, a lubricant to get things moving."

It was a statement likely to appeal to Richard Nixon, whom Perot supported in 1968. A year after the election, Perot surfaced as an official spokesman for the "silent majority," duly recognized by the Nixon administration. He was a natural for White House flattery: a young millionaire who actually believed in the existence of that demographic generality. He was more than willing to lend himself—the crew cut and the unambiguous smile, the tab collars and medallion ties—to this huge, mute constituency. Best of all, he was willing to spend his own money.

Perot founded United We Stand, an organization to fight what was commonly referred to as "social ills," and to provide the silent majority with a unified voice. The organization seemed to consist primarily of Perot and his checkbook, and to be doomed to failure, although the schemes did not lack grandness. The most ambitious was the creation of an "electronic town hall," a series of nonpartisan television broadcasts employing computerized polling techniques to canvass the nation. Some self-promotion was involved, but Perot was genuinely enthusiastic about such an exercise in democracy. Apparently he had not been told about McLuhan, or about the fact that NBC and Gallup had teamed up to perform essentially the same function years before. He had certainly not been prepared for the monumental lack of response from those he considered his ideological brethren.

"I want to put my money where my intentions are," he lamented. "I'm a product of this country, and I feel I have an obligation to the American people to do all I can to make this a better country."

The act of running for public office apparently held no appeal. "I'm a direct, action-oriented person," he said, putting his money in some more obvious places than the electronic town hall. Two and a half million went to the Dallas public-school system, in an effort to prove to the James Astons and Erik Jonssons that he

was proud of being a third-generation Texan, and a
Dallasite. Fair to a Presbyterian fault, Perot gave
$50,000 to a Jesuit high school. When he gave a million
dollars to the Boy Scouts, he immediately bought a thousand acres of land and donated them to the Girl Scouts.

A quiet desperation persisted. "Making all this money
is partly an accident. I had the opportunity to be in the
right place, and I have an obligation to do something
creative."

He made the American war prisoners in Vietnam that
obligation, and United We Stand their savior. No one
but the Communists could impugn the motives of a man
just trying to bring our boys home. Or at least to deliver
Christmas presents to them, along with medicine and
turkey dinners, all loaded into two green 707s and flown
thirty-five thousand miles, never to be delivered. It had
begun with a visit to his office in the fall of 1969 by the
wives of four prisoners who needed money to fly to
Paris, where they planned to ask the North Vietnamese
for information about their husbands.

Perot flew them. Later, one of the wives returned to
his office with her four-year-old son. "This little boy had
never seen his dad," Perot recalls. United We Stand
promptly spent a million dollars on newspaper and television advertisments, and on a massive mailing to drum
up support for the campaign. The answering mail, and
the parcels, formed the ballast for his first trip to Southeast Asia. It was the sort of gesture that could only have
been made by a young man who had earned a great deal
of his own money, who still wore the watch he received
on graduating from high school in Texarkana as proudly
as he displayed on his office wall the American flag that
flew over the White House the day the first man landed
on the moon. He really believed that money administered
in the best faith could move mountains.

Perot continued his efforts to focus attention on the
plight of the POWs, but managed to direct as much or

more on himself. His peers at home were secretly horrified at his extracurricular activities. Nothing was more abhorrent to the new Lone Star corporate uniformity than for a newly rich Texan to act like one. And his fervor aroused some skepticism in other quarters, where his frequent visits to the White House appeared suspicious. Perot's anguish over the POWs didn't prevent him from fully supporting Nixon's policies in Vietnam, or EDS from accepting its richest accounts from defense contractors.

"I just want to see the war ended at the earliest possible time," he said, in a statement that somehow lacked candor. To prove his sincerity, he began to fly around the country, speaking to women's groups, granting interviews, even posing on a horse in his three-piece Neiman-Marcus suit. He made trips abroad, took part in a vigil outside the North Vietnamese Embassy in Vientiane, Laos, appearing in a photograph with his hands clasped reverently behind his back, his face betraying fatigue and, in that unguarded moment, unrelieved boredom.

"As you put on your socks each morning," Perot would later say about this experience, "ask yourself, 'What am I going to do for these men today?' As you remove your socks in the evening, ask yourself, 'What have I done for these men today?' "

The American press provided Perot his exposure, and made a genuine, though futile, effort to understand him. There were photographs of Perot wearing his socks, sleeping rough in his 707, between sessions with reporters and minor diplomats. His "negotiating teams" around the world were reported to be making no progress with the inscrutable North Vietnamese. Perot named the effort the "Village Campaign," a McLuhanesque vision rooted in H. L. Hunt's utopia—a rich man marshaling electronic impulses for absolute good.

Although the campaign appeared to be a failure, Perot

would later claim the opposite. "Our efforts have not generally been understood, because we could not state our real objective—to change the treatment [of the prisoners], and at the same time publicly pursue tactics designed to mobilize world opinion against the brutal treatment. . . . The North Vietnamese made significant changes in the treatment given the men, and virtually ceased the brutal treatment of the men shortly after our campaign began."

Perot's vision of himself leading the campaign was only expressed once—and inadvertently—when he was describing the North Vietnamese who would never meet with him. "They couldn't get over the fact that anyone could go around the world and knock on the door of another nation. Here was a capitalist supposed to exploit the workers, working his heart out to bring relief."

In an age of declining heroism, the decline of the heroic capitalist was the most precipitous. The notion of such a hero was particularly strong in Texas, although Perot was something new, at variance with the image of the strong, silent man who operated above the public arena. Prototypes like Herman Brown and Sid Richardson gave money, when they gave it at all, to the most obvious institutions—hospitals, colleges—without any interest in effecting change as such, or for recognition. Perot was their contemporary counterpart, open, avid, yet lacking the stature of his predecessors in the eyes of the state.

Perot's causes tended to obscure the origins of his fortune. Editors and readers were content with the knowledge that he had helped bring about the Southwest's computer boom, and was an advocate of hard work and self-reliance. The role played by government contracts in the success of EDS was largely overlooked, and it was this that made Perot so similar to his peers among wealthy Texans.

The source was state and federal welfare funds, and

the Medicare program. Early in his career, Perot established a special relationship with Blue Cross and Blue Shield, which won him subcontracts to administer Medicare and Medicaid programs in eleven states, including four out of five of the biggest revenue producers. The EDS charges for the electronic data processing alone would become one of the largest items in the Medicare administrative budget.

EDS had not soared from the very beginning. The first years were lean enough to prompt the recollection from a Perot assistant: "We had to have two full years' salary in the bank to work for Ross." Perot himself moonlighted by running the Texas Blue Shield computer department. He had first become acquainted with Blue Shield officials while working for IBM. The enactment of the 1965 Medicare and Medicaid laws proved a windfall because of this relationship. The Social Security Administration awarded Texas Blue Shield a contract to develop a computerized system for making payments, and EDS was the obvious recipient of the contract, since it had already developed such a system—at government expense.

EDS was able to strike out on its own partly because of the influence of James Aston, president of Dallas's Republic National Bank and also a Blue Shield director. The contract awarded EDS was used as collateral for a loan to Perot from Republic National. Initial local money helped a Texas comer lay claim to later federal funds in all their enormity, part of which could be diverted to the lender in the form of stock dividends. Aston became chairman of Texas Blue Shield; Perot became a director of Republic. It was a neat arrangement, and one that a respected member of the Dallas establishment could live with, although it typically received no publicity. It was only later, after Perot's "Village Campaign" brought him so much notoriety, that Aston would severely judge the younger man.

EDS grew, with Medicare and Medicaid contracts coming in from all over America. The publicity Perot received in other connections helped push up the value of EDS stock; there was never any mention of the fact that the majority of the business done by EDS was for government. Tons of paperwork were processed by EDS, the information codified and channeled through the computers, the costs spiraling along with profits. The fact that the fortunes of EDS were so closely linked to state welfare departments, the Social Security Administration, and Blue Shield remained only a potential embarrassment.

The biggest Blue Shield contract for EDS came from California in 1969. EDS did the data processing for California's Medicare and Medicaid, and received almost half the administrative costs for that state's Medicare program. (An influential official for California's Department of Health Care Services later went to work for Perot.) California Blue Shield eventually became an adjunct of EDS, with Perot's strict code of behavior and dress prevailing, which meant no beards, mustaches, or long hair, and no discussions of sex.

In New York, Governor Nelson Rockefeller personally intervened to keep Perot in the running for a contract to administer New York's $3.7 billion welfare and Medicare program. Originally nine firms had submitted bids for a $40,000 contract to study the existing systems, and EDS was not one of the finalists selected. Then Rockefeller announced that the rejection of the EDS bid had been a "mistake." EDS was selected over the other firms, and the state Department of Social Services awarded EDS a $125,000 contract for consultation.

Perot's support in the White House was helpful. Testimony before the House Intergovernmental Relations Subcommittee revealed that in 1970 EDS cleared up a backlog of 150,000 claims against Iowa's Medicare system simply by approving them all. The testimony also indicated that in Iowa, California, New York, Pennsylvania, Massachusetts, and Indiana EDS inflated its workload for Medicare contracts, resulting in a million dollars' worth of overcharges. The Social Security Administration held up five Medicare contracts between 1969 and 1971 worth $60 million because EDS would reportedly have been making an inflationary 100 percent profit. It was only after Perot agreed to take over an ailing brokerage firm, at President Nixon's behest, that the contracts were approved, over staff objections.

Perot now claims to be the victim of conspiracy. "A group within the Bureau of Health Insurance decided to build a system to compete with EDS. The cost overrun in developing the government sponsored system was in excess of fourteen times planned cost. This group, in spite of virtually unlimited access to funds, has produced the worst performance in Medicare. This group also plays a key role in approving EDS's contracts. This dual role has produced a predictable conflict of interest."

In late 1970, Perot began to get telephone calls from John Connally, Secretary of the Treasury. The subject of the conversations was the dismal state of the stock market, and what relief might be found. Many big Wall Street investment houses nearly foundered in the wake of the bear market. Goodbody & Company had announced its imminent demise, and Merrill, Lynch agreed to take it over, provided no other major firms went under during the negotiations. A panic was thus avoided, although Wall Street was left extremely edgy.

Trouble became evident at du Pont, Glore, Forgan & Company in early 1971. It was feared that if the firm were allowed to fail, then half a million investors would lose their savings, and some sort of stock-market crash would be precipitated. The true condition of Wall Street would be revealed because of the discrepancy between du Pont's value on paper and its real assets, said to be about $15 million less in securities than its customers owned.

"The President would consider it a decent and patriotic act," Connally told Perot, "if you would intervene in the du Pont mess, and help save the country from economic chaos."

The administration had correctly read its mark. Perot valued his friendship with Nixon, and displayed on the black leather top of his desk in Dallas a garish photograph of the President that was inscribed, "To Ross Perot, with deep appreciation and best wishes from Richard Nixon." Perot supported Nixon in both Presidential campaigns; and he met with him several times to discuss the prisoners of war. Perot was a member of the board of the Richard Nixon Foundation, along with H. R. Haldeman and John Ehrlichman. His financial support apparently set the tone at EDS, where executives know that propriety is not limited to trimming one's sideburns above the level of the ear hole. Three of them donated $180,000 to Nixon's 1972 campaign.

Connally's request was echoed by Attorney General John Mitchell, and Presidential Assistant Peter Flannigan. It was all very flattering for a man who believed in authority, and a Texan with little regard for or knowledge of Wall Street. He confidentially inquired of a friend if it really mattered if Wall Street failed, and was told that it might. The advantages of Perot's involvement were not limited to the enhancement of his image. There was still $60 million worth of Medicare contracts to be released, and an $8 million contract EDS already had with du Pont, a palpable argument for his intervention as Sunbelt savior, and the greatest crusade yet.

It was the return of the son of Daddy Warbucks. Perot immediately put up $5 million, without any indemnification, against losses from legal suits over du Pont's assets. A few days before the deal went through, he was told it would take $10 million to save the firm. After an uncharacteristically angry reaction, he made a typically expansive Texas gesture and doubled his stake. The Social Security Administration released the Medicare contracts, and the nobles of Gotham breathed a sigh of relief.

Perot soon discovered that ten million dollars was only about a quarter of the amount needed to save du Pont, and it was too late for him to withdraw. Worse, the du Pont interests were expected to raise $15 million, which they failed to do, leaving Perot theoretically in control of 90 percent of the firm, out of the hands of the du Pont family for the first time in its forty-year history.

Perot brought some of his best men from Dallas to New York, and installed them in top positions. This further annoyed the old hands who still had a small interest in du Pont. They wanted to pull out, but Perot refused to put up the money. Relations between the Patriot and Wilmington's first family became strained. "An elaborate game of chicken was being played," said one observer. "You had this feeling that you were watching two cars running down the white line at terrific speed toward each other, and that the worst was inevitable."

The enmity of the du Ponts was to be matched by their colleagues on Wall Street. The fact that Perot made some sense of the du Pont debacle, and actually managed to produce some profits, was resented as much as the reshuffling, the computer techniques, and the staff of crew-cut whiz kids. They also resented Perot's rampant humility, the self-deprecating champion of the little man, whose company happened to be grossing $20 million a year in sales, and some of that from Wall Street.

Perot also commented on the lethargic state of the investment industry, a preachment not calculated to win

friends there. He started his own school on the West
Coast to train analysts and salesmen; he hired ex-
military personnel to peddle stocks to Middle America,
and tried to rebuild confidence in the market. He became
known, inevitably, as a super-Boy Scout, an avid, provincial, and egocentric dust-eater too naïve and self-
absorbed to resist the President's outrageous request.
Nixon detested Eastern wealth, and it gave him great
pleasure to be able to call upon an ally from the Southwest to bail out the pinstripes. A similar request to them
from Nixon to perform "a decent and patriotic act" would
have been met with restrained derision.

When Perot began pouring money into the nation's
second-largest brokerage firm, Walston & Company, his
colleagues in Gotham decided it was time for the Dallas
computer softwareman to get a lesson in Eastern quietus.
Perot's sales force was raided continually, his actions
systematically denigrated. EDS stock began to drop, as
had that of another Dallasite, Jimmy Ling, after Wall
Street decided that Ling was getting too big for his conglomerates. Perot essentially became an enemy.

In January, 1974, he announced that du Pont, Walston,
Inc., was unloading its costly network of branch offices
and closing its doors. The firm had incurred a $23 million
loss in the previous five months. "All we needed was a
reasonably good period in the stock market," Perot now
says, "in order to allow du Pont time to regain strength
as an organization. Instead, the market deteriorated as
the economy deteriorated. In addition, the Arabs dealt
the securities industry a major blow when they increased the price of oil."

The "wounded deer" returned to Dallas, having lost
18 percent of EDS business that came from Wall Street.
The price of EDS stock had fallen from its 1970 high of
162 to 15 by mid-February. Perot lost a fortune in personal assets, which slid to a mere $130 million, an im-
pressive enough figure for a forty-three-year-old Texan.

But his losses on paper amounted to more than half a billion dollars.

"No great tears are being shed on Wall Street" was a representative comment from the other side of America.

Perot's habits have changed. He reads more—favorite books include *The Travels of Marco Polo* and *Survive the Savage Sea*—and he has stopped undertaking popular and unlikely causes. He rarely grants interviews.

"I can understand," he says, "why persons who do not fully understand what our objectives and plans were in the prisoners-of-war and Wall Street efforts might label me as a Don Quixote, because of the size, complexity, and risks of failure involved in both undertakings. Both tasks needed to be done. We were in a unique position to take these risks. Not many people were. We succeeded in one, and failed in the other."

What is surely one of the most difficult burdens to bear has been the subdued chortling among Texas's wealthy Democrats. Perot has finally taken on the inscrutable glaze of the mandarins of Dallas and Houston, acquired in a circuitous and particularly painful manner. Shortly before the Federal Campaign Act amendments took effect in 1974, Perot gave $88,400 in campaign contributions. Fifty-five thousand dollars went to members of Congress who oversee Medicaid and Medicare, and nearly all of the money was given just after final campaign disclosure reports were filed in the fall, so they did not appear as part of the public record. Eighteen senators and representatives actually received contributions after they had been re-elected.

In the summer of 1975, Perot was sued for $90 million on fraud charges arising out of the merger of du Pont, Glore, Forgan, and Walston & Company. The suit was filed in Manhattan Federal Court by the court-appointed trustee for the bankrupt du Pont Walston against Perot and many of his associates, and the charges also included allegations of deception, concealment, and false pretenses.

Perot is reticent about this, as about most things. Asked what frightens him, he says only, "The possibility that someone might ask me to invest in a brokerage company again."

Interlude

THE STRANGER

"My only regret is that Dean isn't here now, so I could tell him what a good job I did killing him."

He sits cross-legged on a folding chair in the hospital ward of the Harris County jailhouse, laughing and brandishing a Marlboro. White fatigues hang open at the neck, revealing a sunken chest and the colorless flesh of the restricted prisoner. Rubber thong sandals dangle from grubby toes; gone are the wispy beard and shoulder-length hair of those blurred news photos, replaced by dark, oily curls pressed against his head. Bluish acne scars cover his cheeks and the back of his neck; beneath curving brows lies the intimation of his reputed IQ of 126. The eyes dominate a face most notable for its nastiness, speckled green and too large, conveying an extraordinary distance that continues to impress long after the gaze wanders, the ready smile fades.

"It was," says Elmer Wayne Henley, snapping his fingers, "such cool. Dean had been training me to react, to react fast and to react greatly. That's exactly what I did. There wasn't anything that could have made me more uptight than to have been drunk and stoned and hungover and having withdrawals, and then I just blew his life away. He'd of been proud of the way I did it, if he wasn't proud before he died."

Seated with us in the dentist's office—it affords the only privacy in the ward, where Henley is considered safest from the two dozen people who have vowed to kill him—is one of his defense attorneys, a retired army officer in owlish spectacles. He is obviously pleased with his client's performance. Henley will shortly be sentenced to 594 years by a San Antonio court, but that is a formality. The lawyer and his young partners want to sell Henley's life story for as much money as possible, and they see this exclusive interview as a kind of literary screen test.

"Now, Wayne, tell him how you did it."

There is a coziness here that goes beyond sweating together. Another project entirely brings me to Houston, and yet it seems quite proper while here to be dealing with Henley, a commodity as valuable as a state bank charter or a fast-food franchise. Although I have conducted hundreds of interviews, I am uneasy in the presence of this high-school dropout from Houston Heights. That some things are best left under rocks is not a sentiment appropriate for journalists; yet is there any point in plumbing the random, insane horror known as the "Houston Murders"? Many children buggered, tortured, strangled, and discarded with fiendish intent—a process that took *years*. Was Texas—was the country—honeycombed with the decomposing victims of some hidden force so demonic that it eluded ordinary perception and even memory lay buried?

"I had Dean in a corner, see, and he told me, 'You won't kill me.' I shot him—coolly—until I ran out of bullets. I shot him once in the forehead; my hand went down, and I shot him twice in the shoulder. I stepped aside, he ran through the door, and I shot him once in the back of the shoulder, and twice in the small of the back. To make sure he stayed shot."

"We've got this problem of culpability," the lawyer had said earlier, when the two of us were seated outside in his dusty Cadillac, the windowsills too hot to touch. "From what Wayne says, there may be more bodies out there."

He gestured vaguely in the direction of the Gulf of Mexico, where in August, 1973, police discovered the remains of seventeen teen-age boys beneath the dirt floor of a boat shed, wrapped in plastic shrouds and laced with lime, and subsequently dug up ten more along a lonely stretch of beach.

"Maybe there's not just twenty-seven murders. Maybe there's forty, maybe more. If I were you, I wouldn't want to know."

I don't want to know. I am interested in confronting the decade's surviving monster with some banalities about motive and remorse. I want to know what he reads, how he grew up in Texas. His lawyer signed me into the lockup as a special investigator, with the flourish of a true Lone Star entrepreneur. The junior partner is considering selling information about their case to the newspapers, the senior partner rents Henley's mother a house. They plan to share profits from any book about Henley with the family.

"You're going to like Wayne, he's a real engaging kid," the young partner assured me back in their windowless office.

The prosecution seems determined not to be surpassed in ineptitude. For weeks after Henley called the police and confessed to killing Dean Arnold Corll in self-defense during the final orgy, and led them to various graves, officers appeared in court to embellish their statements. Henley's confession began to resemble a Harris County oral-history project. The district attorney wasn't satisfied, however, and a police sergeant was sent into the jail as an undercover agent, according to other inmates, and Henley's lawyers. He befriended Henley, then wrote out more confessions as a kind of parlor game, and asked Henley to sign them. According to the inmates, this sergeant spent considerable time trying to convince Henley to star in a pornographic movie that would make them both rich. He obtained a Polaroid camera, and took snaps of Henley in his daily prison routine—brushing his teeth, playing checkers—and sent them off to be sold in Los Angeles.

Henley is Houston born and bred, the protestations of his neighbors notwithstanding. Thirty years of continuous boom have lent the city an inescapable hard edge —a kind of concrete surface of the soul that creeps across the low, alluvial plain. Houston shares the littoral taint of some other Southern states, where the heat and the oppressive sameness of the land breeds decline, moral peculiarities, and sudden excesses of the blood.

Houston Heights is a seedy, lower-middle-class enclave with horizons limited to once-fashionable homes divided into low-rent apartments, and guarded by pickups on concrete blocks. White adults drink Pearl beer in Billie's Gold Brick, and more than a few teen-agers risk mind-dissolving highs by "bagging"—spraying acrylic paint into paper sacks, and breathing the fumes. Here Henley and a schoolmate, David Brooks, failed the ninth grade together, "skipping, smoking a little weed, shooting pool."

Brooks introduced Henley to Corll, a heavyset employee of the Houston Power & Lighting Company, who was twice their ages. Corll's apartment provided a place "to waste time." Henley realized that the candy shop operated by Corll's mother—where her son constructed a giant frog with red eyes that lit up when the telephone rang, for the amusement of children—was a store he had visited earlier.

"I admired Dean because he had a steady job. In the beginning he seemed quiet and in the background, and that made me curious. I wanted to find out what his deal was. The fact that he did work, wasn't a wild drunk, got along with kids and people in general—that's what started it."

Much of that first year was spent driving aimlessly about the Heights in Corll's car, drinking beer and smoking marijuana and planning petty theft. Henley suspected that Corll was homosexual—"I just figured David was hustling himself a queer"—a fact that had remarkably little influence upon his opinion of Corll.

"Dean's front was wholesome and masculine. He had a big build, but he was flabby. He never really impressed me as masculine unless he was lifting something. He was a loner in his own right. He could be around people, but still you never knew what Dean Corll was doing. No matter how much you talked to him, you didn't know him."

So Corll not only provided an address—a curious sense of belonging to his fictitious "crime ring"—he was also an inspiration, an intimation that life held some mystery beyond the Heights. His homosexuality played second fiddle to this aura of experience and latent power, as viewed in the boys' narrow perspective. Brooks became emotionally dependent upon Corll, and played a passive role in later, demented exaltation, for which he would be sentenced to only 99 years. But Henley wanted money. His other needs would prove too complicated for ordinary sexuality, hetero or otherwise, and would match those of his mentor, but with a deadlier lack of passion.

"Sex didn't become a factor until later. There were rumors going around school about Dean, but he was never overt. Besides, I liked him personally. By the time he finally made an advance, I was an accomplice."

Fellatio was just another antidote to boredom, no more disagreeable than bagging. Dean was a "personal" friend, as well as a source of income. When he instructed Henley and Brooks to bring him boys, instead of stolen television sets, to be sold to a fictitious white-slave market in Dallas for $200 apiece, they complied. Delivering up friends was easier, less risky, more prestigious.

Henley's view of himself at that time is instructive.

"I was known as a playboy, a party person. I got along with everybody. And people knew that if you ran around with me, you ran around with broads."

An ideal procurer.

"At first I didn't sense that Dean might be a murderer, but later I did sense it. He brought out a little blade, you know—and it wasn't a little knife, either. It was a great big knife. He was still talking about organized theft, and wanting to know in case was I cornered, was I willing to off the guy. Of course I said yes—ego would dictate that.

"I stayed around because there was no reason for me to leave. I didn't have to do nothing but steal. Before kids started coming around, we got money from Dean for thieving, for setting up places to rob. I didn't think there was anything to it, but at least I did get money for it. That's what kept me around before he started talking about killing people. Later, he got down to the fact that we was going to be killing people.

"At first I wondered what it was like to kill someone. Later, I became fascinated with how much stamina people have. I mean, you see people getting strangled on television and it looks easy. It's not. Sometimes it takes two people half an hour."

Henley's earliest memory is of near-suffocation. Acute asthma attacks were overcome with the aid of his grandparents, who tended Henley while his mother was occupied with younger children and an unpredictable husband. Henley remembers sitting on his grandparents' bed in the morning, while they drank coffee and read the

Houston *Post*—his fondest recollection, set close to that
of survival.

"They had a little dinner tray they put on the edge
of the bed to hold the cups. I liked being there. I owe
my life to them."

He describes his grandfather—a hard-working baker
who died when Henley was only seven—with a term
that for him is close to adulation. "He loved his children
and his grandchildren, he was *sharp*."

Not so Henley's father.

"We didn't get along. Dad was always beating up on
my little brothers. He overreacted, out of meanness. He
beat up my mother, he beat up my mother and my grandmother once, at the same time. Maybe that's what
started it, the divorce and all. I frapped him over the
head with the vacuum cleaner, and called the police."

Wayne Henley's father also beat him, once fired a
pistol at him. The son attempted to assume the role of
surrogate provider, worked at odd jobs and gave some
money to his mother, took a proprietary view of his old
man.

"Dad just wasn't straightening out. He was getting
drunk too much, getting too rowdy. I thought divorce
was a good idea, and I told him so. I hated to lose my
father, but since then we've just had a little friction.
He and I can get along for a little while, when he's half
sober and I'm half sober."

Henley's mother told police that Dean Corll was "like
a father to Wayne." Corll was himself the product of
quarreling parents, who divorced when he was young,
remarried, divorced again; his mother traveled around
the South in a trailer, started a candy business with the
help of a dutiful son. Corll was an average, submissive
student who played the trombone in the Vidor school
band, on the outskirts of Beaumont.

His mother married a salesman, divorced him, later

married a merchant seaman and divorced again. Corll stayed with her through it all, obtaining a hardship discharge from the Army to return to the family candy business, this time in Houston. There he gave free candy to young boys, and entertained them in a back room outfitted with a pool table and the big green frog whose eyes lit up when the phone rang. His mother moved to Colorado, but this time Corll didn't go with her.

If there is a common theme, it's the old saw: rootlessness. David Brooks's parents were also divorced, so were the parents of most of the victims. The Houston police claimed they were runaways, in an attempt to cover up what must be one of the grossest displays of inadequacy of any police department. If a child in opulent River Oaks had disappeared, the force would have mobilized, but those reported missing in the Heights were considered simply trash, and expected to drift.

The truth is that some of the victims were traveling no further than the corner store (one on his bicycle), that for three years Houston authorities did nothing but add names to a list on a clipboard. No one seemed impressed by the fact that the unusually large number of "runaways" in the Heights involved teen-age boys who attended the same schools. No one had the energy to discover what was common knowledge among students: that any kid who wanted could turn on and pick up a few bucks by allowing a certain fat electrician to go down on him—and that some who had done so were no longer around.

Hunter and prey were products of divided families that owed more allegiance to the hard-scrabble farms of the past than to the pavement of the present. Their parents seemed unwilling or incapable of providing direction. Murderers and murdered all drifted in a common miasma of thwarted desires, vague longings, sordid gratification—a quest of sorts. "Dean searched for a climax he never found," says Henley. He was not the only searcher—just the most cunning and desperate, and quite mad.

Four days before his death, Dean telephoned his mother in Colorado and told her he was in trouble, feared he was losing his mind, and might commit suicide. She sent him a box of candy, and an inspirational book entitled *This Thing Called You*. She inscribed it: "From your 54-year-old mother who has just begun to live. Read this book and help me make up for the things I was too ignorant to teach you when I was in my twenties."

Henley represents a larger problem because he is demonstrably sane. Corll provided him inspiration, and a program, but at some point the apprentice seems to have surpassed the master. "Wayne seemed to enjoy causing pain," Brooks told police, a fact Henley readily admits.

"You either enjoy what you do—which I did—or you go crazy. So when I did something, I enjoyed it, and didn't dwell on it later."

It is not incidental that one of Henley's favorite books is Robert Heinlein's *Stranger in a Strange Land*. He likes Arthur C. Clarke, Isaac Asimov, Harold Robbins, but his appreciation of Ayn Rand reveals that Texas individuality resides in unlikely places: "I like *The Fountainhead* because the hero is a loner who does what everybody said he couldn't do. In *Atlas Shrugged*, I liked the little utopia of the working people. They made their billions, but they weren't going to be controlled by the government."

Henley is the compleat American punk, the kid your mother warned you against becoming if you let smoking stunt your growth. He is also a perverted product of some of those frontier values, degraded in social transition, and emerging in the crime of the decade that seems too utterly contemporary to warrant further examination. Henley may represent the bottom of the barrel in

Texas, but there is a disturbing resonance to his words.

"I feel remorse because I'm supposed to," he says, and he is laughing. "That's something I've tried to build in me. I don't really feel about it, you know. I wished I hadn't done it. I'm glad I got it over with, telling. I'm glad now I'm not hiding it, waiting, and Dean ain't out there killing little kids. But as far as any emotion to it, there's no heartfelt emotion."

Visiting time has expired. Henley exchanges a few words with his attorney, and shuffles off down the hall.

A muscular white guard in tennis shoes leads us to the elevator.

"Good security," the attorney observes.

"Tighter'n a bull's ass in flytime," says the guard. He unlocks the gate.

"Want to buy a jeep?"

The attorney says, "Yeah. What kind?"

They discuss a shipment of Army surplus the guard has mysteriously obtained.

"I'll be gettin' fifty," the guard says. "You watch the papers for the ad."

The old elevator begins to rattle down the shaft.

"He's into everything," says the attorney. "Cars, real estate, you name it. Actually, he's a millionaire."

8 ☆ LAW IN HOUSTON

The New Paladins

Connally's corner office on the twenty-first floor of the First City National Bank offers a privileged view of America's fastest-growing big city. Order is apparent in the furnishings—matching antique desk and cabinet brought back from England, a pair of oils by Melvin Warren, a dollar bill with Connally's face substituted for George Washington's carefully displayed on a side table, an arrangement of books on Texas history, a copy of *Foreign Affairs*.

Connally reclines in a leather-covered swivel chair, looking out over the deep green coastal plain and the monoliths of concrete and glass. He is in his shirt sleeves, blue cuffs secured by silver links. A pair of half-moon spectacles with rims of brushed silver rest near the tip of his nose. Before him on the desk is a stack of papers he says represents a day's work for Vinson, Elkins, Searls, Connally & Smith. The telephone rings for the third time in five minutes, but he ignores it, for he has been asked which Americans he most admires.

"Richard Nixon," he begins, "for his scholarly discipline. Johnson for his compassion, and ability to get things done. Kennedy for his flair, and ability to inspire. Eisenhower and Truman for their ability to inspire confidence during hard times. Billy Graham for his great sincerity, and his ability to draw untold millions to religious fervor. Einstein and Edison," he adds, as an afterthought, "for their great dedication. But I wouldn't want to emulate them—they missed too much in life."

I then ask him to describe himself.

"I'm ambitious. Not toward any particular goal, mind you, but toward solving problems. I'm a kind, compassionate person. At times I'm impatient, restless. I'm hard-working, tolerant above all else. An understanding person."

He pauses, and swivels round to squint at me.

"These all sound like admirable traits. I'll have to give you the other side. I'm suspicious of people who try to take advantage of me. But I respond to people. I *love* people. I'm self-confident, but my restrained egotism doesn't make my judgment bad."

He pauses again; this time his eyes almost disappear.

"Well," he says finally, "I've got a temper."

He is the best interface between big government and private interests, the type of attorney described by Joseph Goulden in *The Superlawyers* who "accepts government as an existential fact and tries to direct what it does to the benefit of his corporate clients." Until the advent of Leon Jaworski as Watergate special prosecutor, Connally was the most visible member of Houston's shadow government, made up of members of the big law firms whose influence extends far beyond state boundaries.

The growth rate of these firms has been phenomenal. Vinson, Elkins, Searls, Connally & Smith barely leads its two closest competitors, Fulbright, Crooker & Jaworski and Baker & Botts, with a force of more than two hundred lawyers. A substantial proportion of these were hired shortly after Connally joined the firm in 1968, fresh from the Governor's Mansion. He is said to have brought with him accounts that included the Halliburton Company, Occidental Petroleum, Pan Am, Avis, and to have added the governments of Algeria, Puerto Rico, and Indonesia.

The advantages of Connally's close contacts in Washington to these and other clients is obvious. His firm also represents such varied interests as Shell Oil, La Gloria Oil, Gulf Resources, Brown & Root, Texas Eastern Transmission, Texas Instruments, Mitchell Energy & Development, American General Insurance, Southwestern Bell, Quintana Petroleum, the Cullen Center Bank & Trust, and Hamburgers by Gourmet.

Until recently the pervasive power of the Houston firms has effectively remained hidden, reflecting the concerns of their founders. None is more famous than the late James Elkins, the county judge who came to Houston in 1917, founded the City National Bank, and linked its rise to that of his adopted law firm, Vinson & Townes. Judge Elkins had the foresight to concentrate on the most promising industries—oil and gas, and insurance.

He was an indomitable personality, whether as a member of the 8-F Crowd, or as a senior law partner. Winning was the objective of business, politics, and play. At the race track with Herman Brown or Gus Wortham, Judge Elkins might bet a hundred dollars on a favorite, but he would also bet minimum money on each horse in the race, so that he might always be able to hold up a winner's stub. In 1958, he called a man to his office who had unexpectedly been elected to a judgeship the day before, and handed him an envelope containing a sizable campaign contribution. When the man pointed out that he had already been elected, Elkins told him, "You've been busy, and I've been busy. Take it now, and I wish you luck." During his stewardship, all lawyers in his firm wore hats, and worked on Saturdays. He lived to be ninety-three.

One reason for the success of the big law firms has been their intimate association with the prominent banks of Houston. "Any corporation needing money automatically gets sucked up into one of the big firms," says a lawyer with his own small firm, who has seen some of his more successful clients do just that. Many of the big banks are controlled by the same men who run the big law firms. "The banks are a huge source of business for the firms, and it has multiplied over the years. As soon as a growing business applies for a loan, they're hooked."

Both the law and banking have changed since Judge Elkins's early days. "The bank is a completely different animal," says his son James Elkins, Jr., a dapper man in his fifties who wears a computer wristwatch, and uses his cigarette holder with an unabashed flourish, a gesture not expected from the president of First City National. "We don't just take deposits and lend money now. We perform financial services, we're a holding company. . . . Vinson, Elkins is just our general counsel. The senior partners own bank stock, but it's purely a client relationship with historical roots."

The other law firms have similar roots. They are less competitive than they might seem. "What is good business for one is good business for another," according to a senior partner of Baker & Botts. One area of competition is recruitment, however, and David Searls brought to Vinson, Elkins some of the best legal talent in Texas. Lawyers and their wives began to woo graduates from UT Law School with all the ardor of a fraternity rush.

Aside from the intimate associations between senior partners and members of state and national government, the big firms offer other advantages to clients. They can lend instant good repute to a new business; the firms' names alone lend confidence. The legal services offered are thorough, and of excellent quality. They include tax, anti-trust, patent, and securities. (Divorce, personal injury, and criminal defense work are all considered tawdry, and except in special instances are not available.) Manpower is never a problem.

Most of the rivalry between the large firms is a matter of style. A partner of one firm, for instance, serves as president of the Houston Bar Association during the odd-numbered years, and a partner in one of the city's lesser firms will serve as president during the even-numbered years. Although the office is only symbolic, the honor is jealously guarded.

Prestige naturally accrues to members of the big firms. Quitting after one has been accepted is considered unwise from a financial point of view, as well as vaguely disreputable, for one has been trusted with the inner workings. More than half the members are only associates, who sometimes work as much as seventy hours a week, waiting for that time when they will make partner. At Vinson, Elkins, a sheet listing the billings of each lawyer is circulated every month, so the partners may check the ratings of the apprentices.

There is no disagreement about the object of the law: it is to produce revenue for the firms. The common bond among them is that they mediate the economic life of the state. *Pro bono* work is discouraged on the grounds that lawyers shouldn't go around stirring up litigation that could possibly prove detrimental to their bigger clients. Many of the huge corporations have problems with environmental standards that have to be met by manufacturers, and it would not do to have lawyers from the same firm representing both sides. Senior partners also do not want any plaintiffs' rulings used as a precedent in other cases against their other big clients.

"Conflict of interest," wrote Griffin Smith, Jr., in the
Texas Monthly, "is a convenient excuse for refraining
from doing anything that would impair the interests of
corporate defendants *as a class,* regardless of whether
there is an ethical conflict in a particular case."

Partners almost never actually run for public office.
Participation in government is frowned upon, except in
such an exceptional case as Connally's, where a partner's
star quality reflects upon the firm itself, and his association with government can provide invaluable advantages.

The firms' power is derivative. They have access to
the money, and to the people who head the empires in
oil, insurance, real estate, utilities, contracting, ship-
ping, and petrochemicals. Any political candidate who
wants to be introduced to a potential wealthy contributor, or to a man of obvious influence, can approach one
of the big law firms and, if approved, receive his introduction. And most elected officials—particularly judges
—will feel great pressure from the firms in subsequent
elections.

Since James Allred, no Texas governor who was unacceptable to the firms has been elected—a period of some
forty years. The offices of Attorney General, State Treasurer, the Texas Supreme Court, the Railroad Commission—all are of great importance to Houston's banker-
lawyers. Judgeships are elected, but vacancies occurring
by death or resignation are filled by appointment by the
governor. If the governor wishes to repay a large contributor by allowing him to suggest the appointee, one
of the big firms gladly acts as the intermediary. If the
contributor also happens to avoid trouble in the courts
because of the firm, then the firm's influence is even
greater. And the fact that the firms outlive all candidates and issues—and have long, sometimes vindictive
memories—is not lost on the best politicians.

The big firms produce lawyers who are specialists in their fields, obsessed with their own careers. Usually they have little time for or interest in the state of the law in Texas or in America, or in the society in which they live. Economic productivity has become an end in itself.

"Lawyers used to serve as chairmen of the symphony," laments an attorney in a big firm who has managed to carve out a redoubt in an essentially alien environment. "They belonged to the school board, the Democratic organization. They were tied to the affairs of the city. Now they're just tradesmen. Lawyers have become the servants of the propertied class, as well as members of it. Instead of lawyers being the best-read and wisest people in the community, they have become technocrats."

Hard work and absolute conformity are requisite at the big firms, where dress and even office décor are as carefully regulated as is access to clients. Control extends to private life, where an associate's home is considerably less than his castle. A reporter doing research into the lives led by lawyers' wives interviewed the wife of a lawyer at Vinson, Elkins, and was taping the interview when her husband called from the office. He became angry when he heard of the interview, and demanded a transcript of it and the right to delete quotes of which he disapproved, although the reporter had agreed that his wife's name and that of the firm would not be mentioned. A few minutes later the husband called back and told his wife that he had spoken to a senior partner, and that she had been *ordered* by the senior partner to stop the interview. The wife complied.

Such dedication is not limited to the big law firms; it is the prescription for success in Houston. A young lawyer who manages investments for a rich, older entrepreneur describes with some trepidation the world he has chosen, after first insisting upon anonymity with a concern that is unsettling. "I went to school up East, but I came back because Houston offered the opportunities I wanted. I saw those graduates of Harvard and Yale, and I knew I was better than they were. But I didn't want to spend years sitting in an Eastern law office behind some rich boy. Houston is still young, you can make yourself what you want. Business is definitely part of your definition. Performance is very important. You can't bullshit your way through, but if you're good, you can reach the very highest levels of finance and power."

His working day often begins at the office at seven in the morning. He goes to lunch at 11:45, and is back by 1 P.M. Some days he eats no lunch. Wherever he is, whatever he does, he is always mindful of his reputation, of what effect his actions—and those of his associates—will have upon the opinions of other, wealthier, more influential men. "If you come to town and make millions —enough millions—you might get into the River Oaks Country Club. But if you make less than millions, if you're poor but intelligent, and civic-minded, and if you work hard and do well over the years, you might get into the Houston Country Club. You see, River Oaks is big money, but the Houston Country Club is the place. . . . There's one thing you never forget: you can make no mistakes."

Lawyers at Vinson, Elkins, Searls, Connally & Smith are fearful of publicity. They fit, roughly, into two categories: those who do the work, and those who bring in clients. Connally is the epitome of the second category. His influence was not limited to the substantial clients he brought to the firm in 1968, for a year later, in his Houston corner office, he could still telephone his appointees on the Parks and Wildlife Commission and obtain rulings favorable to land development projects.

Connally was a welcome addition to the firm, even though he bounded directly to the top, attaining just the sort of position he had envisioned when he first decided to run for governor. He fitted easily into Vinson, Elkins's authoritative routine, and quickly won over the skeptical members of the firm. Managing partner A. Frank Smith, white-haired and uncompromising ("I will not talk about clients in any way"), describes Connally as a "topflight" attorney, at the same time cautioning, "John's politics are not necessarily the firm's politics."

A younger member of the firm who has worked with Connally says, "He's the best I've seen in terms of assimilating facts, and then advancing a position. Any position." But an oil-company lobbyist and lawyer, who has known Connally for years, says, "John couldn't write an oil and gas lease if he had to."

Connally is known as the resident "internationalist" at Vinson, Elkins. He was the primary force behind the firm's bid for an international clientele, and the decision to open an office in London. At meetings of all the firm's lawyers, Connally often stands up and delivers a speech about "economic diplomacy" and other matters relating to financial opportunities beyond the borders of Texas, and America.

The extended influence of the big Houston firms is greatly attributable to that Texas amenity, the jet airplane. The accessibility of Washington and New York has provided an entirely new market since the late '50s, when the trip from Texas took three days on the train— or, at best, flying in a relatively slow and uncomfortable DC-6. Now the lawyers needed to appeal to various regulatory boards, or to help in the seeking of subsidies, can leave Houston in the morning, be in Washington for a noon conference, and be home by dark. The Houston firms are active competitors of their Eastern counterparts that once dominated New York and Washington.

Connally has little to do with the dynamics of Vinson, Elkins. The firm is not as monolithic as it was during the old days; the dual structure is organized around clients, and departments, the principal of these being insurance, tax, corporate (securities), municipal (bonds), and general litigation, which is the most esteemed. The lawyers who concentrate on clients simply make deals— real estate, buying and selling securities, any of a hundred entrepreneurial transactions.

The lines are not definitely drawn; Connally's duties are quite vague. He is used most effectively before government commissions, and as either a presence or a principal in the making of the biggest of deals. The publicity he has generated is beneficial for the firm— the protestations of some of the partners notwithstanding—and has been a substantial factor in its extraordinary growth.

His own financial dealings are varied; they usually involve a large investment on the advice of a friend, made with borrowed money, and a quick turnover. After leaving Treasury, he was, among other things, a director of the First City National Bank, Gibraltar Savings of Houston, Pan Am, Texas Instruments, Halliburton Company, and Falconbridge Nickel Mines of Toronto. His investments include real estate, insurance, banking, cattle, and have been as dissimilar as a Sunday-supplement magazine and a drive-through zoo.

Connally's trip around the world at the end of his short stay at Treasury greatly enhanced his stature as a lawyer and mediator in the private sector. He visited every major oil-producing nation, and enjoyed an unscheduled visit with the Shah of Iran; what Connally and the Shah discussed was never reported. These contacts would attract many new clients to Vinson, Elkins in an age of burgeoning power among the oil-producing nations, who had a great deal of money to invest and valuable concessions to grant.

One such client was Armand Hammer, president of Occidental Petroleum, the sort of person who would value the unique qualifications of Connally and his firm. Hammer was already a legend among American entrepreneurs, the son of a Russian Jew who emigrated to America. Hammer was a physician who had never practiced, a personal friend of Lenin's who brought medical supplies and then wheat to the famished Russia of the early 1920s. Hammer became the first foreign concessionaire with the Bolsheviks, and went on to establish his own business domain within the bureaucracies of successive Soviet regimes, representing various American companies and dealing in commodities ranging from bourbon to Impressionist art to oil-well machinery.

Hammer became a symbol of Lenin's proclaimed objective: the achieving of Russian revolutionary "success" by employing the best American business methods. It was fitting that the two lawyers in Hammer's employ most highly valued by him were Sargent Shriver and John Connally, contemporary men whose avocational politics were opposed but whose vocations in business found a common objective.

A proposal to import Siberian gas to the United States involved Hammer and some other corporations with which Connally and his firm were intimately connected. Negotiations took years, involved great expense and tedium, and promised millions of dollars in profits. It was determined that two billion cubic feet of natural gas was available, to be transported by pipeline to the sea, and carried to this country in specially constructed tankers costing $100 million apiece. The construction work was to be done by Brown & Root, specialists in shipbuilding. The pipelines would be laid by Texas Eastern Transmission. (Newport News Shipbuilding & Drydock Company, a subsidiary of Tenneco, was also involved, along with Occidental.)

"It's a three-legged stool," said Connally, "involving supply, transportation, and marketing. The Russians have the first leg, but we have the other two."

There were difficulties to be overcome from the beginning. The Federal Power Commission had to be impressed with the fact that natural-gas prices should rise, one of the oldest objectives of America's oil lobby, and one that finally seems imminent. The federal government had to provide unprecedented amounts of hard-currency credits, and subsidize the shipbuilding—another instance of public money making the difference between a reasonable profit and a bonanza. And a liberalized trade bill was needed, one without restrictions, so that Export-Import Bank credits could be obtained.

It was a deal worthy of the principals. Connally's unofficial role in the billion-dollar transaction was dual. He was to hold the companies involved together, to keep them from bidding up the price of the gas, and he was to run interference through the Nixon administration. That depended solely upon the availability of money for contributions, and there was a sufficiency. The Republican financial statement made public in the fall of 1973 revealed that executives of Texas Eastern gave $30,000 to Nixon's re-election committee just before the campaign finance law went into effect, and Texas Eastern employees generously donated another $30,000. Hammer contributed $46,000, and James Elkins, Jr., gave $15,000, which may have been connected to the fact that First City National Bank planned to provide some private financing for the Siberian gas deal. In spite of these and other embarrassments, that deal is at this writing still alive in Washington and in Houston.

Hammer and his executive vice-president, another Texan and aide to Lyndon Johnson, Marvin Watson, saw Connally as the ideal advocate for Occidental in Saudi Arabia. Connally's intimacy with Nixon seemed to be the necessary currency for obtaining Saudi oil concessions, thus threatening the incumbent cartel. Connally and Hammer traveled to Saudi Arabia together, and met with Faisal at the time when crude-oil production was expected to increase dramatically. Connally's ambivalent role, played out in the nether world between supposed high-level diplomacy and private trading, was never explained. Significantly, his advocacy was denied by both the Nixon administration and Occidental officials, at a time when Vinson, Elkins, Searls, Connally & Smith counted among its clients the Permian Corporation, a subsidiary of Occidental, and El Paso Natural Gas Company, Occidental's partner in the seeking of Soviet oil concessions. The fact that Occidental failed to obtain the Saudi concessions did not prevent a considerable fee from being paid into Connally's firm.

The end justifies the means. Government exists to enhance private enterprise, which provides jobs, which, in turn, provide votes for the candidates dedicated to keeping the ball rolling. The corporation must endure, according to the new technocrats, by whatever means, and at the expense of ideological niceties. In advocating the $250 million loan guarantee to Lockheed, Connally reportedly said, "What do we care if they perform?" There was no longer a question of priorities.

A simple appearance in the interests of a client was often all that was asked of Connally. Testimony before a federal regulatory agency, or a chat with businessmen, government representatives, or even state legislators often provided the necessary grease for the deal to roll.

As the representative of Vinson, Elkins, Connally became involved in an attempt by Iowa Beef Processers to merge with Missouri Beef Packers in 1973. The merger would have boosted Iowa Beef's annual business to $1.5 billion, making it the General Motors of the meat industry. The firm had no need of Connally to work out the finer details in this proceeding. He was hired because of his contacts in government, particularly in the Justice Department. An anti-trust suit had already been brought against Iowa Beef for acquiring a smaller packer (which it eventually, in 1975, agreed to divest itself of), and Iowa Beef decided a reversal of "political attitudes" was necessary.

After Vinson, Elkins had been retained, Iowa Beef was able to issue an addendum to its annual report announcing that the company had obtained a pricing exemption under Phase Three of Nixon's price controls that it did not enjoy under Phase Two. Iowa Beef was no longer required to obtain advance approval of increased prices from the Price Commission, which granted the company a so-called "volatile" pricing exemption.

The merger, if it had been allowed, would have relocated the beef-processing industry of America in the Texas Panhandle, rather than keeping it in the Midwest. The fact that several officials of Iowa Beef were indicted in New York for alleged price-fixing delayed the crucial decisions in Washington, and the company claimed the merger was not at the proper stage for consummation. "Too many concrete steps have been taken to make that claim very credible," said an attorney representing one of the smaller packers bringing suit against Iowa Beef. "And whoever was betting half a million dollars on the merger . . . on the American Stock Exchange must have had some grounds that far back for plunging so heavily. More likely . . . Iowa is waiting for Connally to spring the necessary approval in Justice."

So interested in the merger was Connally that he interrupted a trip overseas to fly back for consultation at Iowa Beef's offices in Dakota City, Nebraska. Later, however, the firm withdrew the merger proposal.

"I'm not a wheeler-dealer," says Connally. "I don't know any wheeler-dealers. What the hell is a wheeler-dealer?"

☆ ☆ ☆

Connally's embracing of Nixon after the facts of Watergate became known was a calculated risk that the President would pull through, and Connally would be the direct beneficiary in 1976. Some of the advice he offered Nixon struck at the base of constitutional democracy, as did his statement that a President in some circumstances would be right to disobey an order of the Supreme Court. "Suppose somebody sued against waging war," he told me, "and the Supreme Court said the President should pull out the planes. That would be interfering with the conduct of the country."

His recommendation of Leon Jaworski as Watergate special prosecutor was a public-relations gesture after it became apparent that Nixon was doomed and this was his only possible extrication from an unhappy association. Jaworski was a known quantity. He and Connally were political associates; they were Texans, and senior partners in two big Houston law firms. Connally had appointed Jaworski as chairman of his Governor's Committee on Public Education after Jaworski helped Connally get elected. Connally hoped that after Nixon's fall he could point to his recommendation of Jaworski, claiming he helped pull the country out of the Watergate mess after realizing too late that the President was in fact guilty.

Connally's own indictment changed all that. He was charged with two counts of accepting a bribe, one count of conspiracy to commit perjury and obstruct justice, and two counts of making a false declaration before a grand jury in the case involving campaign contributions by milk producers and his old friend Jake Jacobsen. Such indictments would seem not only to have wrecked what political career he had left, but to have rendered him unwelcome in the new administration.

Yet as late as February, 1975, Connally was still a member with security clearance of the President's Foreign Intelligence Advisory Board, appointed by Nixon. The board is charged with advising "the President concerning the objectives, conduct, management and coordination of the various activities making up the overall national intelligence effort," and with conducting "a review and assessment of foreign intelligence and related activities in which the Central Intelligence Agency and other government departments and agencies are engaged." President Ford finally announced Connally's resignation from the board, after his continuing membership became publicized.

But Connally's contacts in Washington apparently remain unimpaired. Within weeks of the resignation announcement, Ford flew to Houston to address a group of prominent businessmen concerning his proposed tariff on oil, and afterward met alone with Connally for forty-five minutes. A White House aide later said that the President had not planned to meet with him, but "Connally just hung around, and the rest left." The aide added that the President and Connally had not discussed his indictment, but had talked of economic and energy matters.

Among those things discussed were almost certainly Siberian gas, and the deregulation of the price of natural gas in America, a cause Connally seems about to win. In a country where the mere handshake of a President can easily be translated into hard currency, the value to a man such as Connally of forty-five minutes spent alone with a new President simply cannot be calculated.

"That's what life is all about," says Connally, "taking advantage of what you do best, what you know. . . . When you get up there in government and start viewing these problems in the broad perspective—why, you don't give any thought to the economic advantages. You call 'em like you see 'em. Later, what are you supposed to do? Go off and hide?"

He is standing now, one hand extended in a forceful

gesture reminiscent of those old photographs of productions by the Curtain Club. The eyebrow is arched, the tone pleasantly dismissive. There is too much to be done, too many people to see, too much money to be made, too many things to acquire.

"You can't deny your own knowledge and experience," he adds, "however it's acquired. It would be a sad day for this country if you ever had to deny it. It's not a question of money, really. It's a question of *creativity*."

Interlude

THE EYE OF TEXAS

The persistence of doctrinaire liberalism in Texas is more a literary than a political phenomenon. Its vehicle for two decades has been the *Texas Observer,* the biweekly champion of the neglected and voiceless in the state, the bur under the establishment's saddle, the scourge of the lobbyists, and the victim of the continuous defeat of its endorsed candidates. The *Observer* often offers readers the only critical reporting in the state on political and economic issues. Its contributors display a brand of Lone Star Existentialism, whereby the literate fling themselves unremittingly and with little effect against the jeweled hide of the leviathan right and other apparent evils.

"We will serve no group or party," reads the paper's credo, boldly printed above the masthead, "but we will hew hard to the truth as we find it and the right as we see it. We are dedicated to the whole truth, to human values above all interests, to the rights of humankind as the foundation of democracy; we will take orders from none but our own conscience, and never will we overlook or misrepresent the truth to serve the interests of the powerful or cater to the ignoble in the human spirit."

Such exuberance still belongs to the '50s, the golden
years of the Texas liberals. McCarthyism, Lyndon's
rightward waffling, and Shivers's leadership of the tory
Democrats into Eisenhower's camp provided unequivocal lessons in American political Machiavellianism; it
was so obvious which way justice lay. The Shivers-Ralph
Yarborough contest for governor in 1952 was seen by
the liberals as an elemental struggle between evil and
good. The backbone of Shivers's campaign was a film
entitled *The Port Arthur Story,* supposedly revealing
the terrible effects of organized labor upon that city. A
public-relations team ahead of its time arranged for the
streets of Port Arthur to be filmed at dawn so they would
appear appropriately empty of people, and the striking
retail clerks—and Yarborough—could be blamed.

Yarborough was narrowly defeated, largely because
he could not get adequate coverage in the press. The
liberals stayed in high gear after the election, and the
Observer became the creature of that outrage and that
energy.

The idea of a liberal journal was originally put forward by a collection of more than a hundred Democrats,
most left over from the New Deal. They included Bob
Eckhardt, and Mrs. R. D. "Frankie" Randolph, heiress
to vast holdings in cotton and lumber country in the
eastern part of the state, and an effective liberal organizer. Frankie Randolph eventually underwrote the
Observer's early losses, and was part of the flexing of
liberal muscle in 1956, when she was elected national
Democratic committeewoman from Texas. That year
Connally, acting as Johnson's political extension, had
barely captured the convention for Johnson from the
Shivercrats. B. A. Bentsen, Lloyd's wife, was their
choice for committeewoman, and Connally arrogantly
assumed he had the necessary votes. He did not have the
votes, and he never forgave Frankie Randolph for her

victory. Johnson was placated after he saw to it that the Harris County liberals were refused entry to the second state convention, but Connally nurtured his grudge for years, and finally persuaded Johnson not to attend a conciliatory dinner given by Frankie Randolph.

Ronnie Dugger, the man chosen to serve as editor of the *Observer*, was a student of UT's graduate school of economics, and former editor of the *Daily Texan*. He was a native of Chicago, but he grew up in San Antonio, taking an early interest in government and its excesses.

"I began to cover the legislature while I was in college," he says. He is a chunky, intense figure in black-rimmed spectacles who has carried into early middle age an air of quizzical, boyish indignation. "People started telling me about bribes. Bribes here, bribes there. . . . A House public health committee member told me everybody on the committee was bought, with the exception of half a member. I decided to look deeper."

Dugger agreed to take on the editorship, after first stipulating that the *Observer* would have to be independent. It was a promising time in Texas. The liberals were influential enough to tempt LBJ to co-opt them; there seemed to be a real chance that Texas would become a two-party state—an event predicted too often in the *Observer*'s pages—with the tories driven into the Republican ranks by the determined and articulate loyalist brigade. Dugger wrote about the workings of the state legislature and the racial and cultural extremities of the state according to the ordinary precepts of journalism, which in Texas were considered radical.

"The paper was first denounced as propagandist. We were called left-wing nuts when we were just liberal Democrats on the national scale. We were really quite mild, but we were considered extremist. People like Connally read the *Observer* as political pornography."

Dugger was an unusual blend of political zealot and scrupulous observer; he remained fair, and untempted by the blandishments of the powerful. No less a person-age than Lyndon Johnson, who read the *Observer* care-fully, and took its criticism to heart, subjected Dugger to a personal audience, and sonorous snow job, only to see the meeting written up in the pages of that little liberal weekly. Johnson interpreted Dugger's imperti-nence as a failure of imagination. "You check that boy's family line," he complained, "and you'll find a dwarf in there somewhere."

Willie Morris, who later served as editor of the *Ob-server* when Dugger took a rest, wrote fondly of the experience in *North Toward Home*. While he was still editor, according to Morris, Dugger would leave Austin after the paper was put to bed, and "take out for some-where in a woebegone 1948 Chevrolet, crowded with camping equipment, six-packs, notebooks, galley proofs, old loaves of bread, and sardine cans. Whenever the Chevrolet broke down, which was often, he would have it hauled to the nearest town and stay there, talking with the people in the town and taking notes on what was going on there."

Dugger's *Observer* attracted many young writers, and provided an apprenticeship for some who went on to success, and larger audiences. These included Morris, who became *Harper's* youngest editor, investigative re-porter Robert Sherrill, Bill Brammer, Larry King, Larry Goodwyn, and others. The experience marked many of them: there was so much to write about, the issues were so unambiguous. Never again would the act of reporting seem so inherently heroic. If such rectitude would later produce a tendency toward self-celebration, at the time it produced some of the best local reporting in the coun-try. The *Observer* gained the reputation of crusader, the importance of its contributors enhanced, ironically, by Johnson's growing influence.

"The worst blow to the liberals in Texas," says Dugger, "was Kennedy's naming Johnson to be Vice-President.

It was very discouraging. From discouragement you can proceed to despair, or you can continue. We appeared to lose so frequently, but we cut new ground. By God, we were changing the context of elections. . . . Now the establishment is just a term of convenience. The whole United States is a corporate system interconnected through the law firms. I stopped thinking about Texas as a state years ago. It's all the same now."

The *Observer* became a springboard for some to more important and more lucrative positions outside Texas. But a bond remained among the early contributors; the writing of the definitive biography of Lyndon Johnson at times seemed part of the credentials. Only Dugger remained behind, spelled occasionally as editor, but always the moral force behind the *Observer*.

Working for the *Observer* in the '50s and early '60s represented, according to Goodwyn, a loss of innocence. But such a loss "is not coterminous in time with the beginning of profundity. . . . Though the sheer buffeting of experience on his journal wore out any number of energetic young writers in the prime of youthful resiliency, Dugger has continued year after year to expose himself to the fissures and crevasses that define so much of the democratic landscape in Austin."

Those fissures and crevasses have taken their toll. "Dugger has wasted his talent," Stuart Long says, in a frank appraisal. Long is by now a seared old journalist. The state's stark diversity has always presented its writers with a problem of focus; it is better dealt with from a distance. If Dugger's prose has lost its edge, if it is occasionally maudlin, that may represent a very different sort of coming of age. There is still so much to write about in Texas, so much to reveal, so many to convince. But the prospects have changed.

"I started the *Observer* 20 years ago," Dugger wrote in the paper's special anniversary issue, "in moral rage that Texas politics was so corrupt. . . . It seemed to me then that you could hope, by finding and telling the truth and developing a moral position about it, to get people to change their politics, and thus the system."

In practical terms, the *Observer* has never put a candidate in office; it has uncovered no major scandal, although its steady reporting of the Sharpstown scandal forced other Texas papers to take notice. It has offered an alternative view to the twelve thousand Texans who subscribe. It has sometimes tempered the powerful and, in the case of Sharpstown, helped bring them down. But the efficacy of the liberal cause in Texas remains in question. Some believe that the liberals, by assuring the polarization of the party, enabled the tories to become so entrenched. Leaderless with the defeat of Ralph Yarborough and then Sissy Farenthold, they face the obsolescence suffered by the extreme right wing a decade ago, contentious on the political periphery, and a little sad.

The fate of the crusading liberal has been mirrored in the *Observer* itself. Since Dugger last relinquished the editorship, the paper's quality of writing and perspective has declined. It is still billed as a window to the South, although the panes bear the fashionable tint of the moribund New Left. The free voices sound remarkably similar. Humor has been replaced by facetiousness, good clean writing by clichés and a precious, folksy idiom. Worse, there are few people left in the pages of the *Observer*—the living portraits that once gave it so much vitality.

"I thought that moral force could be enough," Dugger wrote. "In this I was wrong, and I gladly apologize for my part in the romanticism of liberalism. . . . The reason we failed was not in our hearts, but in the substance and forms of power. We had not been prepared, by our educations, by the ruling civil axioms, by enough disaster, for the weakness of politics and the strength of corporations. We were set-ups for the hope, spawned by the

New Dealers whom we now see to have been so profoundly conservative, that the federal government could be trusted with the public good."

But his real farewell came earlier, in a piece he wrote for the *Observer* shortly before Sissy Farenthold's second defeat as a candidate for governor, a long lament in a changed and indifferent world.

"My thoughts turn this evening to the fighting liberal movement of the late Fifties. . . . I must stop reciting their names because there were thousands of them and memories of that pride and struggle are not apposite to our now and worsening time. Where is the new generation of the caring?

"Where are you? Did Vietnam so disenchant you, you don't care to try anymore? . . . Is it that you are so discouraged by the trend of things, you have given up on democracy in Texas? Even in America? . . . This kind of movement, revived by new people with strong will and firm values, can elect Farenthold, and if it does not . . . the corporations will control . . . this state in the bicentennial presidential election and the bored and the cynical will have to answer for it on the long downside of the future."

9 ☆ THE ELECT

Bentsen's New Deal

". . . Now this Baptist sought me out, and he told me that Senator Bentsen appealed to him. He's a Baptist, *and* a Mason. He said he could take Senator Bentsen before his board of deacons, and not be ashamed of him."

The speaker, a large one-legged man known as Tiny, is wedged into a seat next to me in the rear of a private jet flying between Washington and Newport News. Tiny is an aide to Virginia's First District Congressman Thomas Downing, and a seasoned political adviser, and he feels that Virginia is ready for Lloyd Bentsen.

The other passengers are seated forward, socializing after a long afternoon in the capital. They are Bentsen, some brittle Tidewater Democrats, and the president of a plumbing-supply manufacturing firm, who has provided the plane and the whiskey. Only Bentsen drinks Coke. He exchanges amenities with his hosts, while reviewing a speech he must deliver before the Peninsula Chamber of Commerce in Hampton that evening.

Tiny's assessment is no doubt sound. In Virginia, Democrats faithfully vote Republican in national elections. Federal money makes the difference in Downing's district between reading about the recession and experiencing it. Tidewater conservatism involves the familiar equation of self-made and government-made, with such benefactors as the United States Navy, NASA, and the subsidized Newport News Shipbuilding & Drydock Company.

As the plane prepares to land, Bentsen carefully fastens his safety belt.

The usual entourage guards the airport. The campaign workers and the hired bodyguards are all double-knit and the dry look, ambitious young men with bright, indecisive faces who enjoy driving fast in the company of the candidate—any candidate. "Tac One to Tac Two," mouths one into a walkie-talkie. "Rollin'!"

And indeed we are, tires squealing as we head for Hampton's combined sports arena and ice rink. Bentsen sits rigidly in the back seat, between his advance man, Donald Ward, and me. Ward has advanced such a luminary as Hubert Humphrey, and is good at his job. He hands Bentsen a list of important people he will meet tonight, without interrupting his briefing. "They haven't been hurt too much down here by the economic situation," Ward explains. "Remember, they've got the military, and the shipbuilding. . . . Some of the Republicans are a little upset because a Democratic candidate's coming. The invitation was issued before you announced. . . ."

Bentsen glances at the list of names; later, he will bring them up like old beer, effortlessly and with a smile. There is an ascetic quality about him that is both arresting and deadly dull. His elegantly cut gray suit is padded in the shoulders, obscuring a lankiness that is his only apparent link to the elemental reaches of south Texas. His gray hair is modishly long, his broad crinkly smile a tribute to the best of Houston's orthodontia.

Already today Bentsen has delivered a speech in Washington, to the National Association of Counties, and spent several hours on the floor of the Senate, where he voted more money for the Penn Central Railroad. "We can't save it with free enterprise, which is tragic," he said afterward on the ride out to National Airport, between long-distance telephone calls made from the front seat of his two-tone, chauffeur-driven Monarch. "Business can't do the job of stimulating the economy now. Government has to step in during a time of crisis." But he shows no signs of wear.

A press conference has been scheduled before the mixer, and Bentsen submits himself to the local press as if to stockholders. Asked to name his supporters in his race for the Presidency, Bentsen says they are legion, and laughs at his own joke. When a young woman asks him about his "LBJ image," Bentsen says he didn't know he had that image, then switches easily to his stimulated-economy routine.

Even the Chamber's Republicans, gathered for cocktails in the concrete foyer, admit that the candidate is a handsome man. Bentsen moves easily among them, armed with his smile and the mannerisms of one coached in professional sociability. The men he meets receive a hand on their shoulder too deft to be categorized as a slap; for women, Bentsen clasps his palms together like a champ.

"This time last year I wouldn't have recognized you," admits a blonde in a pink halter. "But I do now!"

"That's just wonderful," Bentsen says, with no trace of a Texas accent, and the hands come up.

"We like the way you sound down here," says her husband. "Us Democrats had to go underground four years ago, but we're risin' again."

Bentsen feigns a left hook to the man's chin, his gesture of exuberance. His responses have been carefully practiced in thirty-five states during the first lonely year of his campaign, and one must look closely to see the effort required to cover the distance between himself and others that is very much a part of Bentsen's private landscape. "I'm not gregarious," he will later venture in the darkened fuselage of the homeward-bound plane, the first Scotch of the day in his hand, as he struggles to differentiate himself from two other Texans. One is under indictment for allegedly accepting a bribe from milk producers; the other, a famous Texas senator who became President, is dead. "Money doesn't mean as much to me." In his voice there is more pain than self-revelation.

Tidewater political ambivalence is apparent in the Chamber's choice of entertainment. Two dozen middle-aged Negro men in matching yellow blazers sing a thunderous version of "The Battle Hymn of the Republic" with unmistakable Southern intonations. Bentsen watches them from the head table, chin in hand, touched neither by sentiment nor humor: he is thinking about his speech, a call for "confidence," government money for massive new projects.

"Let's bring back the old RFC," he says when his time comes, referring to the Reconstruction Finance Corporation, and FDR's "cheerful" pragmatism. "Let private enterprise put up twenty-five percent of the investment on projects like coal-gasification plants, and let private enterprise take the top twenty-five percent of the risk. . . ."

And presumably the top 25 percent of profits. Such reverberations of the New Deal please some Chamber members, but others have apparently felt the chill of the ice through the temporary flooring.

"It's time to roll up our sleeves," says the candidate, and his hand dutifully goes to his own sleeve, "and get back to work." He adds, "We've got to get this Navy modernized," and concludes with a plea for nonpartisan politics. "I believe a little bit like Hemingway, who said we'll bend, and we'll be stronger than the broken places."

The modernized Navy, not Hemingway, earns a polite standing ovation.

"He's a mixer," insists Ward as Bentsen leads the entourage back toward the door. "I've watched Scoop Jackson, and he's not a mixer. If there are six hundred people in a room, Scoop will turn off six hundred. But this man," and he gestures toward the ramrod-straight figure striding without an overcoat out into the night, "this man can be merchandised!"

Sam Houston, the first president of the Lone Star Republic, and Texas's first United States senator, saw his state as the guardian of the country's southwestern flank —a buffer between America and the territorial ambitions of Mexico and other countries. Houston once said, "Texas could exist without the United States, but the United States cannot, except at very great hazard, exist without Texas." Today his encomium has been reversed. Texas is heavily dependent upon the United States; in spite of its ongoing boom, it remains a poor state. Cut loose from the United States, deprived of federal funds and federal regulations, Texas would probably devour itself within a decade.

Texas once had its own fleet, its own money, and its own ambassadors. Only the last remain, politicians whose influence is in sad shape by Texas standards. The glorious days of Sam Rayburn and Lyndon Johnson are gone; no one figure represents the state, no man may intercede with the assurance and the results Texans have come to expect.

Most states would have been happy with the representation in Washington that Texas enjoyed on the eve of America's bicentennial. A Texan was chairman of the national Democratic party; another, head of the Senate Republican Policy Committee. Texas's congressmen were strong. George Mahon headed the Appropriations Committee and its subcommittee on the defense budget, Olin

Teague was chairman of Science and Astronautics. Jack Brooks was in charge of Government Operations, and Ray Roberts, from Rayburn's old district, chaired the Veterans Affairs Committee.

On a less exalted plane, Omar Burleson was seventh in seniority on Ways and Means, Brooks was second on Judiciary, and Representative Jim Wright third on the Public Works Committee. A Texan owned the afternoon newspaper in the capital; two Texans—Walter Cronkite and Bill Moyers—were among the most influential journalists in America. Texas could boast of the most visible black member of Congress, in the person of Barbara Jordan. The Texas delegation still had lunch once a week in the Speaker's private dining room, although no Texan was Speaker.

But none of them seemed destined to lead Texas back to that mythical state of "greatness." The fields of home lay fallow. Governor Briscoe could only offer support to more promising men; Lieutenant Governor Hobby and Attorney General John Hill belonged to the power structure of Democratic politics in Texas, and were basically uninspiring. Connally had taken the big risk over the short term, and lost.

Only the Senate offered some encouragement, and that not from Texas's senior senator—John Tower was not only too academic to meet the demand, he was also a Republican, and short. The task was left to Texas's freshman Democratic senator, traditionally a willing breed, and early on he received the support of the men who count in Texas. Lloyd Bentsen had two strong assets: he was one of them, and he had never lost a contest.

The first was in 1946, three decades before, when the young veteran announced his candidacy for the office of judge in Hidalgo County. At just twenty-five years of age, he was a strong candidate—a lawyer and a former bomber pilot, recipient of the Distinguished Flying Cross, and son of a large landholding family in the Rio

Grande Valley. He had graduated from high school when he was only fifteen, served as president of Sigma Nu at the University of Texas—the Greek society that a poor boy like his friend Connally could never aspire to—and was married to a beautiful Texas girl who had been a model in New York. He had about him, people said, an uncommon air of responsibility for a man so young, and so rich.

Bentsen won that first race for the judgeship, and two years later he was running for Congress. Wearing baggy trousers with pleats, a white shirt with collars that curled in the heat of the Valley, his dark hair slicked back and his tie tucked into his waistband, he stood on various platforms and denounced the "machine" —a euphemism for the ruling personages of George Parr and Mannie Raymond. He won again, becoming the youngest congressman in America when Texas power was in flow in Washington.

House Speaker Sam Rayburn welcomed such patrician promise into his "board of education," the select few who regularly met in his office to plot strategy, drink, and talk politics. Bentsen was the only freshman congressman so honored, and seemed destined to conform to the aphorism about Texas pols: "We pick 'em good, we elect 'em young, and we keep 'em there." He fraternized with Johnson and Connally, learned how to make government work and an appreciation of the art of the possible as personified by Rayburn. Bentsen voted with the Democratic majority—for implementation of civil-rights laws, low interest rates, Roosevelt's innovations —largely because Rayburn did.

But when on his own, Bentsen showed another side. He defended the use of wetback labor by Texas farmers, and opposed the federal employment anti-discrimination law. In 1950, during his second year in Congress and shortly after the outbreak of the Korean War, he stood up on the floor of the House and advocated dropping the atomic bomb on North Korea if North Korean troops were not pulled back behind the 38th Parallel.

"There are those who will recoil in horror," he said, "and condemn such action. But to those I say it is deserving of these people who are so morally wrong as to attack peaceful neighbors in the dead of night. . . . Better to let those who would destroy free nations know . . . the atomic bomb awaits. . . ."

Bentsen's colleague Representative Frances Bolton of Ohio asked, "For what purpose? To kill a lot of Koreans just because they are communists? Would that stop the war? . . . Do we not know that . . . one atomic bomb dropped by the United States of America would open us to atomic bombing? But more than that, it would prove to the Oriental mind the validity of the propaganda . . . that we really are against Asia . . . that destruction is our purpose."

Bentsen would later regret his words. He now claims they were meant solely as a threat to be used in eventual peace negotiations, indicating resolution in Congress. He never withdrew the proposal, and a year later said the United States had "taken a real shellacking in Korea," as a prelude to advocating universal military training.

The debate over states' rights to tidelands oil and the detestation of Adlai Stevenson by the Shivers Democrats in Texas split Bentsen's loyalties. He made some antagonistic speeches about Stevenson, but followed Rayburn's advice and remained within the Democratic fold. He also showed the proper respect for oil, for military preparedness—antidotes to Shivercrat enmity—and for a vigorous anti-Communism.

In 1953, before McCarthy's censure by the Senate, the Corpus Christi *Caller-Times* reported that Bentsen was "atune [*sic*] to the growing resentment against a Civil Service system under which spies and traitors can ply their trade and escape dismissal from government jobs.

He said he will introduce legislation in the next Congress to change the system in such a way that those who are unworthy can be fired without all the costly litigation. . . ." After McCarthy was censured, Bentsen was quoted by the same newspaper as saying that Americans must "increase our efforts to ferret out the reds."

Bentsen's conservatism at the time is best understood in terms of his heritage—the vast, arid stretches of the Rio Grande Valley that touched him in a different way from that of his father. Lloyd Bentsen, Sr., simply bought large tracts of land and then sold them at huge profits; Lloyd, Jr.'s, view was part that of Anglo survivor and part *petite noblesse,* for by then the family was one of means.

His father came to the Valley with his brother Elmer during the First World War. The land was uneventful and ugly and parched, compared with that of their home in South Dakota, the Rio Grande unworthy of a river. But the soil was good. The Bentsens worked ten acres of it, and began driving cars on tours of the Valley. By 1930 they had their own real-estate company. Within two decades they had made $100 million, and were among the first Texans to prove that land could be as big a bonanza as oil.

Land wasn't the sole basis of the Bentsen fortune: there were also banks, citrus groves, cattle, even some oil. But land was the source in freewheeling times, and there were casualties among the staunch Midwesterners who came to the Valley and submitted to the Bentsen tour. They put up cash for what they thought were potential vacation homes and fruit farms, and later found out there was not enough water, sometimes no water, or that the water was salty. In 1950, several lawsuits were filed charging that the Bentsen interests had defrauded buyers.

One couple from Iowa claimed they had been sold a ten-acre tract north of McAllen for five times what it was worth, after being put up free in a nearby clubhouse, and assured that the land was irrigated by a system of underground tiles and would support citrus trees. The water was actually run off from other irrigation projects, and salty enough to kill the saplings. The Iowans also charged that dummy corporations had been set up to protect the sellers. For instance, the clubhouse used to house the potential buyers was owned by a company with the reassuring name of Tip O'Tex Realty. It was owned not by Lloyd Bentsen, Sr., the acknowledged patriarch of the speculators, but by his brother. Lloyd, Sr., did have an interest, however, in a $2.5 million mortgage that Tip O'Tex owed to the Bentsen Development Company.

The judge awarded damages to the Iowa couple; fifty more such lawsuits followed. Most of these were settled out of court, and neither of the Bentsen brothers was ever found guilty of conspiracy or fraud.

Another land deal linked the Bentsens with Allan Shivers in 1946. Then the Democratic nominee for lieutenant governor, Shivers was able to purchase after his nomination an option on 13,000 acres from Bentsen Development for only $25,000. Six months later, after Shivers had been elected, he sold the same option for $450,000 to a firm called the Texas Realty Company. The deal was transacted in the office of Lloyd, Sr.

These facts were not revealed until Shivers ran against Ralph Yarborough for governor. A federal judge ordered his clerk to unseal a deposition Shivers had given in the Valley land fraud cases two years before, and the deal came to light. In any other state, the discovery that Shivers had made a $425,000 profit in the few months between being nominated and elected lieutenant governor would have ended his political career—but not in Texas.

Young Congressman Bentsen revealed his origins most unequivocally when dealing with labor issues. In upholding the practice of hiring wetback labor in the Valley, he objected to the rounding up of illegal aliens to be sent back to Mexico, and to the establishment of detention camps. He defended the farmers who hired wetback labor, opposing legislation that would make it a felony to hire Mexicans who illegally crossed the Rio Grande, and said it was charged that the farmers of the Valley "discriminate against and abuse these people. The facts are that we pay from five to at least ten times more in wages on this side of the Rio Grande than are paid to the same laborers in Mexico, and that we furnish them better housing and living conditions."

Bentsen's two terms in the House convinced Rayburn that he had great promise. "He told me," Bentsen recalls, speaking fondly of the man whose portrait hangs in Bentsen's Senate office, "that in another twenty-five years I could be Speaker. And I thought to myself, *Another twenty-five years*."

He announced unexpectedly that he was leaving politics to enter private business. The methodical pace of government bored him; the idea of running for governor of Texas, as some encouraged him to do, was equally unappealing. The year before, he said in a speech criticizing high interest rates, "My sympathies lie with the farmer, the workingman, the small businessman." Less than three weeks after his leaving Congress, the Bentsen family chartered the Consolidated American Life Insurance Company, which had assets of $7 million, and Lloyd, Jr., joined the bankers and the undeniably big businessmen.

The next sixteen years in Houston would serve as a kind of second emergence for Bentsen, crystallizing a personality that was already single-minded, and reserved. He came out from the corporate process nearly untouchable, skeptical in a way only men accustomed to

money can be, and driven. His ambition and his aloof-
ness seemed to spring from the same source; there would
be no more advocacy of atomic bombing, no more lapses,
and no emotion.

Land speculation had provided the seed money for
Bentsen's second career. The incorporators of Consolidated American were Lloyd, Sr., and Elmer Bentsen,
who put up the cash, and Lloyd, Jr., who served as
president. He had planned ahead, anticipating action
by the Internal Revenue Service to tax the transfer of
personally held mortgages within the family. Bentsen
promptly sued the federal government, and won—a case
that brought about the landmark decision in the development of huge financial holding companies, now the backbone of banking in Texas. Today the big banks—First
City National, Dallas's First National, Republic, Texas
Commerce, Bank of the Southwest—are no longer the
drab institutions that service the entrepreneur, but are
themselves the big operators. They acquire other banks,
merge, and build broadly based empires of their own.

Bentsen quickly established a reputation for hard
work, and a high degree of maneuverability. He demanded long hours and dedication, and inspired his
tightly knit, uncompromising staff. He was no purveyor
of insurance policies. The excess capital of Consolidated
American provided a base for ambitious schemes, and
he multiplied his stakes by merging with Lincoln Liberty Life, with headquarters in Nebraska, and became
president of the much larger Lincoln Liberty. This allowed him to avoid the restrictions of Texas banking
laws, and he began to collect bank shares and other investments for the company's portfolio.

He also anticipated the full value of data processing,
and the kind of cost-effective, sophisticated management
techniques that became standard with the burgeoning
Houston corporations. When the Sheraton-Lincoln Tower
opened in downtown Houston in 1963—twenty-seven

stories of sleek black executive efficiency—Bentsen was known in financial circles that extended far beyond Houston.

Four years later, Bentsen was ready to combine his insurance cover and the myriad other endeavors into Lincoln Consolidated, Inc., a huge, diverse holding company that included financial services and investments, from funeral homes to savings and loan institutions. Banks were the Bentsen stronghold in Texas—in McAllen, Mission, Pharr, Edinburg—with the Bentsens sitting on the boards, and on the board of Lincoln Consolidated. The company's share of bank stock was kept below 25 percent to avoid regulation under the Bank Holding Company Act, which would have required divestiture. Bentsen joined the boards of large, multinational corporations, including Continental Oil, Panhandle Eastern Pipeline, Trunkline Gas Company, and Lockheed Aircraft Corporation.

With encouragement, Bentsen speaks enthusiastically of the environment in which he made his own way: "Texas is willing to dare, to try new things." But a question about values other than material success brings a long silence. "We got together with some friends in Houston," he says finally, to illustrate the fact that Houston is not without a soul, "and set up a group to buy paintings. They were good paintings. We moved the paintings from home to home, and every three months we'd have a party to look at the paintings. Now I think that's an innovative idea."

He remained close to the Democratic party in Texas, as always. In 1960 he had raised more money for the Kennedy-Johnson ticket in Houston than was raised in any other area of the state. He was one of the select few to attend the planning session for Connally's first gubernatorial race, and produced a great deal of cash for that campaign. An important figure for years in the Johnson-Connally wing, Bentsen became the Robert Strauss of south Texas, and when he decided to oppose Ralph Yarborough for senator in 1964, he had all the establishment backing—with the exception of that of the President of the United States.

Johnson was seeking re-election, and did not want national attention drawn again to the ugly divisions in his home state party. Bentsen succumbed to Johnson's blandishments, and two years later his wife was made national committeewoman. Bentsen was solicited to fill the lacuna left by the departing Governor Connally in 1968, but he wisely refused, biding his time for a shot at Yarborough in 1970. Johnson advised him a second time not to oppose the incumbent, but this time Bentsen discounted the counsel.

The name Yarborough automatically opened purses all over Texas on behalf of his opponent, and set influential men to making telephone calls and crucial endorsements. Bentsen suddenly became the new hope of the right. Connally gave him full support—and his mailing list— and assigned him the services of his own packagers and advisers, notably George Christian. The Bentsen strategy was simply to portray Yarborough as a radical out of touch with his constituency, and maybe his reason as well.

The primary campaign was a dirty one. Yarborough was a master of the broad, vituperative attack. But he lacked the subtlety required of a television candidate in a new kind of race, and an appreciation of the virility of the law-and-order atmosphere.

Bentsen knew his basically conservative Texas voter. "If Mr. Yarborough wants to join Eugene McCarthy," Bentsen said, "George McGovern, Edward Kennedy, and the other Senate doves, this is his privilege." Yarborough, Bentsen pointed out, supported "unbridled government spending," the Vietnam Moratorium, busing, and the ban on prayers in public schools. Yarborough's vote against the nomination of G. Harrold Carswell to the

Supreme Court was "disgraceful." And Bentsen called for repeal of the 1968 Gun Control Act, "the first step toward registration of law-abiding citizens' guns."

His television advertising was considerably less tame. Christian practiced the technique he would later use in the television spots for Democrats for Nixon. One of the more questionable of the Bentsen commercials showed color film of the 1970 May Day riots in Washington, complete with tear gas, Weathermen, shrieking people and sirens, and an NLF flag flying across the screen. Then a calm voice asked if Ralph Yarborough had represented "your views" when he contributed to all this disorder.

Yarborough lacked the money for an effective media campaign as well, and he lost. He had lost some of his natural constituents—the urban minorities and labor—who wanted a larger slice of the Texas economic pie and less rhetoric. Bentsen carefully avoided including labor in his attacks on Yarborough, and had quietly sought the support of labor leaders. In spite of the shifting alliances of some traditional liberals, Yarborough's defeat by Bentsen set Yarborough on the path to martyrdom.

In the general election, Bentsen beat Congressman George Bush by the same margin he did Yarborough, 53 to 47 percent. Bush was a fellow Houston businessman, but Bentsen portrayed him as a Connecticut Yankee and latter-day carpetbagger whose support for open housing and gun control made him too liberal for Texas. Both campaigns were subdued. Bentsen's terminated with a television special dealing with the "Republican recession," narrated by "my good friend John."

Connally's support meant the difference between victory and defeat for Bentsen. Their friendship was years old, and more than professional. Bentsen visited the Connallys' home in Jamaica; B. A. Bentsen, Lloyd's wife, sat between Connally and Jake Jacobsen at the Democratic National Convention in Chicago in 1968. During Connally's tenure as Treasury Secretary, Bentsen and Robert Strauss were his closest friends in Washington, and it was Bentsen who testified so warmly at Connally's confirmation hearings before the Senate Judiciary Committee.

"We are personal friends," Bentsen said. "That in itself has special meaning to me, because John Connally understands and respects friendship. . . . He certainly has not shunned controversy when his principles and viewpoints were at issue."

Bentsen resigned from the Lockheed board before running for the Senate. He insists that he and Connally never discussed the $250 million loan to Lockheed, and Bentsen disqualified himself from the Senate vote on the loan, which passed anyway. Asked now if he would have voted against the loan if he had not disqualified himself, Bentsen takes a deep breath, then says, "That's part of investor risk. I would have voted no."

The intervening years have not done much for the reputations of either Lockheed or Connally. But Bentsen did move decisively after being elected to establish his own independence, after Nixon and Agnew proclaimed him part of their "ideological majority." Bentsen promptly called a press conference, expressed surprise at being embraced by the Vice-President, and identified himself as part of the loyal opposition. He then voted to ease the cloture rule shutting off debate in Congress; he also voted to reduce funding for the supersonic transport, sponsored mass-transit legislation, and even favored cutting the oil depletion allowance, except for those independents producing less than 3,000 barrels a day—the best source of campaign financial support.

Their names appear often in the lists of Bentsen's campaign contributors. The most prominent names leave no doubt about the origin of Bentsen's support: George Brown, Perry Bass, James Elkins, Jr., John and Clint

Murchison, Jr., H. Ross Perot, H. B. Zachry, Walter Mischer, Monty Moncrief, Ben Carpenter, John Stemmons, Amon Carter, Jr., Pat Rutherford, Michael Halbouty, and many others in the roster of the Texas establishment.

They are the same people who backed Johnson and Connally, but Bentsen is the first figure of national prominence since the New Deal to be *of* the Texas establishment. He is a transitional figure, a further development of the corporate statesman begun by the person of Alvin Wirtz, and most widely symbolized by Connally. But Bentsen does not act like a Texan, and he doesn't sound like one. Connally may use colorful four-letter words for emphasis, but Bentsen's strongest expletive is "crud."

Bentsen's aides would like Americans to forget that the candidate has a past in Texas. "He'll be judged by his appearance," said Ben Palumbo, Bentsen's Presidential campaign manager (who was later to quit for "personal" reasons). And he'll be judged by what he stood for in the Senate, where he gets middle marks from both sides."

He wanted to join the Finance Committee when he first arrived on the Hill, but instead was assigned to the Research and Development Subcommittee of the Armed Services, a traditional Texas stronghold. It provided Bentsen an opportunity to prove his independence, and to gain the respect of Senator Mike Mansfield. Bentsen found himself sitting in for the chairman during a $2 billion request from the Pentagon for the accelerated development of the Trident missile. The admirals who testified were confronted with substantive questions, of a type they were not accustomed to. Bentsen's knowledge of finance, and his boardroom manner, caused them some embarrassment, and he obtained a narrow vote for a 50 percent reduction in the request. (This was later reversed.)

Bentsen began running for President almost as soon as he entered the Senate. His votes against the SST and the war in Southeast Asia countered his obvious association with Texas. Not so unexpected was his opposition to the use of highway trust funds for mass transit, and to taxation repellent to the oil industry. He favored deregulation of natural gas, and development of the Alaska pipeline. The fact that Bentsen sat on the board of a large oil company was not the best recommendation for a Presidential candidate in 1976.

He gained praise for his work on the pension-reform bill, as well as the support of labor. For years Congress had been trying to reform private pension plans to protect the investor, and after becoming a member of the Finance Committee, Bentsen was able to bring his financial acumen to bear. Of the four bills presented to the committee, Bentsen's was the most complicated, and the one that eventually passed.

His moderate voting record did not hurt him appreciably in Texas, where a $200-a-plate affair brought $365,000 into his campaign fund from oil, construction, and banking interests. The setting was Houston, the guests as varied as Shivers and former Supreme Court Justice Abe Fortas. The fact that Strauss made Bentsen chairman of the Democratic Senatorial Campaign Committee enabled him to travel all over the United States meeting the most powerful people within the party structure. And he was invited back. By the end of 1974, Bentsen had spent about a million dollars on the campaign, and had accomplished his goals: to identify himself with economic issues and to get to know the people who count in Democratic politics.

He chose the Senate Caucus Room for his formal announcement. Surrounded by Texas congressmen, Lyndon Johnson's older daughter, and Jack Valenti, president of the Motion Picture Association of America, Bentsen pledged "to restore the meaning of America's two great promises—opportunity at home, and moral leadership."

Just two months before, he attended a luncheon in Los Angeles, and met informally with Ronald Reagan's closest Republican backers, and a few Democrats. The rich Republicans were signaling their displeasure with the policies of President Ford, and Bentsen was signaling that his appeal is broad enough to include the extremities of the Sunbelt.

While Bentsen was calling for moral leadership and opportunity, his supporters in Texas were attempting a power play in the best tradition of the state. The object was to secure passage in the legislature of a bill that would have virtually the same effect as the unit rule, so dear to Johnson and Connally. The party primary bill was introduced by a carefully chosen representative from Fort Worth, and given such establishment support that it became known as the "Bentsen bill." The bill set up a mechanism by which the candidate could appoint committees to designate his delegates. Proportionate representation was again being replaced by the winner-take-all primary, regardless of how small his plurality. The bill passed, and was signed into law by Governor Briscoe.

Bentsen was already assured of at least 60 percent of the Texas vote in a primary. Briscoe's heavy establishment backing in 1974 was part of the big Bentsen push at home, where the Governor was his willing promoter. But no matter who was nominated at the Democratic National Convention, Bentsen wanted to be certain of carrying his state, which would make him a strong candidate for Vice-President.

Bentsen's chief campaign advisers are almost all fellow Texans—and men who would find themselves in positions of great authority if he were elected: George Christian; Don Bentsen, Lloyd's brother, a prominent businessman;

Joe Kilgore, who represented the Valley in Congress and is a member of Alvin Wirtz's old Austin law firm; Ben Love, chairman of the board of the Texas Commerce Bank, which holds Bentsen's assets in a blind trust; Bill Lane, a Houstonian, member of the board of Lincoln Consolidated, and president of Riviana Foods; and George Kozmetsky, dean of the UT Business School and a key financial adviser who helped Bentsen bring more industry and business into the Valley.

Others close to Bentsen include Ted Strauss, an attorney and fund-raiser for the tory Democrats, and brother to Robert Strauss; Warren Woodward, LBJ's man in Houston in the 1950s, a chief recruiter, and president of American Airlines; Jack Valenti; and Lloyd Hackler, a Texan and one of the most astute political advisers in Washington, who served LBJ and who worked in Bentsen's Senate office until he accepted an offer to head the American Retail Federation.

There is a familiarity about some of the names and faces, just as there is about Bentsen's "progressive" rhetoric—his harking back to the New Deal. Among his proposals is the creation of an "energy bank" to counter dependence on oil by the development of alternate energy sources.

"We're the Saudi Arabia of coal," Bentsen says, and he could include Texas among the states with large reserves of strippable coal. "We need to build gasification plants, but they cost a billion dollars. I've got a friend who came to me and said, 'Look, a hundred million dollars is about my choking point. I can't go any higher.' Well, let the federal government put up three-quarters of the seed money on these massive projects."

The major new works project for corporate money is research and development of energy sources—a project that will consume billions of federal dollars over the next two decades, and could become as big a financial drain as Vietnam. The biggest recipient of that money will be "private enterprise"—those bureaucracies within the private sector already involved in energy, and structured for the most ambitious projects. The oil industry will be the direct beneficiary of such a brave new program, and Texas would be its logical focus.

Financing would be arranged through a renovated Reconstruction Finance Corporation. The RFC was originally established by Congress in 1932 on President Hoover's recommendation as a pump-priming device to help counter the Depression, loaning money to agricultural, commercial, and industrial enterprises. The RFC was greatly expanded under Roosevelt, with $11 billion worth of loans made to banks and trust companies. The life of the RFC was repeatedly extended, covering construction, and the operation of war plants. It was headed by Jesse Jones.

Texas appears to have come full circle. The establishment that Bentsen represents grew out of the New Deal, preserving the reliance of business upon government, but dispensing with the social concern that grew out of the Depression. More than forty years later, faced with an ailing economy, and no war to counteract it, these men look insistently toward the federal government. New Deal rhetoric once again becomes fashionable. Bentsen's version may lack the scope of Roosevelt's, but it is an open-ended proposition. The difference is that Bentsen's New Deal would not create a new class in Texas, but would simply advance the existing corporate welfare community.

It is late when the plane returns from Virginia to Washington. Bentsen's chauffeur drives us in from National, and Bentsen calls his wife to tell her he is on the way to the Shoreham. His voice is devoid of emotion. He sits bolt upright for the rest of the trip, eyes forward, and makes one final attempt to satisfy a reporter as interested in personality as in strategy.

"I'm telling you as candidly as I know how that I want to be President of the United States."

The candidate does not turn his head, does not even say good night when his chauffeur stops in Georgetown to let me out. Bentsen has already forgotten the interview, the evening in Hampton, his vote on the Senate floor; he is thinking about tomorrow.

The present elect of Texas is an austere profile and a gray suit riding slowly up Wisconsin Avenue.

Epilogue

The day Richard Nixon left Washington in disgrace, John Connally was arraigned there in a simple, blond-paneled U.S. District Court for allegedly accepting bribes, perjury, and conspiring to obstruct justice. Connally was the fourth member of Nixon's former Cabinet to be indicted, or to plead guilty to a criminal offense, and the last major figure to be brought to trial by the Watergate special prosecutor.

Connally was said to have accepted $10,000 from Jake Jacobsen for his efforts in convincing President Nixon to raise the support price of milk. Jacobsen had been an attorney for the Associated Milk Producers, Inc., the nation's largest dairy cooperative, which was under investigation for making illegal political contributions. Jacobsen agreed to testify against Connally if the government dropped other, unrelated criminal charges against him.

Connally's services in behalf of the milk producers were recorded in the Oval Office in March, 1971, when he briefed Nixon on the methods used by the dairy co-ops to raise political funds from farmers, and urged him to raise the support price before Congress did.

"Very frankly, they tap these fellows," Connally told the President. ". . . It's a check-off, no question about it. And they're amassing an enormous amount of money that they're going to put into political activities, very frankly. . . . I wouldn't judge it on a moral basis. . . . The economics of it are just beyond question."

Within minutes, Nixon had ordered the price increase, and the dairy co-ops in return donated $632,500 to Nixon's re-election effort.

At the time of the arraignment, the government's case against Connally appeared to be strong. He was specifically charged with accepting two payments of $5,000 from Jacobsen, concocting a false story to thwart investigators, and lying to the grand jury. It was widely reported that Connally had accepted the money, and then decided to return it after Jacobsen was called to testify about dairy co-op contributions. The case was built around the sordid details of money movements so familiar from previous Watergate trials.

Connally's prospects had never seemed bleaker. He had been the country's most influential private citizen, and a contender for its highest office. The indictment and his shift of political affiliation were obstacles no average man, or candidate, could overcome. He symbolized most of what was wrong with business and government in America.

Yet his support among his peers at home had never been stronger. They blamed Jacobsen, not for criminal misconduct but for turning against another Texan, and they blamed Special Prosecutor Leon Jaworski for not blocking Connally's indictment, no matter how blatant such a stroke would have been. (The fact that Jaworski removed himself early from the case was interpreted as practically treason.)

"If I had been the special prosecutor, and had known something good on a fellow," said Walter Mischer of

Houston, chairman of Allied Bancshares, Inc., "I'd have said to that staff, 'Now, this guy has a heck of a reputation, and you'd better proceed with care.' Maybe Jaworski did that, but if so, we don't know it."

A no less extraordinary statement was made by the managing partner at Vinson, Elkins, Searls, Connally & Smith. "We believe completely in his innocence," said A. Frank Smith, and he added, "If a jury were to find him guilty, I wouldn't mind being left out on a limb with John."

Connally would in fact be acquitted of the bribery charge by a predominantly black jury, unimpressed with the testimony of an admitted perjurer. The other charges against Connally would be dropped by a curiously inept prosecution, after a trial that answered none of the questions it raised. And Connally would again demonstrate his remarkable regenerative power, to awe friends and enemies.

No one remembered Connally's testimony before the Senate Finance Committee in early 1971, when he said, "The demands of people basically are insatiable." Among his friends in Texas, the question of whether or not he took a bribe, lied, or acted to obstruct justice lacked essential relevance. For a man's forthrightness was measured by his ability to survive.

Connally would enjoy his greatest popularity in Texas since surviving the wound he received in the assassination of John F. Kennedy. He would renew his efforts to become President of the United States, speaking vaguely of leading a third force in American politics. Ironically, he would be regarded as the Republican challenger most likely to win Bentsen's Senate seat in 1976, and he felt that Bentsen had deserted him when he was most needed. Connally would again become a contender.

But for the man who stood in full view of the court that morning of his arraignment, carefully groomed and self-possessed, the future did not look bright. His plea, nonetheless, was delivered in true Texas style. It served not only himself but also the rich, genial men who had gathered at Picosa three years before, those who lived by the expediency of his words, applying to all charges a firm and resounding "Not guilty!"

Index

A Note about the Author

James Conaway grew up in Memphis, and graduated from South-western University in 1963. He subsequently worked for news-papers in the South, and in Europe. As a free-lance writer, he has published articles in many magazines, including *The Atlantic* and *The New York Times Magazine.* An Alicia Patterson Fellow in 1974, he wrote about the effects of strip mining on the rural communities of eastern Montana, and about related energy matters. He lives in Bucks County, Pennsylvania, with his wife and three children.

A Note on the Type

This book was set on the linotype in Century Expanded designed in 1894 by Linn Boyd Benton (1844–1932). Benton cut Century Expanded in response to Theodore De Vinne's request for an at-tractive, easy-to-read typeface to fit the narrow columns of his *Century Magazine.* Early in the nineteen hundreds Morris Fuller Benton updated and improved Century in several versions for his father's American Type Founders Company. Century remains the only American typeface cut before 1910 still widely in use today.

Composed, printed and bound by The Book Press,
Brattleboro, Vermont.
Typography and binding design by Susan Mitchell